SF
613
.H44
B78
1997

Brunsdale, Mitzi.

James Herriot.

$35.00

DATE			
	WITHDRAWN		

BAKER & TAYLOR

James Herriot

Twayne's English Authors Series

Kinley Roby, Editor

Northeastern University

TEAS 534

JAMES HERRIOT
Mitzi Brunsdale

James Herriot

Mitzi Brunsdale

Mayville State University

Twayne Publishers
An Imprint of Simon & Schuster Macmillan
New York

Prentice Hall International
London • Mexico City • New Delhi • Singapore • Sydney • Toronto

Twayne's English Authors Series No. 534

James Herriot
Mitzi Brunsdale

Twayne Publishers
An Imprint of Simon & Schuster Macmillan
1633 Broadway
New York, NY 10019–6785

Library of Congress Cataloging-in-Publication Data

Brunsdale, Mitzi.
    James Herriot / Mitzi Brunsdale.
        p.   cm.—(Twayne's English authors series; TEAS 534)
    Includes bibliographical references and index.
    ISBN 0-8057-7835-7 (hardcover : alk. paper)
    1. Herriot, James.   2. Veterinarians—England—Yorkshire—
Biography.   I. Title.   II. Series.
SF613.H44B78   1997
636.089'092—dc20
    [B]   96-43137
                                                                       CIP

10 9 8 7 6 5 4 3 2

Printed in the United States of America

To Duke, one in a million,
and
in fondest memory of Merle Dix,
who gave me Joey and Duke,
and changed my life.

Contents

Preface

But ask now the beasts, and they shall teach thee.

—Job 11:10

Just before Christmas of 1972, the New York publication of some gently funny reminiscences by a fiftyish rural Yorkshire veterinarian launched one of the most phenomenal literary successes in the twentieth century. Thomas McCormack of St. Martin's Press sensed he had a winner when he introduced James Herriot's *All Creatures Great and Small*, claiming, "I am about to present a book that will be in print 100 years from now,"[1] but no one could have predicted the amazing popularity of Herriot's work. By the time Herriot died of cancer at age 78 on February 23, 1995, *All Creatures Great and Small* and its successors had sold more than 60 million copies worldwide and had given rise to three motion pictures and an enormously popular BBC television series that has run since 1978, each year bringing new readers to Herriot's books.

The secret of Herriot's literary achievement, I believe, lies in the moral dimension that undergirds his deceptively simple stories: how should we treat our fellow creatures and one another—and the world we all share? How does loving contact with animals help us face the bewildering mixture of triumphs and tragedies that we call the human condition?

The answers Herriot gave in his witty, touching books emerged from the Yorkshire traditions he cherished and his lifetime of tough veterinary work there, work he took up willingly and to the end bore with grace. Because he was first and always a deeply caring physician, he was the better writer for it: his stories glow with a bright spiritual beauty that overcomes the ravages of aging; they radiate wisdom and wonder at creation where mankind and animals play out their intertwining roles; and they are anchored in the faith that a God worthy of human worship nourishes and sustains every living thing, all creatures great and small. Herriot's values are not old-fashioned, they are eternal; and they help heal the paralyzing hurts we human beings continue to inflict upon ourselves in the increasingly unforgiving world we foolishly pride ourselves on making.

James Herriot was singularly unimpressed by the lures of fortune and fame. Because he wanted to maintain the privacy he deserved, he preferred not to give an interview or comment on this study, and so I have tried to let his writings and interviews speak for themselves in the context of the dramatically changing times that shaped them. As I reread Herriot's stories now, they are even better than I remembered—funnier, deeper, and richer in insight. His introductions to the various collections of his work are more revealing, perhaps, than he originally intended; and his published interviews offer some rough-hewn Yorkshire stiles over the boundaries he set around his personal life and his attitude toward his writing.

Herriot described the British county he made his home as "the wide green roof of England,"[2] a phrase that sums up the indispensable role Yorkshire played in his life and work. As Yorkshire sculptor Henry Moore remarked, "our surroundings are part of what we are," and he said his sculptures would have been very different "if the shapes of Yorkshire had not existed first."[3] Like Moore, Herriot shared the continual struggles Yorkshire's farm folk wage in barnyards and pastures swept elementally clean by the bracing Northern winds, observing the most primitive shapes of Yorkshire closely and then molding his experiences into art. Even though his veterinary work daily reminded Herriot that both we and the animals who bless us with their friendship and sustain us with their lives must perish, Yorkshire's green world taught him what his stories teach us, that despite—or because of—its hardships, a simple life close to nature warmly shelters humanity with an undemanding goodness that never dies.

James Herriot, I think, would have been the first to insist that his books are "popular," not "literary," works. A few years into his writing career, he declared he was astonished at "Americans who seem to get very intense about my writing. They read into it all kinds of weighty humanitarian, sociological meanings"[4] generally disregarded by the villagers around Thirsk, where Herriot spent his life. As to why he began to write at around the age of 50, Herriot replied that "Extra income was part of it. But what I really wanted to do was record something of Yorkshire life that was almost gone—the old black magic era of practice" (Gonzalez, *M*, 37). He also wanted to write about "the beauties of the area, and most important, about the Yorkshire people, about the hardy farmers and what a tough breed they are . . . to use a cliché, the salt of the earth."[5] All of Herriot's tales ring true to those intentions. The best of his stories reveal his unerring ear for dialogue and his easy command of the language, his economical ability to convey experience without elaboration, emotion without sentimentality, and a gentle, earthy humor, self-directed as often as not, that lends zest to his short anecdotes about people and their animals.

The man who created the "James Herriot" we know, of course, was James Alfred Wight. I have chosen to refer to him by his pen name because I am primarily seeking the reasons for the popularity of "James Herriot" as author and self-created literary character through closely reading his books and observing his literary reactions to his times. Furthermore, no autobiographer can be definitively distinguished from the literary image he creates of himself without drawing on all possible resources—his correspondence, memoirs by his family and friends, access to his manuscripts and notes, and so on, materials that in Herriot's case are not presently available. For now, at least, we cannot accurately estimate the degree to which Herriot fictionalized his experiences; what we see of James Herriot in his books is what we get.

Accordingly, while I unabashedly possess a typically American affection for Herriot's writing, I have attempted to discuss Herriot's literary achievements objectively, bringing appropriate but not stuffy tools of literary analysis to bear upon two "James Herriots": the canny, grandfatherly author and the engaging images he created of his younger self. Herriot's work presents a dual fictional perspective, two autobiographical stories developing concurrently through his five major books, an unusual situation that demands a two-layered chronological treatment.

Herriot wrote from about 1968 to 1994, describing events in his veterinary practice from 1938 to the mid-1950s. Between the lines of the "young vit'nery's" struggles, we can glimpse another Herriot—a genial, older writer and busy physician, husband, and father who had to snatch 15 minutes at his typewriter here and a half hour there between his evening calls. Telling the stories of the intertwined James Herriots demands a balancing act between studying literature and history, stabilized whenever possible by the horizon of Herriot's own words.

While tracing Herriot's experiences, I have discovered fascinating byways as seemingly random but every bit as useful and fascinating as Yorkshire's many walking paths and twisting stone fences: Herriot's literary lineage, drawn from intriguing sources; the history and mystique of Yorkshire folk medicine; the intangible curative powers of companion animals; the impact of technological changes on veterinary medicine; and, sadly, the price that veterinarians pay for serving their profession. I have also looked into adaptations of Herriot's work, such as the children's books he himself drew from his major books and the cinema, audio, and video versions others have made of them. For the sake of familiarity and consistency, I refer to Herriot's people and places by the names he gave them in his stories unless a situation demands otherwise.

I also bring to my study of Herriot's work a strong appreciation for the values of vanishing rural life. I was born in North Dakota, on the sparsely populated northern border of America's mostly bountiful, often cruel Great Plains, where for more than 30 years my husband and I have raised our daughters, our crops, and our animals on a working Red River Valley farm among folk like Herriot's, sturdy descendants of the Vikings. Like Herriot's people, North Dakotans are constantly beset by foul winter weather, agricultural miseries, government regulations, and daunting distances from "civilization"—but at the same time, many of us rejoice in the companionship of our animals, the integrity and hard work of our people, and the generosity of our land. Around me in the Midwest's small white churches and towns I still see sunburned farmers who, like Herriot's characters, are farming for their sons, and capable wives like Helen who run homes, hold outside jobs, and find time to help their neighbors. Despite disappointing human failings, despite the sour threshings of some critics, the people of the plains remind me that the values Herriot celebrated are not only real, but also still alive with us. Herriot's stories testify that honesty and integrity, self-reliance and self-respect, dignity, the value of hard work, and humility in the face of providence endure, often most clearly discernible in people who live close to their land and their animals. I could not have written this book without knowing them.

Acknowledgments

My deepest gratitude to the memory of James Herriot, for the wise and wonderful work he gave us all, and my heartiest thanks to

Christopher Timothy, for the invaluable insights into his most famous role that he has generously shared for this book;

The North Dakota Humanities Council, for a 1994 Larry Remele Memorial Fellowship to trace parallels between Herriot's milieu and our Northern Plains;

Ann Zavoral and the Fargo-Moorhead Communiversity, for showcasing my research for this book in their 1995 program;

Paul S. Conklin, for photographs with special meaning to all those who love our dogs as Herriot did;

Joan Higgins of St. Martin's Press, for showing galley proofs of Herriot's last piece of writing;

Ken Nickel, for his assistance and kind encouragement;

Dr. Alan Hoverson, for veterinary care second to none;

Dr. Del Hlavinka, for more information about brucellosis than I ever dreamed existed;

Dr. and Mrs. Harold Balas, for their recollections of Herriot Country and a priceless photo of Brian Sinclair, Herriot's Tristan;

Dr. Esther Lesér, for her devotion to art, scholarship, and dogs;

Dale Nelson, for books and music loaned and for demonstrating hard work and integrity every day;

Sheree Kornkven, for her generous help;

Merle, John, and Kathy Freije and Kris and Kurt Litke, who give dogs the kind of home we all should have;

My family—John, Margaret and Norb, Jean and Maureen—for their support;

Sally and David Harmon and Reta Riely, for above-and-beyond dog care;

My friends, two- and four-footed, of the training floor and the show trips and the field tests, for their generous help and encouragement: Jeanine and Mark Feist, Genna, Bozz, and family; Deb Bremer and Chip; Deb Winkler, Jackson and Cinder; Kathy Rust and her Vizslas; Mary

Ellen and Wally Steinhoff and Teak; Doug Spieker and Rudy, Penny, and the lovely memories of Bibi and Buck; Jeff and Sandy McMaines and the special memory of Tanner; Pat Quiggle and Woody; Marvin Roth and his late wife Mildred and Josh;

Oliver and Ethel Hoff, for heading Duke's fan club;

Everyone who generously contributed valuable insights into Herriot's work: the late Bob Adams, Betty and Ken Blankenship, Marge DeChant, Jane Ann Dosland and Dr. Julie Dosland, Dr. Alan Hoverson, Donna Johnson, Anne Jones, Carolyn and Jim Kastella, Dr. V. Knudson, Kermath H. Kornkven, Toni Magelky, Darlene and Ed Randel, Marvin Roth, Kathy Rust, Lorraine Sarek, Delores and Angie von Ruden, Cindy Wambach, and all those who prefer to remain anonymous;

Ed Touchette, "Uncle Ham," for celebrating the incorrigible Labrador sense of humor;

Janette Blake, for sending us Angel;

Winifred Dix, for her loving puppy care;

And most unforgettably of all, Anne Jones, for breeding marvelous Labradors and never forgetting what Labradors are for.

Chronology

1916   James Alfred Wight born October 3, in Sunderland, England; only child of James Henry Wight, a musician, and Hannah Bell Wight, a professional singer; moved after three weeks to Hillhead, a suburb of Glasgow.

1929   Reads article on veterinary medicine in *Meccano Magazine* and decides to become a veterinarian because of his love of dogs.

1930   Attends Hillhead High School and is influenced in career choice by visit from Principal of Glasgow Veterinary College; English veterinary profession in very low esteem.

1938   Graduates from Glasgow Veterinary School and takes position as assistant to Yorkshire veterinarian J. Donald Sinclair ("Siegfried Farnon") at Thirsk, Yorkshire.

1939   Takes additional position as veterinary inspector in the Ministry of Agriculture, Fisheries, and Food; about 55,000 tractors now in use in Britain and milk being hauled to dairies.

1941   Marries Joan Catherine Danbury on November 5 and the same day is made a partner in Sinclair's practice; lives at 23 Kirkgate ("Skeldale House") until mid-1950s.

1943   Is called up as RAF aircrew trainee; trains mainly at London, Scarborough, Windsor, and Manchester.

1944   Son Nicholas James ("Jimmy") is born February 13.

1945   Receives medical discharge; returns to his Thirsk practice and a revolution in veterinary medicine—antibiotics, vaccines, new surgical techniques, and artificial insemination; about 200,000 tractors make the British draft horse, mainstay of veterinary practice, obsolete.

1949   Daughter Rosemary is born May 9.

1950–1960   Herriot family moves to a smaller town house, "Rowan Garth"; assistant Calum Buchanan works for a few years in the practice, which shifts from large-animal to small-animal work; automobiles become common in the Dales.

1961   Takes trip from October 28 to November 6 via ship to USSR as sheep veterinarian.

1963   Takes short trip August 8–10 via plane to Turkey as cattle veterinarian.

1966   At age 50, Wight begins writing and tries unsuccessfully to be published.

1970   *If Only They Could Talk* published in England under pseudonym "James Herriot."

1972   In United States, St. Martin's Press publishes *If Only They Could Talk* and its sequel, *It Shouldn't Happen to a Vet,* as *All Creatures Great and Small.*

1973   Serves as president of Yorkshire Veterinarian Society.

1974   *All Things Bright and Beautiful* published; Herriot has U.S. book-promotion tour and plans move to bungalow in country (eventually "Mire Beck," at Thirlby, near Thirsk); David Susskind produces first movie version of *All Creatures Great and Small.*

1975   *All Creatures Great and Small* airs on Hallmark Hall of Fame, February 4; Herriot receives American Veterinary Medical Association's Award of Appreciation; Herriot and his wife make his second and last U.S. book tour.

1977   *All Things Wise and Wonderful* published.

1978   First BBC television series of *All Creatures Great and Small.*

1979   *James Herriot's Yorkshire* published; television series *All Creatures Great and Small* airs on U.S. PBS-TV; movie *All Things Bright and Beautiful* (BBC-TV); Herriot receives Order of the British Empire and honorary Litt.D. from Heriot-Watt University, Edinburgh.

1981   *The Lord God Made Them All* published.

1982   *The Best of James Herriot* published; Herriot made fellow of the Royal College of Veterinary Surgeons.

1983   Herriot receives honorary D.V.Sc. from Liverpool University.

1984   *Moses the Kitten,* Herriot's first children's book, published.

1985   *Only One Woof* (juvenile) published.

1986   *James Herriot's Dog Stories* and *The Christmas Day Kitten* (juvenile) published; 1983 BBC film *All Creatures Great and Small* released on video.

1987   *Bonny's Big Day* (juvenile) published.

1988   *Blossom Comes Home* (juvenile) published; fourth television series of *All Creatures Great and Small* in process.

1989   *The Market Square Dog* (juvenile) published.

1990   Deaths of Brian Sinclair ("Tristan Farnon") and Calum Buchanan, a few weeks apart; *Oscar, Cat-About-Town* (juvenile) published.

1991   *Smudge, the Little Lost Lamb* (juvenile) published.

1992   *Every Living Thing* and *James Herriot's Treasury for Children* published; Herriot diagnosed with cancer.

1994   *James Herriot's Cat Stories* published; Herriot suffers broken leg while defending garden from sheep.

1995   Herriot dies of cancer on February 23 at his home at Thirlby.

1996   *James Harriot's Favorite Dog Stories* (new edition) published; its brief introduction is Herriot's last piece of writing.

Chapter One
"A Marvelous Life"

It is not doing what we like to do, but liking what we have to do, that makes life blessed.

—Goethe

Not long after the New York publication of *All Creatures Great and Small* in November 1972, its 56-year-old author remarked, "Nothing important has ever happened to me . . . my life is merely the framework for a series of animal incidents."[1] James Herriot, a genuinely modest man, did not see that something very important indeed was beginning to happen to him—an enormous literary success that probably astonished him more than anyone else. Based on "animal incidents" Herriot experienced as a rural Yorkshire veterinarian just prior to World War II, *All Creatures Great and Small* sold 37,000 copies, was chosen by two major book clubs, and was considered by three film companies—all by January 1973.[2] By his golden wedding anniversary in 1991, Herriot's books—five major story collections, several gift volumes, a Yorkshire travel book, a decade of Yorkshire calendars, and several illustrated children's books—had sold 50 million copies worldwide and had also inspired three motion pictures and the immensely popular BBC television series also titled *All Creatures Great and Small*. By the mid-1990s, Herriot's popularity was fortified by the 1992 publication of *Every Living Thing;* a video version of *James Herriot's Yorkshire* was in production; and in October 1994, *Publishers Weekly* reported that St. Martin's initial 600,000-copy printing of *James Herriot's Cat Stories* was "blowing out of the stores, with stronger wholesale sales and independent reorders than they've had for any Herriot title." By the following March, *Cat Stories,* the last Herriot book to appear during his life, had sold 829,724 copies, placing it among the top 12 U.S. best-sellers of 1994. A new edition of *James Herriot's Favorite Dog Stories* appeared in September 1996 in a first printing of 850,000 and was chosen as an alternate by three major U.S. book clubs.[3] James Herriot had become an international industry.[4]

The outstanding success of *Cat Stories* proves that an audience buffeted by brushfire wars, continent-spanning plagues, voice mail, E-mail, lost

1

mail, MTV, and the Information Superhighway can still find solace in the disarming tales of a gentle veterinarian from a Yorkshire town he called "Darrowby" and a past he called "a sweet, safe place to be"[5]—a world far removed from the horrors of the nightly news, yet as intimate as the decency and compassion of the human heart. Herriot himself was well aware of the distance between his fictional world and our all-too-real one; he insisted on it. In one of his last interviews, he declared, "My books are a restatement of old values: hard work and integrity. You can see them on the farms here in Yorkshire all the time and it's quite a contrast to what one finds in city life today" (Gonzalez, *SR,* 89). Firmly based on those old values, James Herriot's work charms his readers with a healthy nostalgia for what used to be best in our world as well as an unquenchable hope for what we want to think—in spite of ourselves—remains a constant good in what Mark Twain called "the damned human race."

James Herriot's real name was James Alfred ("Alf") Wight. He was born on October 3, 1916, in Sunderland, near England's northeast border with Scotland. Three weeks later, his parents moved to Hillhead, a western suburb of Glasgow, where Herriot spent much of his boyhood rambling the green hills that rise around the city, with his Irish setter Don always at his side.

Glasgow, Scotland's largest city and the center of the broad industrial belt that extends across southern Scotland, seems to have always possessed a unique and powerful personality. Originally a settlement near a convenient ford in the river Clyde, Glasgow molded itself into "a medieval centre of piety and learning; then develop[ed] successively into an expanding centre of international trade, a place of rapidly growing manufacturing importance, a powerhouse for international heavy engineering products and a cradle for the construction of a major proportion of the ships that sailed the seven seas throughout most of the nineteenth century and into the early years of the twentieth."[6]Although Herriot was always reticent about his family (except for stories he wrote about his courtship, the early years of his marriage, and his children's youth), he felt he probably inherited his preference for solitary, windswept spaces from a long line of British sailors in his ancestry. His lifelong love of classical music came from his mother, who sang opera in Glasgow, and his father, an organist and pianist. Throughout his life, Herriot himself enjoyed playing the piano, though in later years, much to his family's relief, he abandoned efforts to teach himself the violin.[7]

Glasgow set its lasting stamp on Herriot, and his grandfatherly baritone never lost its distinctive Glaswegian burr. Another literary son of the city, Maurice Lindsay, describes the majority of his fellow middle-class Glaswegians as " 'couthy' and kindly, easy-going and tolerant, perhaps not ultra-sophisticated by the standards of London, Paris or New York" (Lindsay, 282)—a thumbnail sketch that suited Herriot well. Glaswegians take a justifiable pride in their practicality—after all, a Glasgow shoe manufacturer, A. P. Somerville, invented the square-toed footwear that let Glasgow men stand closer to the bar (Lindsay, 281)— and they possess a characteristic humor whose flavor, Lindsay claims, "today is much the same as it was half a century ago" (Lindsay, 281–82). To illustrate that unmistakable Glaswegian tang, Lindsay uses an earthy anecdote that Herriot, a passionate fan of British football (soccer), might have roared over in a country pub:

> A middle-class father had been persuaded to take his football-daft son to the annual ritualistic Rangers versus Celtic match.
>
> Those who have never attended a football match along with perhaps 30,000 others may not have had cause to appreciate that the sheer press of numbers makes the provision of normal sanitary arrangements impossible.
>
> To this particular father's dismayed astonishment, a little Glaswegian beside him suddenly stopped shouting, unbuttoned his fly and relieved himself. The father, a little startled, instinctively stepped back.
>
> "Whit's the matter wi' you, heh?" came the indignant query. "Shoes leakin' or somethin'?" (Lindsay, 283)

During Herriot's childhood, Britannia, fueled in great measure by heavy industry and shipbuilding, was still ruling the waves—but only barely. In the late nineteenth century, when Lord Macaulay wrote his polished *History of England,* a text that remained the model for student essays during Herriot's school days, Great Britain was the richest country on earth, and its landowners were some of the wealthiest people in the world. Between 1880 and 1914, 4.5 million square miles were added to British-dominated areas of the world's map, while at home, about four-fifths of Britain was owned by seven thousand people[8] and worked by nearly all the men and women of the countryside as tenants and laborers. When Herriot was born in the midst of the Great War, though, enormous changes in British society were afoot. The veto power of the House of Lords had already evaporated in 1911. In World War I, Britain lost 850,000 and had 2,000,000 wounded, of which the relatively few landed families bore a proportionately heavy share, and British taxes tripled to help pay the vast costs of the "war to end all

wars." Consequently, between 1918 and 1921, one quarter of England—
a million acres—changed hands; waves of strikes disrupted traditionally
orderly British life; and by 1921, according to *The Economist,* Britain was
laid low by one of the worst depressions since the industrial revolution.

Between the world wars, it was no wonder Herriot loved to walk the
green Scottish hills south of Loch Lomond. He was growing up on the
outskirts of "a grey and grimy city, encased in the sooting of an obsolete
coal-burning age . . . street after street of grim, crumbling nineteenth-
century tenements [with] . . . weeds and discarded rubbish disfiguring
the back courts [and] frustrated and hopeless urban illiteracy" (Lindsay,
15). Britain was declining because of a "fundamental rottenness [in gov-
ernment] . . . a stagnation under a frightened, lazy and nostalgic elite."[9]
In the 1930s, America and Japan were devouring Britain's world trade,
and at home the British working class and the unemployed were facing
the worst of the economic disaster.

Even in the depths of the depression, however, Britain's gloomy outlook was lightened by a few gleams of progress that arose from technological advances achieved during World War I. New industries were
turning out trendy new consumer products such as automobiles and
electrical gadgets, and the British middle-class could afford them, as
well as cheap mortgages and private education. General health in
Britain was also improving because of a better diet, increased social services, and new medical treatments such as penicillin (discovered in
1928) and vaccines, which for the first time were bringing diseases such
as pneumonia, tuberculosis, diphtheria, and syphilis under control.

While Herriot was attending Glasgow's Hillhead High School, winds
of change were also sweeping British agriculture. By 1930, 42 percent
of Britain's arable land was in 100- to 300-acre farms, but experts were
already proposing farm units of 2,000 to 3,000 acres for maximum efficiency.[10] On the horizon, too, was the rapid disappearance of the draft
horse, once the backbone of veterinary work. Herriot would see draft
horse numbers reduced nearly to a trickle in the first three years of his
practice.[11]

Herriot said horses had always intimidated him; his love for dogs
led Herriot to veterinary medicine. He described his choice of career in
the introduction to *Dog Stories,* a 1986 volume collected from his first
four books. In 1930, when he was 14, Herriot's "vague desire" to
devote his life to dogs crystallized when he read a *Meccano Magazine*
article, "Veterinary Science as a Career."[12] A little later, Dr. White-
house, principal of the Glasgow Veterinary College, visited Hillhead

High School to drum up recruits, and by his own account, Herriot "was hooked" (DS, xiii).

Significant obstacles lay in his way. As a high-school student, Herriot, who from the start seems to have enjoyed an innate way with words, was studying English, French, and Latin, not science and mathematics, subjects he dreaded. In order to enter veterinary school, he had to get two "highers" and two "lowers," qualifying scores for matriculation, and he knuckled down to business. By dint of two years' ferocious labor, he even managed to get a third "higher" in Latin (for which, he said, school authorities would grant anything) and a "lower" in mathematics, at which he claimed to be a "total numbskull" (DS, xiv).

Other circumstances were beyond Herriot's control, however. The most ominous threat to his youthful ambition was that in 1930 the Glasgow Veterinary College seemed to be on its last legs, the result of the profession's decline in the early twentieth century. Veterinarians had enjoyed an honorable reputation in ancient times—the Greek title for the veterinarian, *hippiatroi,* emphasizes the knowledge of the horse and its ailments—but Great Britain did not establish its first veterinary school until 1792, spurred by a century of epizootics (the animal equivalent of epidemics) that wiped out two million British cattle because at that time no British practitioners knew how to cure or prevent such diseases.[13] Scottish educational institutions traditionally led the British Empire in practical areas such as medicine and engineering, and Edinburgh's veterinary training soon outshone London's. However, in eighteenth-century Britain, only the lowest and most ignorant men were "horse doctors," giving that term derogatory connotations that unfortunately persist: "Even today," observed American veterinarian B. W. Kingrey in the 1970s, "when we think we have finally laid to rest the old unhygienic image of the profession, it kicks off its tombstone and again rears up in television in the horse doctor as town derelict."[14] As if that sorry public image was not a bad enough career prospect, Britain's economic problems after World War I nearly broke all of the country's veterinary schools. Herriot recalled that during the depression most animal-loving Britishers could not even afford to keep pets (DS, xii), and even worse for prospective veterinarians, the 1931 Model A trucks rolling off Ford's Dagenham assembly lines heralded the coming obsolescence of the noble Clydesdales and their kin, stalwart veterans of British haulage and farm draft work. According to Herriot, the British government had slated Glasgow Veterinary College to close and had withdrawn its financial support just before he entered, and consequently in the early 1930s the institution was barely being kept alive on a star-vation budget (*DS*, xvi).

Herriot said that he spent some of his happiest years at college, although a fair number of his classmates took more interest in gambling than in their studies. In addition, many of his instructors were woefully superannuated; and the material they offered, overwhelmingly focused on the horse, seemed depressingly medieval even to him. Despite all its drawbacks, however, Glasgow Veterinary College gave Herriot one priceless advantage that can make or break hopeful candidates for gru-eling professions: plenty of hands-on learning outside the classroom, which for Herriot mostly involved dogs because of the growing scarcity of horses. After five years' training, Herriot graduated from Glasgow Veterinary College in 1938, the height of the depression, only to dis-cover that jobs for new vets were frighteningly scarce. The few available positions paid as little as 30 shillings a week plus board and room, then the going wage for farmhands, and in some desperate cases, qualified veterinarians were even reduced to working for just their bed and board.

According to Herriot's fellow Yorkshire author J. B. Priestley, several different Englands coexisted in the 1930s,[15] and certainly two dramati-cally different Yorkshires awaited young James Herriot in 1938 when he leaped at an advertisement for a veterinary assistant placed by Donald Sinclair, who would come to be known in Herriot's books as "Siegfried Farnon." Sinclair was six years Herriot's elder and became Herriot's life-long partner and closest friend. As he traveled south from Glasgow, Her-riot, dismayed, viewed Yorkshire's dismal manufacturing cities before he arrived at Sinclair's practice, in sight of the Yorkshire Dales, a beautiful remnant of safe old prewar England.

One of the English counties hardest hit by the depression, industrial Yorkshire suffered 60 percent to 70 percent unemployment on average between 1931 and 1936,[16] and 31 percent of the county's working-class families lived in severe poverty on a weekly wage that workers grimly called "a fodder standard" of two pounds, three shillings, and sixpence. This allowed one shilling for getting to and from work, seven pence for the newspaper, and sixpence for the cost of the wireless, not much improvement over the bare-bones subsistence level of British workers in 1901, when "Nothing must be bought but that which is absolutely nec-essary for the maintenance of physical health, and what must be bought must be of the plainest description"—in short, no toys, no savings, no fresh meat, not even a burial allowance.[17]

Regardless of the condition of the British economy, the people of rural Yorkshire have always faced difficult living conditions. Farm laborers in 1937 were earning 30s. a week, whereas Herriot's first wage from Donald Sinclair was four pounds a week plus room and board at Sinclair's practice at Thirsk, a market town of a few thousand people. Herriot's duties seemed to have lasted 25 hours a day, eight days a week, in a sparsely populated area of short summers and fiendish winters that in Herriot's day could strangle entire districts and force the "vit'nery" to slog through several miles of deep snow to reach a patient. Though he would learn that making a living in rural Yorkshire was a tough test of body and soul, once he saw the Dales, upland valleys watered by rivers that wind southward from some of England's most harsh terrain, James Herriot fell helplessly in love with them.

Thirsk is the center of "Herriot Country," where Herriot practiced for more than 50 years. The town lies at the junction of several roads about 25 miles northwest of York, midway between two sets of Dales. Directly east of Thirsk, past steep Sutton Bank, which looms over Mire Beck, Herriot's unassuming rural home near Thirlby, the A170 highway to Scarborough forms the southern boundary for Bilsdale, Bransdale, Farndale, Rosedale, and Newton Dale, valleys stretching down from the North Yorks Moors National Park. To the west of Thirsk lies the Yorkshire Dales National Park, established in 1954 and 99 percent privately owned, a picturesque 680-square-mile area that has always been a prime attraction for local vacationers. The popularity of Herriot's books currently brings about eight million visitors a year to the Dales.[18]

Herriot preferred the western Dales, where he spent most of his first months working with Sinclair's first partner Frank Bingham. This mostly untamed "land of green hills, valleys, and purple moors" possesses some of England's legendary scenery, full of "limestone crags, dry stone walls, fast-rushing rivers, and isolated sheep farms or clusters of limestone cottages."[19] Herriot came to know all the Dales intimately, and he used them as the unforgettable backdrop for nearly all his stories.

For Darrowby, the fictional hub of Herriot's practice, Herriot amalgamated several of his favorite Yorkshire towns: "A bit of Thirsk, something of Richmond, Leyburn and Middleham and a fair chunk of my own imagination."[20] Blessed with a keen ear for voices and colloquial speech and a fine memory for conversations, Herriot seems to have filed away mental notes about his work from the start. Later he used a daily diary, and after he became famous, he kept a pad and Dictaphone in his car to record his raw material, eventually shaping two to three years of his recollections into each of his five major books. *All Creatures Great and Small* covers the period from Herriot's 1938 arrival in Yorkshire through his courtship of and marriage in 1941 to Joan Danbury ("Helen" in his books), the daughter of a Dales farmer, when Sinclair made Herriot a partner in the practice. The book's sequel, *All Things Bright and Beautiful,* covers the years from late 1941 to Herriot's 27th birthday, in 1943, when he was called up to serve in the RAF.

Idyllic as the Dales appear in picture postcards (the photographs are usually taken on sunny summer days), a veterinarian's life there just prior to World War II was enormously taxing. North Yorkshire rains are less heavy than those of the west coast of England and Scotland but are just as frequent, and the skies remain overcast for much of the time between October and March. The short Yorkshire summers are preceded by weeks of night-and-day lambing, Herriot's favorite season, from April in the lower areas, where twin lambs are common, to mid-May on the upper farms, where the shorter pastures due to the higher altitude drop the sheep's average fertility rate to one lamb or less per ewe. Snow, including the vicious whiteouts Herriot has vividly described, sets in harshly in November, and dairy animals have to be confined to "shippons" where they must be fed hay and silage with barley or oats to survive the severe weather. Ewes remaining from the early September culling spend the winter on the fells, unless heavy snow is likely, when farmers must bring the animals in to shelter (Duerden, 15). In Herriot's first years as a veterinarian, old Dales farmers often shocked him by dismissing weather he considered a screaming blizzard as "a plain sort o'day."[21]

"Young vit'nery" Herriot arrived in the Dales near the end of "a long, dark time when animal therapeutics involved a combination of mystery, superstition, strange recipes and bizarre concoctions. The bleeding, blistering and fomenting to which animals were subjected begged for some humane kinds of restrictions and regulations. But they did not exist" (Kingrey, 115–16).

What did exist when Herriot took up his work in the Dales involved veterinary treatments and procedures that by now have become virtually extinct. Lacking squeeze chutes and hydraulic lifts, veterinarians then manually wrestled formidably horned dairy cows, hulking steers, recalcitrant bulls, snorting Yorkshire boars, and oversexed stallions into position for home-concocted remedies that to Herriot smacked of medieval witchcraft. These probably really were holdovers from such relics of the Dark Ages as the eleventh-century Anglo-Saxon Leech Book, a text based on "Greek knowledge" containing two sections dealing with animals' external and internal ailments as well as an intriguing third section devoted to "more monkish" prescriptions, such as relieving symptoms inflicted by supernatural causes.[22] Being one of England's most remote areas, the Yorkshire Dales have long been the repository for folk cures and curses wreaked by "witches," unfortunate women accused of intercourse with the Devil, or "wise men" thought able to charm evil spirits out of sick beasts or human beings.[23]

Before the veterinary use of cesarean sections became common practice in the 1950s, a veterinarian often had to manipulate calves and foals *in utero,* sometimes for hours, and pull the newborn animals physically from their dams. The sweaty, bare-chested vet might perform this work in freezing-cold stone barns if he was lucky—or out on a windswept hillside if he was not. Besides pneumonia, he usually risked infection from serious long-duration diseases such as brucellosis, from which Herriot himself suffered. In the 1930s, caring for dogs and cats, Herriot's favorite animals, had its own pitfalls, as veterinarians often had to stand by helplessly while cherished pets died because effective medicines had not yet been discovered—and then cope with the misery of the grieving owners. Dealing with the physical and emotional strains in those early years, Herriot learned more about his work and the people of the Dales than books could ever have taught him—or, as Donald Sinclair pithily put it, "Alf, there is more to be learned up a cow's arse than in many an encyclopedia" (Gonzalez, *SR,* 88).

While Herriot was getting his firsthand training in the Dales, the world outside was again caught up in the gathering storm of war. The "peace in our time" Munich Agreement engineered by Britain's 1938 appeasement policy proved to be an obscene sham, and in September 1939 the Nazi blitzkrieg fell upon Poland, launching a new kind of all-out warfare. After that winter's deceptively quiet "phony war," Nazi Germany savaged the Low Countries and France in early 1940, forcing British forces to evacuate from Dunkirk in May, overwhelming Norway in less than one week in June, and bringing France to its knees by June 22. While the British army regrouped, Great Britain depended on its sailors and merchantmen to preserve the country's lifelines against U-boat wolf packs, and in the skies the RAF's badly outnumbered Hurricanes and Spitfires fought the harrowing Battle of Britain. During this crucial period, when Britain fought alone and the outcome of the war seemed doubtful, Herriot and Sinclair volunteered for military service, although as members of a reserved occupation, they were not inducted immediately.

The new war demanded motor vehicles instead of horses and mules, which were kept at home for farm labor. "Horses have ration-books," a contemporary British reporter noted in 1942; "I wonder when they will issue them for cats" (Briggs, 265). After heavy losses had depleted the ranks of the RAF, even veterinarians, Herriot and Sinclair among them, were called up as aircrew in 1943.[24] By the time Sinclair's colorful brother, Tristan (Brian Sinclair), had qualified at veterinary college, though, the Far Eastern theater of war was demanding veterinarians to care for the donkeys and camels in draft use there. Herriot later wryly noted that while as second-class airmen he and Siegfried "pounded the parade ground for weary hours, Captain Tristan Farnon sailed off to the war in style" (*ATBB,* 400).

After his call-up on his birthday, October 3, 1943, Herriot spent about two years in the RAF. His third book, *All Things Wise and Wonderful,* counterpoints his dreary days of marching, physical training, flying lessons, and quartermaster duties with happier recollections of his Yorkshire practice. Although Herriot discovered that he liked flying and soloed to qualify as a pilot, an unspecified operation he underwent, possibly for a hernia repair, necessitated his medical discharge in 1945, allowing him to return to his family and his veterinary work. Herriot's son Jimmy, who now practices as a veterinarian in Thirsk, was born while Herriot was in RAF training at Scarborough, and several amusing episodes of *All Things Wise and Wonderful* treat Herriot's AWOL visits to his wife and child.

In Britain's so-called people's war, "J. B. Priestley's Yorkshire voice was almost as influential as that of Churchill." Both men used traditional historical and cultural ideals to inspire their countrymen, but Priestley anticipated the welfare state, insisting that if all classes of British society were expected to sacrifice equally, then all must share in an equalized society when the war was done. Priestley declared, "We're not fighting to restore the past. We must plan and create a noble future" (Briggs, 269), and much of Britain listened.

Elements of Britain's government actually planned that noble future while the war was raging. Sir William Beveridge's *Report on Social Security,* which appeared in late 1942, became "a symbol of the new Britain," the "welfare state" that would be "the government's legislated thanks to its people for their wartime sacrifices" (Briggs, 273). Because those sacrifices were so enormous—300,000 British combatants,

35,000 merchant seamen, and 60,000 civilians were killed, the last primarily in the Blitz, which extended from Plymouth to Glasgow—the government's thanks would have to be correspondingly huge. London in particular had "taken it" (to paraphrase Churchill) in the worst of the Nazi bombing, but when the war ended in 1945, the embittered British people had "had it" with those they blamed for their suffering. The 1945 election thrust Winston Churchill and the Conservatives from office, and under Clement Attlee and his Labour government the nationalization of British banking, industry, and health care began; large-scale educational reforms ensued; and arts activities aimed at the widest possible audiences increased substantially, promoted by the newly established Arts Council.

These expensive social programs, coupled with the United States's refusal to renew the Lend-Lease Act in 1945 and Congress's imposition of conditions for a postwar loan that Britain could not meet, resulted in a decade of gritty austerity for the British that "proved increasingly depressing as victory in war receded. Indeed, their unacceptability eventually came to outweigh the popularity of the government's welfare measures" (Briggs, 275). As did nearly all of his compatriots, former airman James Herriot came home to miserable conditions. In 1947, the British shivered through a major national fuel crisis; two years later, the Labour government devalued the pound sterling from $4.04 to $2.80. Even bread was rationed between 1946 and 1948, and candy remained on the ration list until 1954. George Orwell's *1984,* published in 1949, extrapolated the welfare state to a dimension that must have sent chills down the spines of many British readers because they suspected it was more truth than fiction.

But the most important thing to Herriot, as it must have been for thousands of returning servicemen, was that he *was* home, with his wife and son and his new daughter Rosemary, born in May 1947. When Herriot came back to the Dales, he discovered that his profession was on the verge of a revolution that would change agriculture and veterinary medicine forever. He later described this period in *The Lord God Made Them All,* his fourth major book, which he insisted for a long time was the last that he would write.

As one of the opening salvos of Britain's twentieth-century agricultural revolution, the Agricultural Act of 1947 idealistically attempted to save farmers, whose profession places them at the mercy of the unpredictable elements, from insecurity. A more practical change was the Veterinary Surgeons' Act of 1948, which stopped unqualified persons from practicing veterinary medicine, as they had legally been able to do until that time. In addition, "miracle drugs" developed during the war, such as antibiotics for infectious diseases and steroids for stress-related ailments, were becoming available for veterinary use, and new cost-effective animal surgical procedures such as cesarean sections were coming into vogue. As a result, high-quality animal-protein food was becoming a bargain (Kingrey, 116), although because of postwar austerity programs British beef eaters would not enjoy all the animal protein they wanted for some time.

In the postwar period, an unusual and widespread visceral reaction seems to have contributed to Britain's increased legislative and scientific attention to agriculture. A British Council booklet published in 1946 noted "a remarkable interest in writing which discussed agricultural planning, and which often went far deeper than the practice of agriculture into a kind of 'religion of the soil' which might arise from a subliminal fear of the destructive power of modern technology."[25] A simpler, more positive, and just as profound explanation might lie in Herriot's conviction that the hard life of the Dales farm folk fostered a fundamental goodness of spirit marked by cheerfulness, hospitality, patience, and above all integrity, a combination that opposed the evils of present-day civilization.

Such evils were becoming rampant in Britain by 1950. Infused with substantial U.S. Marshall Plan aid from 1948 to 1951, Britain was emerging from postwar austerity only to reel from disasters abroad and at home. Former colonies, notably India, demanded and received their independence, while yet another international crisis, the Korean War of 1950–53, erupted. On the domestic scene most of the traditional norms of British life seemed to be disintegrating. By 1950 only 10 percent of Britons were regular churchgoers; wave after wave of nonwhite immigrants was arriving, causing interracial strains in underemployed urban areas; and crime was on a ferocious upsurge. In Yorkshire the rate of indictable crimes reached a new peak, committed by one out of fifty youths between the ages of 14 and 18 (Briggs, 282), a moral breakdown fictionalized by William Golding in his horrifying 1954 fable *The Lord of the Flies*. In 1950, a third of British homes lacked bathrooms, although by 1955, 92 percent of the population had access to television, a proportion of cleanliness to mass entertainment symptomatic of a national spiritual malaise that was typified by the decade's prevalent literary theme, "the outsider" alienated from his society. A sensitive man such as Herriot must have been appalled at the conditions he saw when he visited his boyhood home, "dear old Glasgow town," reeling from urban atrocities perpetrated by "a runted, stunted violent minority of low intelligent quotient; the 'boys' or 'lads' who start fights at football matches, daub bus-shelters and buildings with aerosol paint sprays, slash the seats of railway carriages, scatter litter and broken glass about, and generally indulge in the sort of mindless behaviour that leaps into television features and shouts from newspaper headlines, unjustly smearing the reputation of the whole city in the eyes of the world beyond" (Lindsay, 281).

Physical labor tends to de-emphasize self-absorption, however, and in the hard rural life of the Dales, societal changes arrived more slowly than in Britain's cities and suburban areas. Money was still scarce; by the end of the 1940s, which he described in *The Lord God Made Them All,* Herriot recorded the average rural veterinarian's wage in 1948 as £10 a week (*LGMTA,* 195). He was also just beginning to experience the sort of scientific changes that he could welcome with open arms. In the last years of the 1940s, Herriot could effect astonishing cures with the new "miracle drugs," and he was able to help stamp out such previously fearsome diseases as swine fever with new vaccines. The bovine mainstay of the Dales, the dairy-beef shorthorn breed, was giving way to the higher milk-producing Holstein-Friesians, dehorning was becoming stylish, and artificial insemination was tentatively beginning to reduce the veterinarian's risky traffic with uncooperative bulls. Herriot, who often noted in his books how much he detested change, found himself becoming a pioneer in a small way simply because he and his partners had to try out new things in order to carry on their work.

Despite intermittent attacks of brucellosis, Herriot was living the life he most wanted to live, busy with his growing family, his dogs, and his work. By the early 1950s, he decided he had to get his wife out of the charming but antiquated and "woman-killing" multistory building that housed the practice, so the Herriots moved to a small town house for some years, and in the 1970s, after he had become a famous writer, to the bungalow they called Mire Beck in the hills east of Thirsk, near the village of Thirlby. Tristan Farnon, after practicing briefly at Thirsk with his brother Siegfried and Herriot, left to take a position with the Ministry of Agriculture, and the growing practice made it necessary for Herriot and Siegfried to employ a succession of assistants beginning with John Crooks, a talented young vet who worked with them from 1951 to 1954 and became Herriot's close friend. Herriot never wrote much about Crooks, possibly because Crooks went on to national eminence in their profession. Herriot put his stories about his next assistant, the colorful Calum Buchanan, into *Every Living Thing,* the last of Herriot's major books. *Every Living Thing* describes their practice in the mid-1950s, when life even in Britain's remotest villages, like the towns of the Dales, was being wrenched from its traditional foundations not by war or austerity but by what Kingsley Amis called "the greatest single vulgarizing influence on our national life" (Shaw and Shaw, 13)—commercial television.

In the 1960s, vulgarization had overtaken Britain. The Commonwealth had dwindled away and Britain's once-mighty industry and technology were floundering. The British missile and nuclear programs swiftly proved outmoded; the much-vaunted Comet jet airliner flopped; and though England had pioneered in computer design, microchip development soon fled to Silicon Valley and Japan. In British homes, spending, not saving, became the order of British days, made infinitely simpler and more alluring by the Betting and Gambling Act of 1960, which legalized gaming clubs. Traditionalists bemoaned the threat to educational standards they felt was offered by the new no-entrance-requirements Open University system, which with the host of new state-supported universities—eight had sprung up by 1963—doubled enrollment in higher education while offering a hotbed for the New Left, spawning campus revolts and drug experimentation. The new permissiveness launched such tradition-shattering phenomena as Mary Quant's miniskirts, the Beatles, teddy boys, the first wave of skinheads, and unbridled rioting at football matches. Agriculture felt the culture shock, too: newly body-conscious housewives were clamoring for smaller and leaner cuts of meat, and the development of new drugs and vaccines for large-animal use dropped suddenly because of widespread concern over drug residues and environmental pollution. Rural veterinarians like Herriot and Farnon found themselves plunged into small-animal care instead of the large-animal work to which they had devoted most of their working lives.

Overall, amusement, wickedly defined as "the happiness of those who cannot think" (Shaw and Shaw, 13), had become the product of Britain's popular media-borne culture, but James Herriot did not seem to have been amused in this sense at all. In 1961 and 1963, perhaps in part to escape changes he deplored, and perhaps to pursue a change of pace he felt he needed, Herriot took up John Crooks's two offers of trips abroad as a traveling veterinarian. The first trip took Herriot by ship to Lithuania, then a part of the Soviet Union, and the second trip took him to Istanbul via an antiquated cargo plane that later crashed, killing its entire crew. Herriot included his diary entries for both trips in *The Lord God Made Them All,* though they do not follow his chronology for the rest of the book, which covers his life to about 1950. Midway through the 1960s, faced as were many parents with his children's university expenses, Herriot was casting about for possible sources of additional income, but his second career—however successful it eventually turned out to be—did not come easily.

At around age 50, Herriot returned to one of his first and, as it proved, strongest suits, the talent for writing he had demonstrated during his school days, even while he was grinding his way through science and mathematics. After he became famous, Herriot invariably told interviewers the following story about the birth of his writing career, attributing it to his wife's forthright intervention:

> The life of a country vet was dirty, uncomfortable, sometimes danger-ous. It was terribly hard work and I loved it. I felt vaguely that I ought to write about it and every day for twenty-five years I told my wife of something funny that had happened and said I was keeping it for the book. She usually said "Yes, dear" to humour me but one day, when I was fifty, she said: "Who are you kidding? Vets of fifty don't write first books."

That did it, Herriot said: "I stormed out and bought some paper and taught myself to type" (*SATA,* 170).

Looking back on his books, Herriot also said he had felt compelled to record "a fascinating era in veterinary practice" (*BJH,* intro.), but get-ting his first stories onto paper proved more trying for Herriot than the breech delivery of a Holstein bull calf:

> Then [in 1966] I started to put it all down and the story didn't work. All I managed to pick out on the machine was a very amateur school essay. So I spent a year or two learning my craft, as real writers say. I read *How to Be a Writer* and *Teach Yourself to Write* and I bombarded newspapers, magazines, and the BBC with unreadable short stories. They came back, every one, without a word of comment. Not even "You show promise." There's a special noise that a rejected manuscript makes when it comes through the letter-box and hits the doormat. It's more recognisable than that of a ewe in labour or a cow with a prolapsed uterus. I would call it a sick thud and it was a noise I learned to hate.

Then I read Salinger and Hemingway and Dickens and Conan Doyle, all with a learner's eye. In the end, I got away from my awful Macaulay's essays style, with its beautifully balanced sentences and florid adjectives. And I learned the art of flashbacks from Budd Schulberg's book about Scott Fitzgerald, *The Disenchanted*. (*SATA*, 170)

Herriot had to snatch spare moments for his writing from his full-time veterinary work, typing out his stories in front of the television set as he watched British football, another of his passions. About 18 months after he began writing, Herriot had a book-length manuscript, and he thought first of the London publisher Michael Joseph, who had done a series called *Doctor in the House*. He took a friend's advice, though, and sent the manuscript elsewhere, where it languished another year and a half. "Finally the book came back. . . . I threw it in a drawer and it would have been there to this day if Joan hadn't ordered me to take it out and do something with it" (Gonzalez, *M*, 6). Herriot sent the book to an agent, who placed it within a week with Michael Joseph, and Joseph published it in 1970 as *If Only They Could Talk*, under the pen name "James Herriot"—a necessity because the British veterinary profession considered advertising unethical. Herriot commented, "There was this fellow playing such a good game of soccer for Birmingham that I just took his name" (Gonzalez, *SR*, 58).

If Only They Could Talk sold a meager 1,200 copies, and Herriot's second batch of stories, *It Shouldn't Happen to a Vet* (1972), seemed headed for the same literary oblivion. Later that year, though, America gave Herriot his real breakthrough, which Herriot attributed to a special affinity Americans have for his work. In 1986 he observed that his stories "are not just funny animal tales. They're about tough pioneering days and hardbitten old farmers," and he added, "Because they come from pioneering stock themselves, the Americans saw that at once" (Gonzalez, *SR*, 58).

Thomas McCormack, president of St. Martin's Press, discovered Herriot's work on a buying trip to London in 1972. *If Only They Could Talk* initially gave McCormack "a sinking feeling," and the book sat around his home unread for four months. When his wife finally insisted that he read it, McCormack was entranced. He bought both books from Michael Joseph, combined them into a single volume, and got Herriot to cap it with the perfect happy ending, the story of his wooing and winning his wife. Independently of one another, Herriot and McCormack had both come across an Anglican hymn that each felt might supply a new and more effective title:

All things bright and beautiful,
All creatures great and small,
All things wise and wonderful,
The Lord God made them all.

McCormack wanted to use the second line, but Herriot preferred "All Creatures Great and Small." McCormack observed, "He's such a talented writer, but he just can't do titles"—and the publisher won (Freilicher, 53).

When *All Creatures Great and Small* soared to the top of American best-seller lists early in 1973, Herriot was shocked. After a few months, he claimed "it was almost too much of a success" (*SATA,* 171). Although he did his best to conceal his identity and to disguise his country practice, hordes of Americans began to comb the Yorkshire Dales for Darrowby and their favorite author, leaving Herriot bemused by a degree of fame he never sought and always deplored. "They track me down even though I've never mentioned the exact location of the vet's practice. I've even trained the local people to point in the wrong direction when admirers find the town and ask where I am" (*SATA,* 171). Herriot's wife, now "a handsome white-haired woman," did not put up with tourists and journalists: "Alf is too kind. I send them packing."[26]

In 1974, after *All Creatures Great and Small* had sold over a million paperback copies, St. Martin's brought out Herriot's next two British-published books, *Let Sleeping Vets Lie* and *Vet in Harness,* as *All Things Bright and Beautiful.* Herriot's wartime reminiscences, *Vets Might Fly* and *Vet in a Spin,* followed in 1977 as *All Things Wise and Wonderful,* and *The Lord God Made Them All* appeared in 1981. Herriot had little to do with either David Susskind's filming of the first movie version of *All Creatures Great and Small* in 1974, or the first television serial under the same name, screened by the BBC in 1978, though Herriot deeply approved of the projects and admired the actors involved. In recognition of Herriot's achievements, Edinburgh's Heriot-Watt University made him an honorary doctor of letters, and the Prince of Wales conferred the OBE (Order of the British Empire) on him in 1979, the year that *James Herriot's Yorkshire* appeared. Herriot also began to adapt short episodes from his books as a well-received series of eight illustrated children's stories timed by his publishers to appear for Christmas sales each year, starting in 1984 with *Moses the Kitten* and continuing through *Smudge, the Little Lost Lamb* in 1991.

In the course of two publicity trips in the 1970s to the United States, Herriot had to endure the American literary promotion process, which unsettled him so much that except for private vacation trips he never left Britain again. In 1982, he was named a fellow of the Royal College of Veterinary Science, and in 1983 he received an honorary doctorate in veterinary science from Liverpool University. Until about 1988 or 1989, he continued to practice with his son Jimmy and Donald Sinclair at Thirsk, going out on calls in his modest, cluttered car with his Border terrier Bodie, happily ignoring his accountant's advice to move to a tax haven such as Ireland. Staying home and working as a veterinarian was an expensive luxury for Herriot because doing so forced him to pay about 83 percent of his income to the Inland Revenue.

Herriot claimed that he had always found writing hard (Gonzalez, *A*, 5), but during the last years of his life, writing became much more arduous because he had to watch the picturesque old Yorkshire farming characters slip away and their agricultural-institute-trained sons take their places. Even though he praised the new "generation of scientific agriculturalists" as "the most efficient farmers in the world," Herriot observed, "They are likable and they work harder than any people I have ever known, but they are not as much fun as their fathers" (*BJH*, intro.).

Most of Herriot's friends and the models for his favorite characters also left this world in the 1980s. Mrs. Marjorie Warner of Sowerby, the inspiration for the overstuffed Pekingese Tricki Woo's wealthy mistress Mrs. Pumphrey, died in 1983, leaving £90,000 for the care of needy elderly people in Yorkshire. Denton Petty, known in Herriot's books as "Granville Bennett," the hospitable veterinarian who got Herriot spectacularly drunk more than once, was now gone.[27] In 1989, Brian Sinclair ("Tristan"), who for some time had picked up a few dollars lecturing on his friendship with Herriot, and Calum Buchanan, "the vet wi' the badger," died within a few weeks of each other. Herriot's son Jimmy is now senior partner in the veterinary practice at Thirsk, where Herriot's daughter, Rosemary Page, a physician, also practices, and Donald Sinclair, in his eighties, still lives in the vicinity as well.

Herriot had claimed that *The Lord God Made Them All* would be his last book, but after he "more or less slid out" of his practice in 1989, the television producer of *All Creatures Great and Small* wanted to start the series up again, and Herriot bought a word processor and returned to his memoirs. Besides working on the television story lines, Herriot published *Every Living Thing* in 1992, his last full-length book, which covers his recollections of the mid-1950s.

In his next-to-last piece of writing, the introduction to *James Herriot's Cat Stories,* published in 1994, a collection drawn from his earlier books, Herriot seemed melancholy, referring to his veterinary work—and in the light of the prostate cancer that had overtaken him in 1992, perhaps his life—as "all over."[28] In 1994 he broke a leg trying to drive notoriously ill-tempered black-faced sheep out of his garden, and he must have been in considerable discomfort. Typically, he sustained his family and friends to the very end, and his friend John Crooks, who saw him shortly before his death, remarked that even then "his spirit was tremendous" (Daniel, 33).

However much he might have wanted to, James Herriot, like any living being, could never stop the changes that transformed the world around him, but he wove his life and memories into his stories of Yorkshire's folk and beasts, creating a "sweet, safe place to be" as a comforting and lasting antidote to our hectic times.

Chapter Two
All Creatures Great and Small

> The animals want to communicate with man. But Wakan-Tanka does not intend that they should do so directly. Man must do the greater part in securing an understanding.
>
> —Brave Buffalo, Standing Rock Reservation

In one of modern publishing's great ironies, James Herriot's first books seemed to be headed for polite oblivion when they first appeared in England. By the British literary standards of the early 1970s, the stories that an overworked Yorkshire veterinarian pecked out on his portable typewriter—realistic tales of bygone times, rustic characters, and old-fashioned values—belonged to a genre that London literati considered hopelessly passé after two world wars, when Britain, like the rest of the West, had lost its innocence.

During the dreary postwar years, British living conditions and British art were locked in a fatal embrace that for years showed no tendency to break apart. Shortly before his death in 1946, the historian H. G. Wells deplored "the tremendous series of events [that] had forced upon the intelligent observer the realisation that the human story has already come to an end and that *homo sapiens,* as he has been pleased to call himself, is in his present form played out."[1] Britain's postwar troubles seemed to confirm Wells's pessimism. Shortages and rationing, strikes, unemployment and crime, floods of unskilled immigrants, loss of international prestige, and, most unsettling of all, the atomic bomb in the hands of both the United States and the Soviet Union, former allies now distrusted about equally by some Britons, all contributed to the gloomy atmosphere that permeated British art.

After World War II, British critics recognized no literary successors to the greats who had written in English during the 1920s and 1930s—writers such as D. H. Lawrence, James Joyce, and William Butler Yeats. By establishing the Arts Council in 1946, the Labour government hoped to bring art to the masses, but like most state-supported aesthetic ventures, the results failed to live up to expectations. For years, most council-sponsored productions exuded a sour combination of defeat and alienation summed up in the term "the Midlands disease," which paired deteriorating British morale with the waning of Britain's industrial productivity.

The pessimism and skepticism rampant in British artistic and intellectual life following World War II closely accompanied a general decline in spiritual values. Writing in *The Cambridge Cultural History* (1988), Gilbert Phelps declared flatly, "all post-war English literature has been overshadowed by a sense of social and cultural disintegration and of the ever-present threat of violence and chaos. . . . negative approaches [to art] are clearly related to erosion of former humanistic moral values . . . [with] a marked preoccupation with the forces of evil and the Gothic mode . . . [while] positive affirmations are rare in post-war English literature" (Phelps, 198, 204–5). Many British authors simply flailed at traditional positions and values that now seemed pointless. Evelyn Waugh's *Men at Arms* (1952) debunked the official patriotic myth, Kingsley Amis's *Lucky Jim* satirized British academic snobbery, and Nigel Dennis's *Cards of Identity* (1955) was an early novel of social alienation. A vicious cycle of artistic negativity thus set in; by reflecting only the all-too-true unpleasantness of contemporary life, bitter British novels and plays confirmed and maintained the hopelessness of it all in print and on the stage, in turn prodding disenchanted audiences into further antisocial behavior. Depressing works by angry young artists fueled their peers' protests against authority so ferociously that the prominent Cambridge critic F. R. Leavis, who like his Victorian predecessor Matthew Arnold wholeheartedly believed in the morality of art, insisted that this leveling of society would destroy nothing less than the nation's moral quality (Shaw and Shaw, 9).

As Wells had done in the late 1940s, Leavis came close to prophesying disaster for the anything-goes 1960s. In the dreary literary mainstream of that time, "condition of England" novels such as Margaret Drabble's *The Ice Age,* an exposé of societal greed, and sobering treatments of the empire's disintegration such as Paul Scott's *The Raj Quartet* (later televised as *The Jewel in the Crown*), were widely read, and even books of considerable literary worth depicted a worn-out lifestyle incapable of regeneration. On the outré fringe, British artists were doggedly exploring "the possibilities of sounds, materials, language and locations which had not hitherto been considered appropriate to art . . . [and] This could take extreme forms. In 1965 two artists even discussed the possibility of publicly disemboweling a human corpse and hurling the guts at the audience" (Shaw and Shaw, 26).

Fortunately for the sensibilities of the general public, however, a few positive artistic countercurrents to such revelations also appeared in the 1960s. Optimistic works appeared mostly in popular artistic genres, and several of these works enjoyed soaring sales, demonstrating just how disgusted the common reader had become with unbridled defeatism and sensationalism.

Probably the most widely read category of popular British fiction in the 1960s and 1970s was the fantasy quest, ignited by the immensely popular trilogy *The Lord of the Rings,* which became a cult sensation. The trilogy's author, Oxford don J. R. R. Tolkien, offered his British readers a "new myth for England" that he felt they deserved because they had persevered in World War II, a reassuringly clear-cut conflict between good and evil. Despite the fantasy trappings of his novels and the trilogy's elegiac ending, Tolkien's romantic idealism and his traditional ethical system, harking back to the Allies' "great crusade" against the Axis powers, proved a welcome change for a public dazed by unshorn and unclad young actors and musicians unabashedly committing all sorts of public atrocities in full frontal exposure. In addition, both Tolkien and his friend and fellow Christian scholar C. S. Lewis, author of *The Chronicles of Narnia,* convincingly portrayed animals and other nonhuman beings in novels sharing the traditional theme that all forms of life should exist in divinely established harmony.

The enormous popularity of these fantasy works added impetus to an ecological trend surfacing in the literature of many Western countries, ignited in great part by Rachel Carson's famous *Silent Spring.* Animal lovers and environmentalists believed that humanity would have to pay a heavy moral as well as physical price for destroying the natural world, a message that was soon fortified by unsentimentalized best-sellers such as Richard Adams's *Watership Down* and Russell Hoban's *Turtle Diary,* both told from the nonsentimentalized point of view of animals endangered by humanity's depredation of nature.

The initial stirrings of fictionalized ecology, most written in deadly earnest, coincided with James Herriot's unlikely advent on the literary scene. Herriot, however, had a singular talent that gave him an edge in the popular-fiction market: his unquenchable Glaswegian humor was tailor-made for telling the stories that he had been salting away for years about the earthy doings of animals and country folk. His good friend John Crooks recalled that riding out on calls with Herriot and his children was "a very happy place to be and a wonderful countryside, of course. Alf [Herriot] was always telling stories about what had happened to him that day. He had this wonderful sense of humor, and to be with him was at times absolutely hilarious" (Daniel, 32). Herriot himself commented later about his early years of practice, "There were so many laughs in all of this, so many characters, so many strange activities, that I wanted to put them all on paper" (Gonzalez, *A,* 37).

Because of the heavy pressures of his veterinary work, however, Herriot by age 50 had gotten no further than his occasional "I'll put that in the book one day" to his wife, who finally administered what he called the verbal "kick in the tail" that spurred him into action (Gonzalez, *A,* 37). For the next 18 months, Herriot wrote in "dribs and drabs," only to have his first book rejected. After it languished for another year and a half in a drawer, Mrs. Herriot again took a firm wifely hand, and the rest made publishing history.

Although Herriot's work fell neatly into the 1970s' ecological craze for animal-oriented tales and became a national best-seller in America immediately upon the publication of his first book there, Herriot always tried to shun the limelight. He preferred to ration out his memoirs in his books, and he was notoriously reluctant to give interviews. According to Ken Nickel, who twice tracked Herriot down for *Dog World,* "it is well known that tourists in his surgery are not James Herriot's favorite people. Even so, tourists are a cut above journalists because they take up much less of his time."[2] From the first flush of his unexpected popularity in the mid-1970s to the mid-1990s, when *James Harriot's Cat Stories* rocketed him again to the top 12 of the major best-seller lists, Herriot tried his best to keep clear of interviewers. When they did locate him, however, Herriot's responses were always courteous and consistent; and though he voiced his comments with sensible Scottish economy, they do open the gate to a fraction more of Herriot's private life than he offered in his books.

In 1978, Herriot admitted to journalist Arturo Gonzalez that a desire for "extra income" had been partially responsible for the veterinarian's decision to set his stories down on paper, and understandably so, because on his limited prebook income Herriot was putting his son, Jimmy, and his daughter, Rosemary, through veterinary and medical school respectively. For the most part, however, Herriot insisted in his interviews that his reason for writing was to preserve Yorkshire's traditional animal treatments dating from the prewar era, an era he found so fascinating (Gonzalez, *A,* 37). As time passed, though, money seems to have played only a small part in Herriot's continuing to write, just as well because of the heavy 83 percent tax burden he incurred by remaining in

Britain. Eventually his accountant told Herriot that of his six books, he had written five "for the tax man."[3] In fact, after taxes and a few modest luxuries such as a little yellow sports car for his wife, a high-quality stereo system for himself, and their bungalow-with-duck-pond at Thirlby, Herriot put most of his literary profits into a trust fund for his children, three granddaughters, and grandson.

In the early 1970s, when Herriot's first published books *If Only They Could Talk* and *It Shouldn't Happen to a Vet* arrived upon the confused and unstable British literary scene (Phelps, 207), each sold disappointingly—about 1,200 copies—and British critics politely damned the books with excruciatingly faint praise. In a 1972 portmanteau review called "Oh Sweet Content!" Britain's *New Statesman* lumped *It Shouldn't Happen to a Vet* ("agreeable and very funny") together with an account of the death of an early Arctic explorer ("sudden and fishy") and the memoirs of public hangman James Berry, who "had a store of merry Yorkshire anecdotes with which to tide over awkward pauses."[4]

Herriot knew very well what British reviewers thought of his work, but he was not writing for them. He observed that "Professional critics tend to be nice, but a bit condescending . . . They acknowledge that it sells, but manage to imply that it's all rather lightweight stuff, not too taxing on the intellect. I agree with them, actually."[5]

In 1973, however, torrents of praise were unleashed across the Atlantic for *All Creatures Great and Small,* comprising *If Only They Could Talk, It Shouldn't Happen to a Vet,* and a few additional chapters Herriot added at the request of Thomas McCormack, president of St. Martin's Press. Herriot cleverly rounded off the book with new material, the romantic story of his proposal to his wife, "with the help of a shove from his veterinary partner, Siegfried" (Freilicher, 53). McCormack recalled that he had trouble selling the paperback rights to this book; the paperback houses "thought it would be just another doctor's memoirs, and not even a people doctor at that. But Bantam was extremely perceptive and got reprint rights for a mere $50,000" (Freilicher, 53).

All Creatures Great and Small immediately struck a nerve in the U.S. public. In February 1973, *Time*'s William Doerner rhapsodized over the irresistible simplicity of *All Creatures Great and Small:*

> What the world needs now, and does every so often, is a warm, G-rated, down-home, unadrenalized prize of a book that sneaks onto the best-seller list for no apparent appeal other than a certain floppy-eared puppy appeal. . . . Dr. Herriot . . . clearly and fondly knows the two-footed

creatures on his rounds as well as the four-footed. The result is a collection of word pictures of rural Britain in the 1930s . . . windswept, hard-scrabble farms run by families who need their animals for transport, income, or food.[6]

Almost concurrently, in *The New York Times Book Review,* Nelson Bryant approached a definition of Herriot's formula for literary success:

> Herriot's book is more than a collection of well-told anecdotes and sharply drawn personalities. Laced through it is the author's growing awareness that he is in the right place doing the right thing. . . . Herriot charms because he delights in life, embraces it with sensitivity and gusto and writes with grace. Reading him, one is reminded that there are still . . . country places where the wind blows clean, places where men and women find pleasure in hard work and simple living.[7]

Herriot was amazed at the eruption of praise for *All Creatures Great and Small* in the United States (*SATA,* 112), and because his readers there gave him his first, biggest, and most-lasting fame, he always maintained that "The Americans have been very kind to me" (Nickel, "Trek," 19), one reason he did not close his doors to American fans until his final years. Although he often said that his aim was "to write stories as if they were being told at a country pub,"[8] Herriot also stressed that his stories were "not just funny animal tales" (Gonzalez, *SR,* 58), and Americans usually agreed. Due to Americans' pioneering heritage and their appreciation of the wide-open spaces, a special affinity for Herriot's work seems to run deep in the national psyche. The impressive sales of *James Herriot's Cat Stories* in 1994 and 1995 shows that the American audience is still taking Herriot's stories—his celebrations of the rural life and its values, his portrayals of a wide range of human and animal Dales residents, his devotion to his challenging profession, and his infatuation with the beauty of the land itself—into their hearts.

British reaction to Herriot's work, at least at first, seems to have been tempered as much by ingrained social attitudes as by their reviewers' penchant for understatement. Even in today's Britain, a sizable gulf remains between the horse-riding and the horse-tending (not to mention the horseless) classes. To more democratic American eyes, many of those Britishers who own the land still seem to look down upon both those who work it and those who tend the animals that share the land with them. Although veterinary medicine anywhere is still one of the most exhausting modern professions, it does not enjoy the prestige in

Britain that it does elsewhere, especially in the United States. The average British veterinarian, like his American counterpart, probably does not care much "what door he is shown so long as he can cure animals." However, according to one British observer (who possibly had not witnessed the grueling work most rural American veterinarians still face), the British vet must sometimes wistfully ponder the "main worry" of a colleague who has sought greener transatlantic pastures—that worry being "to find the nearest airstrip for his private plane. He [the emigrating veterinarian] practices in America where everyone calls him Doctor."[9]

The gulf between the social status of British and American veterinarians is not the only factor that contributed to the differing initial receptions that America and Britain gave Herriot's work. The Yorkshire Dales occupy a position in Britain roughly analogous to the northern Great Plains of the United States; both regions are largely made up of sparsely populated rural areas geographically isolated from major cities and endure harsh climatic conditions for most of the year. Many of the people who inhabit these regions still share a heavily agricultural lifestyle, values, and economy, a Scandinavian cultural heritage, and the hardy pioneering impulse Herriot liked to celebrate in his stories. In addition, both the Dales and the Great Plains have seen considerable downsizing of their rural populations. Between 1946 and the 1970s, British policy makers developed "New Towns" as "a tool for redistributing the British urban population," and in the 1960s and 1970s, the British population shifted increasingly from farming areas toward jobs in bustling Southern metropolitan areas and the "good life" of "medium-rise maisonettes."[10]

When Herriot's first books appeared in the 1970s, his descriptions of the simple rural Yorkshire life far removed from such modernities as "maisonettes" coincided with an American craze for all the manifestations of cozy (and possibly mythical) country living. This trend had little to do with leftover flower children still inhabiting rural communes. Instead of blearily contemplating their navels and discussing "life," Herriot's suburban U.S. readers pored over layouts in women's magazines of country kitchens festooned with checked gingham curtains and spotless copper pots dangling over resurrected iron ranges, and they plunged rapturously into crocheted granny afghans and relentlessly combed family trees for agrarian ancestors. Herriot's scenes of prewar rural Yorkshire suited this cheery pattern as neatly as a well-callused hand fits a well-worn gardening glove, and many episodes of his books became *Good Housekeeping*'s annual Christmas gift to the magazine's readers. To an

American public aching for "good old days" that quite possibly never were and fervently wishing that crimes resulting from the drug scene and the horrors of the Vietnam War would somehow vanish from their television sets, *All Creatures Great and Small* offered a welcome reason for shutting off the nightly news, picking up a book, and escaping to the comparative security of the past.

Everywhere in Herriot's Yorkshire there are reminders of a simpler past that strongly appeals to American readers. Over the years, the most distinctive feature that human beings have added to the landscape of the Yorkshire Dales is the crazy-quilt pattern of gray drystone fences, built entirely without mortar, that have marked ownership of Yorkshire farms since the sixteenth century. Today such wall construction is becoming a lost art, but Yorkshire's rambling stone fence lines testify to their builders' skill and perseverance and the straight-shooting work ethic that many Scandinavians brought from Norway and Sweden when they came a-viking to England's northern coasts in the ninth and tenth centuries and settled down to farm in a more hospitable climate than they had left behind.

Scandinavian physical features and personality traits still crop up in Yorkshire's populace, and as Herriot continually demonstrated in his stories, the old Scandinavian traditions of fair play, hard work, and fidelity to one's word—as well as a reluctance to part with hard-earned cash and a hardheadedness that borders on the bombproof—linger on the Dales. Herriot called the farmers he served "the salt of the earth," and he badly wanted to pass his memories of them on to posterity.

When the notion of celebrating humble Dales people encouraged the fiftyish Thirsk veterinarian J. A. Wight to teach himself to write, he gradually created an engaging alter ego for himself. At the very least, he had to take a pen name because the stringent code of professional conduct shared by the British and American veterinary associations strictly barred their members from any sort of advertising. In addition, Herriot, who became president of the Yorkshire Veterinarian Society in 1973, was sensitive to the necessity of maintaining a favorable reputation for his profession, which had struggled for a long time to overcome the unsavory image of the "horse doctor." In 1978, American veterinary historian B. W. Kingrey commented on the profession's "unusual" preoccupation with "the matter of ethics":

[We] may have been a bit stuffy about the subject. If there is an unusual fierceness and jealousy concerning the code of ethics ascribed to by the veterinary profession, however, it might best be understood as a sensitive reaction to an unattractive public image earned by earlier self-proclaimed animal doctors, cow leeches, farriers and gelders with their empirical and often destructive remedies . . . [who] did manage to establish themselves quite firmly at about the bottom of the social order. (Kingrey, 115)

Beyond preserving fascinating stories from his early days of practice and thereby enhancing the reputation for hard work and integrity he felt was basic to his profession, veterinarian Alf Wight had no long-range profoundly theoretical drum to beat when he took on the persona of James Herriot. "As for me," Herriot modestly claimed, "I was the colourless, heavily intimidated character I describe. Damon Runyon had a guy who simply lived on Broadway and observed the life around him and that's me" (SATA, 172).

As it turned out, though, even in All Creatures Great and Small, James Herriot became a more complex literary character than his creator might originally have intended. Herriot the author supplied the grand-fatherly perspective that anchored his recorded experiences on his youthful self, a character who might have begun as a humble observer, but matured and became much more interesting as the books progress. In All Creatures Great and Small, the oldest Mr. Herriot—the author— remained mostly behind the scenes, but his good-natured presence occa-sionally intruded in observations such as "There has always been a 'this is where I came in' feeling about a night call" (ACGS, 482). This unusual dual perspective greatly increases the appeal of the Herriot books. As Herriot the author looked back upon his youth and presented it in the light of his older self, "The young man is made more likable by being blended with the narrator's thirty additional years of aware-ness."[11]

Structurally, the episodes of All Creatures Great and Small roughly fol-low Herriot's first two years of practice, but because he was partial to— and mastered—the flashback technique and generally did not bother to date his episodes precisely, the casual chronology of his tales rambles like the stone fences that wind up and down the Dales. In All Creatures Great and Small, the author occasionally added glimpses of other James Her-riots besides the "young vit'nery" in his first two years of work, includ-ing the teenage Herriot just beginning his veterinary studies in Glas-gow, and the young man a few years further into his practice who looks back to his earliest "vetting" days. After Herriot used this multiple per-spective successfully in All Creatures Great and Small, he continued the device throughout the rest of his major books, giving a multidimensional texture to his autobiographical story line.

Besides the appealing portraits of himself as variously aged young vets, Herriot the new author immediately hit upon what proved a sure-fire formula for his major books, each of which contains about two years' worth of anecdotes. Because Herriot usually had less than an hour at a time to write, his chapters are generally brief. Most of them can stand alone as separate stories, but some, such as the chapters in *All Creatures Great and Small* describing his courtship of Helen, fall into groups, each with its own continuing story line. Herriot sometimes scattered component episodes throughout larger narratives or carried others, such as the continuing saga of Tricki Woo, the wealthy Mrs. Pumphrey's pampered Pekingese, into his later books.

As well as tending to be self-contained units, most of Herriot's chapters usually follow the time-honored literary recipe for successfully unified short fiction. Herriot introduced one central character per episode, often starting out in the traditional middle of things. The arresting first scene of *All Creatures Great and Small* begins with young Herriot sprawled on a freezing stone barn floor, wrestling a calf out of an exhausted cow, and wondering why he had ever wanted to become a vet—an irresistible opening that compelled his readers to turn the pages. In each episode, Herriot caught his characters up in one major action, often humorous, occasionally sad, but always absorbing, in which the youthful Herriot coped with both a veterinary problem and the human complications that it entailed. Herriot posed the difficult lives of his people against one constantly fascinating backdrop, the Yorkshire Dales, an area relatively untouched in literature until his books, and he meticulously intertwined the smaller themes of his individual episodes into one paramount message: wholeheartedly tackling and overcoming the challenges of a simple existence can help heal people from the wounds modern civilization inflicts on them.

Herriot's finely tuned ear for local dialect also added invaluable authenticity to his tales. While recordings reveal the soft, attractive Scots burr that Herriot never lost, he was instinctively able, like Dickens, one of several favorite authors he adopted as his literary guides, to convey the whole range of Yorkshire speech patterns—down-to-earth conversations in stone barns, exclamations proper to the taproom at the Drovers' Arms, and the elevated chat of Mrs. Pumphrey's drawing room. Herriot's facility with language even extended to his patients' vocalizations, sounds absolutely vital to his veterinary observation and practice: the "soft, careful cough" of a tubercular cow (*ACGS,* 297), or the "reassuring bubbling" of a healthy bovine stomach (*ACGS,* 420).

In *All Creatures Great and Small,* Herriot convincingly portrayed interactions between the Dales people and their environment to give the book one of its greatest strengths: "each [tale] bears the stamp of the Dales and an individual's coping . . . The setting of the Dales . . . proves capable of revealing character in new ways, similar to the ways it has shaped each Dales individual" (Gardner, 634). Herriot had a special spot in his heart for the folk of the small Dales farms and villages. The Dales people were almost always touchingly generous despite their poverty. As in many Scandinavians, the stern exteriors of Herriot's people usually hid genuinely friendly hearts, similar to the upper-Midwestern American descendants of the Vikings who, when pressed, will admit to finding something so funny they almost laughed out loud. Even though at first young Herriot was an untried Scottish stranger to them, and his clients tended to be slow in paying their fees, they usually shared what they had with him—a glass of beer, a farm supper, a warm loaf of bread or a slab of home-cured bacon. Sometimes the hospitality of the Dales proved almost more than Herriot could bear. For example, in one case of "life on the old age pension" that Herriot recorded in *All Creatures Great and Small,* when he refused payment for ending the suffering of old Mr. Dean's aged Labrador, Mr. Dean gave Herriot the only thing he had to give, a tattered cigar (*ACGS,* 85).

The higher up in the Dales, Herriot said, the better he liked the people for their hospitality, simplicity, dignity, and independence (*ACGS,* 76). His admiration, however, never caused him to lose his humorous objectivity, which he was able to bring to bear on man and beast alike. During a particularly dramatic rumenectomy on a cow that had swallowed a nail, young Herriot gleefully provided his audience of hired men with a running commentary of such vivid clinical detail that one amateur assistant, a hefty Viking, passed out cold. When another assistant, who aspired to his own veterinary practice, fainted during a problematic pig castration, Herriot accidentally hit upon a surefire socioeconomic means of immediate resuscitation: pretend to shortchange a frugal Dales farmer and he will rise up "ashenfaced but alert and glaring" (*ACGS,* 331).

In *All Creatures Great and Small,* Herriot invariably sketched his minor characters, such as the fainting Viking and the revived swine farmer, with economy and good humor. To Herriot's literary credit, he never took the easy way out of an episode by using stereotypes. He always saw other sides and saving graces to his characters, even the occasional Dales grouch such as the miserly Mr. Skipton, whose motive for laboriously providing a peaceful retirement for two useless old plow horses could, Herriot believed, "only have been love" (*ACGS,* 324). In another vividly unwholesome character, the sullen Mr. Sidlow, who practiced horrifying home remedies and called in the veterinarian only when a hapless beast was about to die, the author still managed to create a convincing three-dimensional personality. As members of a fanatical religious sect, Sidlow and his family could have proven to be young Herriot's nemesis by embittering him about human nature. On the contrary, however, even when Sidlow blasted Herriot's shaky self-esteem and kept him from placing a bet on a hot tip at the racetrack and winning £50—a fortune to a starting veterinarian in the late 1930s—Herriot the author rescued the situation by finding something to laugh at: his own younger self.

Much of the humor Herriot incorporated into *All Creatures Great and Small* stemmed from the fascinating three-cornered friendship between Herriot and the brothers Farnon, characters based on his veterinary partners Donald and Brian Sinclair, a relationship cleverly summed up in "Siegfried" and "Tristan," the affectionately ironic names Herriot gave his partners in his books. German music was, of course, politically incorrect in World War I England. As professional musicians, though, Herriot's parents would have been familiar with the towering works of the German composer Richard Wagner and had likely given Herriot an early acquaintance with Wagnerian opera, the flamboyant quintessence of German romanticism. To many irreverent observers, the vast scale and mythological scope of Wagner's "music-dramas," horned-helmeted gods and grandiosely girthed goddesses and all, convey a whiff of the ridiculous—perhaps the same kind of reaction a magnificently pawing and snorting bull provokes in visitors who are safely behind a sturdy fence. At any rate, Herriot the Scotsman underscored the colorful personalities of two of the closest English friends he made in the Yorkshire Dales with the names of two of Wagner's most dramatic characters.

Wagner's Siegfried was the ideal Germanic hero, the central figure of the mammoth four-opera cycle *The Ring of the Nibelung,* a mighty warrior and magnificent horseman, conqueror of the dragon Fafnir and tragic lover of the redoubtable warrior maiden Brunhilde. Donald Sinclair, who had bought the Thirsk veterinary practice a few years before Herriot answered Sinclair's advertisement for an assistant, was for Herriot at first and always the perfect image of an English gentleman: a loyal friend and consummate horseman, sure-handed with the equine practice that Herriot dreaded; in *All Creatures Great and Small,* a chivalric ladies' man; the stalwart victor in a mighty conflict with his dragonish bookkeeper Miss Harbottle; and an operatically unreasonable older brother driven to larger-than-life distraction by his younger brother, whom Herriot named "Tristan" after one of the most famous fools for love in the world's romantic literature.

Siegfried Farnon is one of Herriot's most thoroughly realized characters, because Herriot kaleidoscopically revealed a different feature to his partner's complex personality nearly every time Siegfried appeared. At their first meeting, Herriot showed his aristocratic boss as being gracefully amused at Herriot's discomfiture when Siegfried literally caught him napping. A little later, Herriot pictured Siegfried as overcome with childlike delight when showing off the trappings of their profession, the drugs in his dispensary and the medieval-looking instruments that veterinarians used at the time. In *All Creatures Great and Small,* Siegfried terrified Herriot with his high-speed driving on the steep country roads of the Dales but also awed his partner-to-be with an intellectual grasp of their profession and its potential. Siegfried's mercurial nature sank to its depths in the fits of temper to which Tristan continually provoked him, a feature of their relationship that Herriot initially found unsettling but later accepted as a game that provided both brothers and himself—and his readers—considerable pleasure.

From 1938 to 1939, the period of *All Creatures Great and Small,* Brian Sinclair was sporadically completing his veterinary studies and helping out in his brother's practice between romantic escapades and protracted visits to local watering holes. Wagner's handsome young Tristan is a dangerous charmer who, while fetching his uncle's bride to Cornwall, quite justifiably provoked his uncle's wrath by inadvertently sharing a magic potion with her and causing bride and Tristan to fall fatally in love. Herriot's high-spirited young Tristan, just as ingratiating as the Wagnerian original to everyone except his long-suffering older brother, constantly earned Siegfried's outraged reprimands but seemed incapable of learning anything from the experiences. After Herriot's books became best-sellers and Brian Sinclair had retired, Sinclair lectured frequently about "his life with James Herriot" (*SATA,* 172). He also jokingly maintained that "ninety percent" of Herriot's stories "are true, [but] the ten percent about me were not."[12]

In *All Creatures Great and Small,* the youthful Herriot often found himself at dead center of Wagnerian, Götterdämmerung-scale explo-

sions set off by Siegfried's volatile reactions to Tristan's escapades, allowing readers to see and appreciate the best and worst of both brothers. In
this book, young Herriot was usually a bemused observer of Tristan's
scrapes, old enough to deplore his friend's exam-failing and pub-crawl-
ing, but young and sometimes restless enough himself to become a
reluctant participant in Tristan's pursuit of wine, women, and song,
with some humorously disastrous results.

For the Siegfried-Herriot segment of this triple relationship, the
author seemed to have adapted a famous partnership from one of his
favorite detective-story authors, Arthur Conan Doyle. In Conan Doyle's
popular mystery novels, Sherlock Holmes was "the dream-paradigm of
the brilliant decadent, cunningly written from a non-decadent point of
view."[13] In *All Creatures Great and Small*, Herriot's younger self often
played a stolid Dr. Watson to Siegfried's brilliant, dedicated, and erratic
Holmes, a literary debt that may explain the inconsistencies Herriot
shows in Siegfried, whom one commentator somewhat testily sees as "an
eccentric, overly intelligent, glib lady-killer who can be absurdly angry,
absurdly patient, or even vicious. He never notices his inconsistencies, is
always confident, yet is often forgetful and inattentive . . . [but] ultimately is a man of principle" (Gardner, 634).

Though Herriot's Siegfried never stooped to the decadence of the
rule-bending, cocaine-addicted Sherlock Holmes, Siegfried's diagnostic
brilliance and acute medical insight resembled Holmes's deductive powers. Siegfried's insight sometimes bordered on the esoteric, as in the
miraculous medieval bleeding cure he effected on a gypsy pony. Written
from Herriot's down-to-earth viewpoint, such episodes also illustrate
one of the aspects of his profession that most intrigued Herriot over the
years. He called it "black magic" or "witchcraft," the often inexplicable
metaphysical element that sometimes enters into the dealings physicians
have with their patients.

Herriot often sighed over those mysterious prewar treatments: "Oh,
those old black magic days with their exotic, largely useless medicines
reeking of witchcraft" (*BJH,* intro.), but his memories of such procedures were necessarily ambivalent. As a veterinarian, Herriot had to
rejoice that the old days when the best a physician could do was stand
by and hope for the best were "gone for good," but as a writer, he said,
"I mourn their passing" (*BJH,* intro.). When Herriot began practicing in
the Dales, he noted that "a veterinarian was practically a practitioner in
black magic. Farmers would stick an onion up the backside of a sick animal hoping to cure it, and the vet would be labeled a miracle-worker

because he'd pull out the onion and the animal would get better"
(*SATA,* 167).

As a matter of fact, witchcraft, in both its sinister black-magic sense
and the white-magic sense of folk medicine for men and beasts, flour-
ished for a long time in Yorkshire, particularly in its more remote northern areas. Thirsk was the site of civil court sessions, held four times a
year, well before 1736, when Parliament abolished the harsh laws
against witchcraft instituted by James I. According to Mary Williams,
an amateur North Yorkshire historian, "We were a lot less cruel to our
witches than they seem to have been in other parts of England and we
were kindness itself compared with Scotland or the Continent where
many thousands of witches suffered a cruel death" (Williams, 64).
Records indicate that the Thirsk quarter sessions were notoriously more
severe in penalizing the white (nonmalevolent) variety of witch. Supposedly God-fearing Christians might be more tempted to consult wise
men or wise women for success in love, good crops, or cures of animal
ailments than the more malignant black witches, thought to be responsible for the casting of potent evil spells (Williams, 22). In one Yorkshire
tale, Edward Kelley, a notable Yorkshire practitioner of witchcraft in the
1570s who was an assistant to the infamous Elizabethan black magician
Dr. Dee, necromantically evoked the spirit of a dead man in the church-
yard of Wootton-in-the-Dale to find a buried treasure.[14]

More recent magical activities were recorded by North Yorkshire historians Richard Blakeborough of Guisborough (1850–1918) and Canon
John C. Atkinson of Danby (1814–1900) who enthusiastically "went
round country districts gathering stories from senior citizens about local
witches who had been around in their lifetimes or whose stories had
been handed down to them from previous generations" (Williams, 5).
Herriot, who always took an active interest in local history, might have
inspected such "magical" artifacts as a doll representing the locally
famous "Old Kathy" that is on exhibit at the Whitby Museum and a
rocking chair in the Marske Folk Museum that belonged to the
redoubtable Nannie Pierson Jr., whom an elderly gentleman in the
1960s recalled stopping farm carts in their tracks by ensorcelling their
horses. Emma Todd's crystal ball is still on view at the Ryedale Folk
Museum in Hutton-le-Hole, a particularly notorious center of the craft,
20 miles or so as the broomstick might fly northeast of Thirsk. Writing
in 1987, Mary Williams declared that, in North Yorkshire, witchcraft "is
remembered even in the 20th century [and] there were still villagers in
the 1940s who weren't entirely sure that witchcraft was a thing of the

past" (Williams, 26). Furthermore, in describing some strange nineteenth-century goings-on involving the magical healing of sick animals witnessed by one John Peacock in the Thirsk-Helmsley-Sowerby area, Williams mused, "Strange things do happen . . . No doubt, John Peacock and his friends wouldn't know as much about diseases to which a cow can fall victim to as, for example, our Yorkshire vet James Herriot knows in these days. On the other hand, Mr. Herriot would be the first to admit that neither he nor his colleagues know everything" (Williams, 49).

The supernatural overtones of early veterinary practice aside, Herriot not only stood metaphorically between his employer Siegfried and his partying friend Tristan, but also, like all veterinarians in general practice, was often an intermediary between his animal patients and their human owners and companions. Although Herriot often claimed that his chief purpose in writing was to entertain his readers with tales they might have heard in the local pub (Gonzalez, *M*, 5), *All Creatures Great and Small* also illustrated the theme of the veterinarian's position in the complex human-animal relationship.

For primitive peoples, the relationship between mankind and animals was straightforward: kill or be killed; eat or be eaten. Once the discovery of agriculture gave rise to what we call civilization, however, men learned to domesticate animals for food and byproducts, and the relationship became morally complex. In 1953, the German behaviorist Konrad Lorenz analyzed humanity's contradictory attitude toward animals raised for food:

> In the case of farmers, who follow a certain age-old tradition, the relation of man to beast is determined by a line of conduct of an almost ritual kind, which becomes so much a matter of course as to relieve him of any moral responsibility or feeling of compunction . . . [but] Morally it is much worse to wring the neck of a tame goose that approaches one confidently to take food from one's hand than it is . . . to shoot a wild goose, which is fully conscious of its danger and, moreover, has a good chance of eluding it. Almost more questionable . . . is [man's] attitude toward those which he uses for other purposes. The coldbloodedness with which calves are slaughtered, and even the cow herself when, milked to the last drop, she can no longer "pay her way" is one of the less pleasant aspects of the associations between man and the domestic animals.[15]

Herriot the author knew very well that by the nature of the profession the veterinarian is caught in an ancient and inescapable paradox.

The rural vet, who usually takes up his work at least in part because of his affection for animals, must fight to maintain or restore the health of beasts that are ultimately destined for the butcher shop; their deaths are economically necessary for their owners, even crucial to the survival of farmers living close to the bitter edge of bankruptcy.

For the central tension of *All Creatures Great and Small*, Herriot balanced his involvement with his patients against the objectivity he had to maintain to serve them well. Being reminded that one's breakfast bacon comes not from an immaculate, impersonal supermarket cooler but from the slaughter of a living being possessing a mind that according to Lorenz "in its inmost workings, so much resembles our own" (Lorenz, xvi) is depressing at best; animal lovers in particular are often hard put to justify humanity's carnivorous nature. From the outset of his writing career, Herriot acknowledged the eventual fate of his farm-animal patients. He keenly conveyed the unfairness that gives dogs too short a life span and forces their owners to confront the mortality of beloved friends and, by extension, their own. Not long before his death, Herriot declared "with a nod to his patients, 'I don't eat meat much . . . I prefer vegetables, you know' " (Brower, 97), an indication of where his own sympathies lay.

In the conclusion of *All Creatures Great and Small*, Herriot supplied a happy antidote to such heavy thoughts by recounting his long-term courtship of his future wife Helen, in real life Joan Catherine Danbury, who had been keeping house for her farmer father and her younger siblings after her mother's death. To young Herriot's dismay, Helen had other beaus, good-looking and well-to-do young men of the area, and she was so notably a catch for an assistant veterinarian with too much to do and too little money that he quaked at the thought of asking her for a date. As it happened, Helen was a perfect match for Herriot. She was well organized (he claimed he never was), she had a fine sense of humor (every bit of which she needed to cope with the young Herriot's fumbling attempts at courtship, as gleefully recounted by Herriot the author), and she had her own fetching pioneering flair: she completely enthralled the smitten young Herriot by being one of the first women in the Dales to wear slacks—marvelously well.

The episode of Herriot's painful first date with Helen, a dinner dance at which everything that could go wrong did, effectively illustrates the author's ability to look back on hilarious missteps of his youthful self and smile along with his readers, one of Herriot's most endearing qualities as an autobiographer. Close to the end of *All Creatures Great and*

Small, Herriot the author followed several dating calamities with young Herriot finally working up the courage to take Helen to a village movie. This date was awful, too: the projectionist showed the wrong picture, and a raucous dissatisfied customer constantly disrupted their hand-holding, but it worked out for the best. Herriot and Helen left together to deliver puppies and in the process arrived at an unspoken understanding so appropriate that readers want to stand up and cheer: the underdog won out after all!

Not all the experiences Herriot chronicles in *All Creatures Great and Small* are humorous, like his attempts at wooing Helen; or humbling, like his accounts of the lessons he learned at the hands of the farmers and their animals; or sad, like the inevitable losses to which a physician never becomes accustomed. The most moving passages of the book are those in which the physical fatigue of his work, its mental strain, and the emotional involvement Herriot cannot avoid all nearly defeat the "young vit'nery." Called out for a difficult foaling, a procedure usually much more exhausting than delivering a calf, Herriot was justifiably outraged: "Once out of bed in the middle of the night was bad enough, but twice was unfair, in fact it was sheer cruelty. . . . What a life! What a bloody awful life! . . . Why the hell had I ever decided to become a country vet?" (*ACGS,* 210–11). But despite such three-o'clock-in-the-morning fits of self-pity, the young Herriot always managed to hang on and rejoice when the new little creature finally took its first breath. Herriot the author attributed his survival to his ability to laugh at himself and his never-ceasing joy at new life, the signature combination that from the start made his books so appealing. Throughout *All Creatures Great and Small,* the youthful Herriot created by his 50-year-old self "is modest, sincere, slow to anger, never pretentious, and often writes of himself as ridiculous and laughable. But foremost, he is likable for his love and appreciation of the Dales" (Gardner, 634).

The sight of a wobbly new foal or calf or lamb that Herriot's skill and hard labor helped bring into the world always remained for him the most satisfying reward for his hard life's work in the Yorkshire Dales. In the births of animals, Herriot must have appreciated the great solace that nature offers for our grief at mortality, the eternal cycle of life that is so much easier to recognize in farming areas than in the dehumanizing urban sprawl of modern cities. In Herriot's Dales, brief spring shades into blossoming summer, followed by fruitful harvest that gives way to another ferocious winter. Finally the middle-of-the-night vet calls of the April lambing season, Herriot's favorite time, begin the wheeling year all over again, the one taste humanity is allowed of immortality. In moments dark and bright, when Herriot lifted up his eyes to the hills that surround his Yorkshire Dales, they never failed to restore his faith in himself and in the humble and demanding way of life he chose when he first took up his work there.

Small anecdotes from his first two years of practice provided the raw material for the literary world James Herriot created in *All Creatures Great and Small,* allowing the older Herriot, as he had hoped, to entertain his first audiences with charming incongruities, such as the pet piglet Mrs. Pumphrey installed in her home as a companion for her cosseted Tricki Woo. The author also dissected the foibles and failures of Siegfried, Tristan, and the young Herriot with a gentle humor all his own. If *All Creatures Great and Small* had simply been a recital of such amusing moments, however, the book's appeal would never have endured. The secret of Herriot's first big success, as in all the rest of his work, lies in his ability to help readers understand the perplexing mixture of grief and delight integral to human life, storytelling shapes altogether more elemental, easier to discern, and more immediately satisfying when Herriot showed them against the clear, windswept landscape and traditional values of the prewar Dales.

Chapter Three
All Things Bright and Beautiful

This thou perceiv'st, which makes thy love more strong,
To love that well which thou must leave ere long.
                                        —Shakespeare, Sonnet 73

While *All Creatures Great and Small* was being prepared for U.S. publication in 1972, James Herriot was moving ahead with his next group of stories, which chiefly covered the two years between his marriage on November 5, 1941, and his call-up by the RAF on his 27th birthday, October 3, 1943. Like *All Creatures Great and Small,* Herriot's second American best-seller was a combination of two books, *Let Sleeping Vets Lie* (1972) and *Vet in Harness* (1973), first published in England by Michael Joseph.

In an October 1973 review for *Books and Bookmen,* British critic David Llewellyn took *Let Sleeping Vets Lie* more seriously than his colleagues had Herriot's first British-published efforts. Llewellyn's review paired off *Let Sleeping Vets Lie* with R. S. Naismith's *So You Want to Be a Veterinary Surgeon* and painted a bleak future for "an earthy profession" whose practitioners were still being "shown the back door" in a class-conscious England. Llewellyn saw Herriot's purpose as "more to entertain than to recruit," but the reviewer also observed that Herriot not only "always ha[d] a phrase for it," but was "a man in love with his job" (Llewellyn, 118).

By this time, American audiences were unequivocally in love with Herriot. When St. Martin's Press brought out *All Things Bright and Beautiful* in August 1974, the book immediately took the U.S. reading public by storm. Noting that "Herriot's first book of reminiscences . . . [had become] an enormous and quite unexpected success" in 1972, the *Washington Post Book World* represented the majority American opinion: "The sequel was expected to be more of the same—charming little stories, many of them heart-warming, some of them genuinely moving—but mostly leftovers. But *All Things Bright and Beautiful* is even better than the first book and was an even bigger success."[1] Other American critics found Herriot's second book "even more appealing,"[2] "the ultimate animal story by the ultimate veterinary surgeon,"[3] and "pick of the litter" for young-adult readers.[4] Writing for the *National Observer,* Michael Putney went further, implying Herriot was the founding father of a whole new literary phenomenon: "If there wasn't a tradition of veterinary literature before, there is now."[5]

Dedicated "with love to my wife and to my mother in dear old Glasgow town" and written more than 30 years after World War II, Herriot's *All Things Bright and Beautiful* deliberately celebrates peace against the threat of war. That paradox gives the book both its unifying theme and its dramatic tension, factors that raise *All Things Bright and Beautiful* beyond the level of pleasant reminiscence to genuine literary achievement.

"Praise God, now, for an English war," wrote that redoubtable Englishwoman Dorothy L. Sayers in the desperate fall of 1940.[6] The Nazis were throttling most of Europe, America was not yet committed to the fight for freedom, and Sayers's country was fighting for its life in the Battle of Britain. Sayers knew that when Britain had to defend itself alone in the face of an implacable enemy, British men and women had always roused themselves to a greatness otherwise unattainable—and would again. If, many years later, Americans who had never had to repel a foreign invasion should wonder where individual Britons found the heart to persevere during the darkest days of World War II, *All Things Bright and Beautiful* offers Herriot's answer: these everyday things, these humble places, these bright and beautiful old values like integrity and honesty, endurance and compassion—these, he felt, are what the British fought so hard to defend.

When Herriot the author looked back from the vantage point of middle age to his younger self a few years into his practice at Darrowby, the author saw that even as a man in his twenties "I was forming a pattern for later life" (*ATBB,* 264). In *All Things Bright and Beautiful,* his comment pertained specifically to his early habit of quizzing his vet student assistants on his own favorite medical exam questions. More generally, however, Herriot as a young husband and veterinarian was evolving not just his lifelong professional style but also the satisfying design of dramatic tension that underlay his most successful writing. *All Things Bright and Beautiful* is a fine example of Herriot's best work, an invigorating balance between the comforting constants of his quiet chosen life and the unsettling variables that continually intruded upon it from outside.

In the early 1940s, the most threatening intrusion on Herriot's peace of mind was the new world war looming just beyond the Dales, and from the beginning of *All Things Bright and Beautiful,* Herriot the author deliberately chose not to discuss the war directly. Becoming a full partner with Siegfried Farnon in the veterinary practice was a sizable stroke of good fortune for a bridegroom who had about 25s.—roughly equivalent to a farm laborer's weekly wage at the time—in his savings account (*ATBB,* 131). In 1939, Herriot had taken a second job as a veterinary inspector for the Ministry of Agriculture, and after a honeymoon spent in the Dales high country tuberculin testing cattle, James and Helen set up housekeeping on the top floor of Skeldale House. They both knew those happy days could not last, because Herriot and Siegfried had volunteered for the RAF and had the sword of deferred service hanging over their heads. At the beginning of *All Things Bright and Beautiful,* Herriot insisted that he intended to write no more about the war: "This book is not about such things which in any case were so very far from Darrowby" (*ATBB,* 11).

Setting those words to paper in his late fifties, Herriot might have been voicing an understandable desire he always felt, both during the war and after it, to keep the whole bitter experience as far as possible from his home. His attitude resembled the British reaction to World War I when Herriot was growing up in Glasgow, an attempt to block the cataclysm from their collective consciousness.

"The First World War was a tremendous strain on Britain's human, economic, and psychological resources ... Losses in the fighting resulted in a failure of confidence that characterized British opinion in the interwar years"[7] and contributed to the appeasement policy espoused by the Chamberlain government, an idealistic theory that proved abysmally wrongheaded. "Some sympathy for Germany existed in Britain from reactions against the Versailles treaty and the belief that Hitler had some justified grievances. Neville Chamberlain held that every effort must be made to avoid war."[8] However, the Munich Agreement of 1938, concocted to defuse the Nazi threat to Czechoslovakia, failed in March 1939. When the Nazis invaded Poland the following September 3, Britain and the Commonwealth immediately declared war. During the "phony war," the winter of 1939–40, Germany consolidated its conquests and Britain and France put their faith in economic blockade and outmoded defensive fortifications such as the Maginot Line, but disaster after disaster descended upon Europe in the spring of 1940. By mid-June, Norway had fallen, the British had evacuated their army from Dunkirk, and the Low Countries and France had surrendered to the Nazi onslaught.

At this crucial time, the patriotism that led Herriot and Siegfried and thousands of British men and women to volunteer for the war effort was not merely a question of national or personal pride, but a matter of survival. In 1940, the war was as physically close to Herriot's home in the Yorkshire Dales as England's Midlands manufacturing centers, and Britain was as near to being invaded as the country had been since Napoleon's time. At first, Nazi strategy relied on U-boat wolf packs to decimate British merchant shipping, and bombing raids of up to 1,000 planes on RAF airfields and manufacturing centers to eliminate RAF air superiority and obliterate British industry. England's industrial cities such as heavily bombarded Leeds, Birmingham, and Manchester were less than 100 miles from Darrowby, and London, target of the savage Blitz, was only 250 miles away, about two hours' flying time for a German bomber.

Winning the air war was critical to Britain's survival, and the RAF was not as humbled as Hitler hoped. After the surrender of France, "Messerschmitt Bf 109 pilots, morale soaring, prepared to take on what they considered to be the beaten Royal Air Force. But by the time bomb-laden Heinkels and Dorniers of the Luftwaffe rumbled across the Channel to start the Battle of Britain, the RAF was anything but beaten. Auxiliary pilots, trained before the war, beefed up the squadrons. Men who had flown for France, Poland, Norway, and other defeated nations switched into RAF blue and set out to avenge their countries. About 700 Hawker Hurricanes were combat-ready. And the new and beautiful Spitfires were now rolling off the assembly lines at a good clip; over 300 had reached the squadrons."[9]

During the Battle of Britain, from July 10 to October 12, 1940, the Luftwaffe tried its utmost to soften up British defenses for Hitler's dream of Operation Sea Lion, the cross-channel invasion, but Hitler made a critical change in priorities on September 7. The Nazi attack shifted from England's industrial midsection to London in the hope of destroying civilian morale, killing and wounding up to 3,500 people a day. After Londoners refused to cave in, the Luftwaffe pounded Britain from Plymouth to Glasgow between the late fall of 1940, when Coventry in the Midlands suffered unspeakable damage, and the spring of 1941, when London stood up to shattering assaults. The price on both sides was appalling. The total British casualties from Nazi bombing raids were a staggering 43,000 dead and 51,000 injured, and during the Battle of Britain alone, Nazi Germany lost 1,733 planes compared to RAF Fighter Command's 915 (Lowe, 316–17). Both the Luftwaffe and the Royal Air Force had to replace large numbers of experienced air crews with new recruits—and James Herriot knew he would soon become one of them. Although the war primarily affected parts of England at some distance from the Dales, Herriot could not have been immune to either the emotional shock of the losses all Britons were sharing, or the sobering probabilities of his own future as an airman.

Prior to his induction, Herriot, who generally considered change an abomination, believed that the worst part of the war for him was the uncertainty it brought to his life. Like many of his fellow Britons, Herriot had no idea when he would be called up, and very little notion of what he would be doing—except that it would not involve veterinary work. So far as the British military was concerned, Herriot's status was vague. At the start of the war, veterinary medicine was a reserved occupation, and despite having volunteered early, Herriot and Siegfried Farnon were inducted relatively late in the war, not as officers but as badly needed aircrew. Tristan Farnon had qualified as a veterinarian some years later than Herriot and Siegfried. By sheer luck, Tristan was called up for draft-animal work in the Far East (a part of the war that the military had not foreseen in 1939), and as an officer, Tristan enjoyed considerably more prestige than his older brother and Herriot received as enlisted RAF recruits. Thus, for several years, Herriot daily faced the unhappy possibility that the mail would bring a summons uprooting him from his new wife and his practice. The summons eventually came as his unwelcome birthday greeting on October 3, 1943. After Herriot and Siegfried Farnon were called up, Helen left Skeldale House to live nearby at her father's farm, and strangers took over the practice until Herriot and Siegfried could return.

Even if Herriot did not want to discuss the war directly in *All Things Bright and Beautiful,* the war's horrible reality lurking just beyond the Dales made up the "antagonist" factor of the major tension that Herriot used to pull his second set of reminiscences together into an artistic entity. War is a condition of rapid, dehumanizing, and usually unexpected change, a situation completely antithetical to the stability and security that Herriot loved in the Dales. In the first years of the war, the real threat of violent change he faced convinced him his duty was to defend his home. As he looked back in *All Things Bright and Beautiful,* Herriot declared that "everything was impermanent at that time" (*ATBB,* 400). Because he had "always abhorred change of any kind" (*ATBB,* 129), he deliberately concentrated in this book on "the ordinary things which have always made up our lives; my work, the animals, the

Dales" (*ATBB*, 11)—ironically, the same three precious elements of his life that the war overwhelmed with changes neither Herriot nor anyone else could halt.

While the world outside the Yorkshire Dales was being torn by momentous struggle, Herriot was solidifying two of his most lasting human relationships, his marriage to Helen and his working partnership with his friend Siegfried Farnon. Both his marriage and that friendship endured throughout Herriot's lifetime, proving the sturdiness of the pattern that Herriot laid down for himself as a young man. The keynote Herriot chose for *All Things Bright and Beautiful* is his transformation from insecure bachelor to happily stabilized married man. Herriot opened his second book right in the middle of the story, just as he had begun *All Creatures Great and Small* with one of his lonely struggles— that famous bone-chilling description of a tough calf delivery in an ice-cold stone Yorkshire barn. At the start of *All Things Bright and Beautiful,* however, Herriot contentedly snuggled up to his understanding wife after returning nearly frozen from a late-night call to a sick sheep, one whose owner had waited until after closing time at the local pub to call in the vet (*ATBB*, 3–4).

Herriot savored the consolation and security of married life that Helen brought him, "a warm infinity, a measureless peace" (*ATBB*, 70) because it anchored his unpredictable life. In *All Creatures Great and Small,* after Herriot had unexpectedly been forced to put a stricken Thoroughbred out of its misery, Siegfried warned Herriot that a country veterinary practice was full of frustrating inconsistencies, "a long tale of little triumphs and disasters and you've got to really like it to stick it" (*ACGS*, 42). In *All Creatures Great and Small,* Herriot had simply though deftly chronicled a succession of his "little triumphs and disasters," but *All Things Bright and Beautiful* allowed him more latitude to develop his characters, especially his own younger self. Now that he had tested out his storytelling techniques in his earlier book, Herriot was probing more deeply his reasons for being able to stick with his demanding practice.

Young Herriot of *All Creatures Great and Small* appeared to be an obliging, well-meaning, but somewhat flat observer against whom Herriot the author played off the colorful personalities of Yorkshire's men and beasts. By the time Herriot the author put together *All Things Bright and Beautiful,* Herriot the bridegroom had become three-dimensional, and therefore much more interesting and convincing. Recalling the farm and house calls rural vets had to make in the 1930s and 1940s, Herriot the author noted that his younger self often became "bell-happy," and in moments of stress tended to lash out even at innocent message takers, even his beloved Helen. Rising in the middle of the night when, as Herriot ruefully observed, one's metabolism is sluggish, wrestling with a large animal when both parties are miserable, and driving home again over dirt roads questionable at best takes its toll every bit as much on a man's disposition as on his physique. Herriot recalled that Helen once had to remind him not to shout at her when she passed on a message for a late call to a sick goat on Christmas Day. He said that he was immediately ashamed of himself and apologized, but he realized his "feeling of goodwill was at a very low ebb" (*ATBB,* 199). When Herriot the younger achieved that kind of self-knowledge, he was demonstrating one unmistakable sign of change—growing up.

Some of the workaday disasters Siegfried had promised were not so small, either, and now that Herriot had married and his personal life had become so much happier, he had a good deal more at stake in his chancy work. Herriot rightly reminded his readers that every day vets have to step "open-eyed" into "rough and dirty" dangerous situations with a high accident rate (*ATBB,* 185). In the period of *All Things Bright and Beautiful,* a great deal of potential injury involved horses, the animals that had always intimidated Herriot most.

Horse work, which was paramount for veterinarians in the early years of Herriot's practice, was and still remains one of the most hazardous areas of veterinary medicine. "In the old days with lots of horses," Herriot commented in an interview, "it used to be really tough, because if a horse kicks you it can mean a broken leg" (Green, 92). As a suburban youth, Herriot had always been nervous around horses, but he had to study them in depth at Glasgow Veterinary College, where everything else he studied took a poor second to horse cases (*ATBB,* 182). Out on the job after qualifying, Herriot always readily admitted that he lacked the rapport with horses that Siegfried and Frank Bingham enjoyed, but every day when the work had to be done Herriot risked life and limb tending 2,000-pound draft horses and high-strung throroughbreds, animals that often possessed a deadly combination of unpredictability and speed; Herriot insisted that when he'd been kicked, he had never seen it coming (*ATBB,* 184). The episode in *All Things Bright and Beautiful* in which young Herriot unexpectedly had to stitch up a huge, lethal-hoofed gelding illustrates both Herriot's gift for humorously penetrating self-analysis and his talent for splendidly concrete images that put his reader shoulder-to-shoulder with the vet at the horse's mighty haunch. Herriot's imagination made him "acutely aware of the dire possibilities," and his mind "seemed to be dwelling voluptuously on the frightful power in those enormous shining quarters, on the unyielding flintiness of the spatulate feet with their rim of metal" (*ATBB*, 183). Such beasts had been the mainstays of premechanized farming, but during the years covered in *All Things Bright and Beautiful*, Herriot watched the majestic draft horses disappear from Yorkshire's fields and roads—the most dramatic change he witnessed in the history of veterinary medicine.

At this time, veterinary medicine was also on the eve of the antibiotic revolution, one change Herriot could not have welcomed more gladly, although he judiciously pointed out two sides to the issue. Today physicians and their human patients have become accustomed to the antiseptic miracles of technology and drug therapy, but before the advent of vaccines and antibiotics, veterinarians, like their family-doctor colleagues, were sadly limited in their ability to prevent and cure diseases. Nonetheless, many bewildered victims of modern technocratic medicine yearn for the combination of insight, simple hands-on physical comfort, and caring nursing practiced in bygone days. American humorist Will Rogers remarked that "if he ever became ill he would go to a veterinarian because you don't have to tell him what's wrong with you" (*W&W*, 30).

In *All Things Bright and Beautiful*, Herriot offered a convincing case for the intangible advantage that the old practitioners could and often did offer: a combination of keen diagnostic ability, patience, and compassion that still "seems to separate the veterinarians from doctors. . . . veterinarians tend to take a little more time and exhibit a little more concern for the patient and for the client.[10] Herriot knew very well that this "black magic" could produce inexplicable cures, and his books reveal that from the start of his veterinary career, for all his humility, he displayed a rich talent for the intangible side of his work, healing by kindness.

In the days before antibiotics, the veterinarian's humane desire to alleviate suffering could sometimes make the difference between life and death, as when, lacking any other remedy, Herriot sedated a dying ewe heavily enough to free it from pain and thereby almost accidentally saved its life. He later put that discovery, as he did others he made by trial and error, to good use saving other animals. However, as Herriot the author looked back on the early years of his practice, his greatest frustration sprang not from his constant fatigue or the dangers he had to face, but from his feeling of helplessness when animals died because the right cure had not yet been discovered. In spite of the best intentions and the hardest labor, Dales farmers of those days, such as the widowed

Mrs. Dalby, who uncomplainingly struggled on against nearly insurmountable odds, often tragically lost their herds to such diseases as husk, a bovine respiratory ailment for which no cure existed until the 1960s. Writing 30-odd years later, Herriot's anguish over these losses was still clear; he thanked heaven that young veterinarians did not "have to stand among a group of gasping, groaning creatures with the sick knowledge that they can't do a thing about it" (*ATBB*, 119).

Despite all the stresses of his work and the limitations of medicine in the late 1930s and early 1940s, "Herriot treat[ed] his ailing animals with skill, gentleness, patience, and solicitude—qualities that he display[ed] toward humans too" (Putney, 17). Herriot's attitude toward his patients accounts for much of his appeal to American readers. A 1991 survey of U.S. animal owners indicates their near-universal gratitude for the kind of qualities that Herriot exhibited, the same qualities animal owners most admire in their veterinarians and wish for in their own physicians: "We have often said that this doctor of animals is so much more caring, compassionate, and willing to go way beyond medical care than another doctor of people we have known. Thank you for the opportunity to pay tribute to this extraordinary person."[11]

Near the end of *All Things Bright and Beautiful*, Herriot set his finger on the pulse of veterinary medicine: "the wondering and worrying about how your patient is progressing; then the long moment when you open that door and find out" (*ATBB*, 408). In this book, Herriot showed his younger self in the process of another growing-up change, his attitude toward his profession. Young Herriot had to abandon some of his idealism and learn the hard way that if a tragedy greeted him when he opened the door to his patient, he had to live with his grief and his sense of defeat and go on to make the best he could of the experience. But some triumphs greeted him, too, such as his "resurrection" of that dying ewe. In those moments, the wholehearted joy of doing one's chosen work well went a long way toward rewarding Herriot for the physical discomfort and emotional pain he often suffered in the course of a day's (and night's) work.

As a rural veterinarian, Herriot was always happiest in the spring, when lambs dotted the Yorkshire landscape. Herriot had small hands, "lady's hands," as the Yorkshire farmers called them, so untangling twin or, occasionally, triplet lambs so that they could be delivered naturally was Herriot's favorite job, and he called birth "the wonder that was always fresh, the miracle you couldn't explain" (*ATBB*, 22). A striking element of Herriot's literary success, one that he enlarged upon in *All*

Things Bright and Beautiful, was his ability to convey mysteriously sacred moments such as birth. In his books, little miracles of rural life, accomplished in the humblest circumstances and—for Herriot—always in the presence of an animal or two, provide flashes of insight into the goodness of nature, insights that light up everyday toil and make it worthwhile.

The animals Herriot wrote about so perceptively fall into two groups, large farm animals, with which he spent most of his time during the early years of his practice, and small companion animals such as dogs, the animals that had first inspired Herriot to take up veterinary medicine. Not only veterinary care but also society's general use of animals was changing drastically at the time he wrote about it in *All Things Bright and Beautiful,* lending a transitional flavor to Herriot's early years in practice. The dual-purpose shorthorn cattle long popular in the Dales gave way to larger, more productive specialized breeds such as the impressive black-and-white British Friesians (known in the United States as Holsteins), which commonly provide six gallons of milk a day—an amazing 2,000 gallons per 305-day lactation period. Just as in the early 1940s draft horses were abruptly phased out in favor of tractors and trucks, wartime meat-rationing lowered demands for beef, pork, and mutton; synthetic fabrics began to cut dramatically into the British wool market; and consequently small-animal work, principally on dogs and cats, occupied increasing amounts of Herriot's professional time as the years rolled on.

One reason the Farnon-Herriot practice worked so well was that each partner's personality and preference in animal patients complemented the other's. Reminiscing in 1986 about his relationship with his chief partner, Herriot declared that he and Siegfried were "exact opposites. He's always energetically trying to change things, while I resist change. A lot of people here think he's brilliant, but not even my best friends would say that of me. His mind relentlessly churns out all kinds of ideas—some excellent and others doubtful. I rarely have an idea of any kind. He likes hunting, fishing and shooting; I'm hooked on soccer, tennis and cricket. . . . we are even opposite physical types" (Gonzalez, *SR,* 59). Herriot identified his partner's main personality traits as generosity, impeccable manners, and enormous patience with animals (*ATBB,* 150), and like Frank Bingham, their much older partner with whom Herriot had first worked in the high country, Siegfried was passionately fond of horses. Herriot was only too happy to let Siegfried take care of all the horse cases he wanted.

Perhaps a little surprisingly in light of Tristan's escapades, Herriot described Tristan Farnon's identifying characteristic as compassion. Herriot particularly praised the younger man's ability to work with cattle and rascally terriers, whose prankish tendencies Tristan often seemed to share in Herriot's stories. As opposed to Siegfried's arbitrary brilliance and Tristan's mischief, both of which Herriot recounted with relish in his first two books, Herriot the author, possibly with tongue fixed in cheek, cited his colleagues' estimate of his own talents with engaging humility: "Old Herriot may be limited in many respects but by God he can wrap a cat" (*ATBB*, 218).

In the same modest fashion, without stooping to the "pathetic fallacy" of attributing human abilities to animals or sentimentalizing them as the Disney films do, Herriot cleverly personalized most of his patients and animal acquaintances, whom his varied practice at Darrowby allowed him to appreciate as individual beings, each reacting to him in its own way. In *All Things Bright and Beautiful,* Herriot's hilarious sequence of flashbacks to his courtship of Helen contains a scene in which Herriot recalls his intense discomfiture when, new to the neighborhood, he found himself judging family pets at the Darrowby Show, the social highlight of the year in the Dales. Passing up his own favorite, a shiny black Labrador who raised a courtly paw each time Herriot passed, and the sleek tabby cats for whom Herriot confessed a longtime affection, Herriot settled on a goldfish because its youthful owner had all the right answers about caring for his pet. To the derision of locals, who thought they smelled a put-up rat, and to the great embarrassment of the "young vit'nery," the boy turned out to be the squire's son.

In that episode, Herriot sketched the Labrador, cats, and goldfish in a cursory if droll fashion, describing each animal strictly from the outside. Harriot concentrated there for humorous effect on the human foibles of the pet owners, the audience, and most of all himself, but in other episodes of *All Things Bright and Beautiful,* he probed the animal psyche more deeply. Jock the sheepdog was one of those astonishingly intelligent Border collies that have always been the canine superstars of the Yorkshire sheep-raising industry. As Herriot told the story, without a trace of anthropomorphization, Jock was a champion performer in sheepdog trials, but his real forte was chasing cars, at which he rapturously excelled—until beaten at his own game, like Oedipus's father, by his younger, swifter offspring. Jock then sank into depression. Not until his rambunctious litter had departed for their new homes was Jock himself again, back to being unchallenged "top dog" (*ATBB*, 11–17).

Appreciating the irony of Jock's situation, Herriot accurately and respect-fully diagnosed Jock's psychological trauma, proving that dogs as well as people have their self-images to maintain, an insight into animal behav-ior that is receiving increasing attention by psychological researchers in the 1990s.[12]

Throughout *All Things Bright and Beautiful*, Herriot again put to ample use the literary lessons he learned from Victorian novelist Charles Dickens, whose popular *Pickwick Papers* were, like Herriot's books, a series of connected humorous sketches that made their author world famous immediately upon publication. Like Dickens, Herriot portrayed characters from all levels of society and gave them peculiar yet perfectly appropriate names that stick in the memory like Yorkshire brambles. Like Dickens, too, Herriot crusaded against abuses of the helpless in his society—in Herriot's case, the horrendous abuse that people, knowingly or not, inflict on animals.

One of Herriot's most vividly realized larger-than-life Dickensian characters in *All Things Bright and Beautiful* was the gifted small-animal surgeon Granville Bennett. Herriot was fond of the works of witty Irish playwright George Bernard Shaw, and the name "Granville Bennett" possibly came from Shaw's protégé Granville-Barker, a solid British dramatist considered even better than the more famous late-Victorian novelist John Galsworthy at creating convincingly lifelike literary char-acters. For personality, Herriot modeled Granville Bennett upon his real-life friend Denton Petty, now deceased, whose widow Zoe still lives near Herriot's home in Yorkshire. In *All Things Bright and Beautiful*, the Bennetts' titanic hospitality regularly overwhelmed young Herriot with volatile combinations, notably beef-and-onion sandwiches washed down by copious amounts of fatally assorted drink.[13]

When a case came to young Herriot so severe that he felt unable to care for the unlucky animal himself and yet could not bring himself to put it down, he drove the animal across the Dales to Bennett. Herriot typically personalized the patient as "little Maudie,"[14] a black-and-white cat whose jaw had been crushed by a hit-and-run driver, "worst of all the eyes filled with the terrified bewilderment which makes animal suf-fering so unbearable" (*ATBB*, 23). As Herriot watched in fascination, Bennett's stubby fingers set down his cigar and whiskey, and his jovial bonhomie dissolved completely into the total absorption of a master sur-geon intent upon taxing reconstructive work. A little later, Granville Bennett metamorphosed again from the gruff barking terror of the operating room into the marshmallow-hearted, self-proclaimed "Uncle

Granville" who proudly showed off his postoperative success with Maudie to an admiring Herriot.

Besides Herriot's ability to capture the eccentricities of his characters while keeping them just on the right side of credibility, a technique he honed by studying Dickens' novels, Herriot also used his stories to denounce abuses every bit as movingly as Dickens had. Dealing with the outrages perpetrated by humans on helpless animals like Maudie must be one of the most distressing aspects of a veterinarian's profession, and though Herriot was far from a wild-eyed animal-rights crusader, he always did his best to help animal victims of human neglect or outright sadism. After Herriot became famous for his writing and as many as 150 visitors a day swamped the waiting room of his surgery, he would politely oblige them with autographed bookplates, "endure their cameras," and then ask them "for donations to the Jerry Greene Animal Shelter" (*Life*, 68).

One of the most powerful episodes of *All Things Bright and Beautiful*, the story of Mrs. Donovan and Roy, the neglected golden retriever she nursed back to health, demonstrates Herriot's growing literary ability to bring people and animals to life on his pages, as well as his ability to enter and understand the animal mind, and his righteous indignation at human cruelty. Furthermore, this episode demonstrates Herriot's willingness to become involved—something increasingly rare in today's impersonal world—and to go the extra mile to bring an animal and a human being into a relationship that helped them both. The elderly Mrs. Donovan, Herriot's springboard for this episode, was a self-appointed know-it-all amateur veterinary practitioner who tended to be a thorn in the young veterinarian's side, one of those women cut out from birth to revel in being the village scold.[15] Outspoken, patronizing, and blissfully unaware of her own ignorance, Mrs. Donovan had been sailing bumptiously on her way, constantly putting Herriot down with her home remedies—until her own little dog was run over. Herriot gave her his standard advice to get another dog immediately, counsel that Mrs. Donovan, like many bereaved dog owners, found intellectually sound but could not bring her broken heart to accept. A month later, though, the village constable called Herriot to a horrifyingly neglected dog: "this patient animal sitting starved and forgotten in the darkness and filth for a year . . . sometimes wonder[ing] what it was all about" (*ATBB*, 83). In a stroke of animal-loving genius, Herriot matched grieving Mrs. Donovan's emotional need to the desperate need of the poor dog, and all came right in the end. In Mrs. Donovan's busy hands,

Roy became "a Golden Retriever in full magnificence" (*ATBB*, 87), and Mrs. Donovan the amateur veterinarian achieved a "blazing triumph that never dimmed" (*ATBB*, 88). Herriot the author modestly attributed the salvation of these two unforgettable individuals to providence, but beyond his understated narrative, the sensitive insight that motivated this small miracle is easily recognizable, a tribute to Herriot's compassion for his fellow man and to his lifelong love of dogs.

Herriot had an unusual skill for depicting the mental workings of all of his animal patients without a trace of sticky sentimentality, but as the story of the golden retriever Roy demonstrates, Herriot was particularly good at getting inside dogs' minds, probably because he always had a special affection for them. From the dawn of civilization, dogs have had a special capacity to bond with human beings, and Herriot, an animal lover who also happened to be an animal doctor, maintained a profound spiritual attachment to all the dogs, whose devotion, he said, warmed and lightened his tough working life.[16]

During the period of *All Things Bright and Beautiful,* Siegfried Farnon, who claimed to oppose the keeping of pets, routinely piled his five dogs into his car when he went out on calls. Herriot took his wife's beagle, Sam, along with him—Sam being one of the most wonderful gifts, Herriot said, that Helen had brought into their marriage. From that time on, Herriot said, his life took on a whole new meaning because Sam was with him, and after Sam, at least one dog always accompanied Herriot on his daily rounds. Herriot's gift for language allowed him to put into words feelings for dogs too deep for many dog owners to verbalize themselves, especially the "abiding satisfaction" he felt upon "giving pleasure to a beloved animal" (*ATBB*, 296), and the pain he still felt years after Sam died. That pain made James Herriot a brother to everyone who has ever loved and lost a dog.

Sam's presence, too, helped Herriot realize the healing power of the Dales, the third of the preoccupations in *All Things Bright and Beautiful* that allowed him to shut away for a little while the upsetting changes World War II was carrying to his Yorkshire doorstep. He claimed that with Sam a simple walk in the countryside always renewed his energy and refreshed his soul. Those walks also provided him with the memories that later inspired his utterly lovely descriptions of the Dales, meticulous choices of words and rhythms now largely vanished from the current best-seller scene. Several commentators have praised Herriot's descriptive passages, which approach poetry when he writes about the Dales: "as lovely as a Turner landscape: 'This was the real Yorkshire with

the clean limestone wall riding the hill's edge and the path cutting brilliant green through the crowding heather. And walking face on to the
scented breeze I felt the old tingle of wonder at being alone on the wide
moorland where nothing stirred and the spreading miles of purple blossom and green turf reached away till it met the hazy blue of the sky' "
(Putney, 17). But Herriot was not really alone there, because his dog
Sam was with him.

When in the first years of his practice the world and his work rested
too heavily on Herriot's shoulders, he sought solace in the high country
north and west of Darrowby, a habit he continued throughout his life. In
All Things Bright and Beautiful, he called his desire for solitude a "self-
indulgence," seeming to feel a little puritanical guilt at his "penchant for
stepping out of the stream of life and loitering on the brink for a few
minutes as an uninvolved spectator" (*ATBB,* 45). More likely, these
respites helped Herriot pursue his work as successfully as he did because
they let him maintain a sense of equilibrium in the face of the sober real-
ities of his profession: most of his large-animal patients would not die of
natural causes but be deliberately slaughtered when needed for food or
when their usefulness was over, and even the most cherished pets,
including his own, lived precarious, too-short lives, inevitably leaving
bereft owners to mourn their animal friends' passing.

In *All Things Bright and Beautiful,* Herriot also showed his younger
self developing another saving grace as man and physician, a sense of
humor that was starting to range over a wider spectrum of irony than is
seen in *All Creatures Great and Small.* As Jonathan Swift, who knew all
about literary satire, put it:

> Humour is odd, grotesque, and wild,
> Only by affectation spoil'd;
> 'Tis never by invention got,
> Men have it when they know it not.[17]

In *All Creatures Great and Small,* Herriot's jokes, except for his accounts
of Tristan's pranks, were mostly amusingly self-directed. In *All Things
Bright and Beautiful,* however, Herriot's humor became more subtle
when aimed at himself and broader in scope when he studied the animals and people around him. In his second U.S. book, Herriot the
author often pitted the incongruities of human behavior against the
more reasonable actions of animals. One notable example was Clancy, a

formidable Airedale cross who had an unquenchable taste for garbage
and an ominous curl to his gigantic jowl that invariably prevented
young Herriot, the human being supposedly in charge of the situation,
from attempting the risky business of taking the dog's temperature.

Even when directing his humor against one of his favorite targets,
human pomposity, Herriot consistently laughed with his subjects, not at
them, and he never resorted to savaging his victims with sarcasm. To
take his capable but inflated veterinary student assistant Carmody down
a peg, Herriot turned Carmody loose to deal with a wild Galloway steer
that promptly dragged the vet-in-waiting through a mucky barnyard.
Decent man that he was, Herriot couldn't help but find Carmody's
tenacity admirable, and some 20 years later, when Carmody was a
famous researcher, Herriot still managed to see a redeeming glint of
humor under the man's starchy exterior.

For some readers, Herriot's humor tended to deflate a bit in those
chapters featuring Tristan "whose escapades border on the fictitious,"[18]
such as the madcap appearances of the "Raynes Ghost," a monastically
garbed role Tristan adopted for the sheer joy of putting the fear of God
into local lorry drivers. Most of Herriot's readers, however, seem to
believe that he brought even such unlikely narratives off successfully.
The Raynes Ghost frightened his younger self nearly into cardiac arrest,
but Herriot the author saved the episode from becoming farcical by
adding his young Harriot's down-to-earth reaction to Tristan's masquer-
ade, a not entirely empty threat to strangle the practical joker, and then
polishing off Tristan's career as specter at the meaty, cudgel-wielding
hands of Claude Blenkiron, the village constable.

In this case, the Dales provided a historical dimension as well as the
picturesque backdrop for Herriot's successful combination of wild fanci-
ful prank and realistic earthy retribution. Yorkshire abounds in romantic
ruins, remnants of once-wealthy Cistercian abbeys whose monks were
dispersed and their holdings confiscated by Henry VIII when he broke
with the Church of Rome in the 1530s. About 10 miles northeast of
Thirsk is the magnificent ruin of Rievaulx (pronounced "Rivers") Abbey,
the first major monastery built in twelfth-century Britain by the Cistercians, a branch of the Benedictine order bent on ascetic reformation.
Herriot first became acquainted with Rievaulx Abbey on a walk when
he was courting Helen. The Cistercians had enormous talent for locating their austere houses in impressive valley settings, and at his first
glimpse of the sternly soaring Gothic arches of the half-demolished
choir, Herriot fell under their spell.[19] Seen by chilly night, though, the

ruins contributed a genuinely spooky atmosphere to Tristan's practical joking.

By the time Herriot wrote *All Things Bright and Beautiful,* he had been in the Dales for about 40 years, and he knew the area and its people intimately. Characters such as Herriot's avenging constable Claude Blenkiron, the "dark, sinewy" folk of the Dales (*ATBB,* 347), had been shaped by generations of struggle with their harsh climate and the demands of hardscrabble farming, and they did not suffer fools gladly. Herriot, a newly arrived young Scotsman, needed some time to become accepted by the Dales people. From the start, though, he appreciated their habitual, uncomplaining acceptance of fate's cruelties: a laconic "These things happen" was their usual response when the best that Herriot could do proved insufficient to save one of their animals—or even the entire herd.

The people of the Dales were almost invariably hospitable. By the time he recorded in *All Things Bright and Beautiful,* Herriot had worked among the Dales people for several years and had married a farmer's daughter, so in this book he is taken into their homes more often than he had been earlier, with occasionally hilarious results. Once Herriot was subjected to a hearty lunch of lard, which he loathed, and piccalilli, a combustible mélange of cucumber, onions, beans, cauliflower, and green tomatoes pickled in vinegar and spiked with turmeric, ginger, and dry mustard (*BJH,* 265). Devouring that meal with an appearance of requisite appreciation, Herriot declared, was one of the bravest things he'd ever done. Anticipating the cholesterol-fearing 1990s, his detestation for dietary fat subsequently became obsessive (*ATBB,* 364), a factor that probably helped him keep his health and his youthful appearance well into his seventies.

Besides the humorous situations Herriot and his readers enjoyed so much, a good deal of the appeal of *All Things Bright and Beautiful* derives from a more serious dramatic irony: the audience knows facts hidden from the young hero—but not, in this case, from his older self, who is telling the story. Throughout *All Things Bright and Beautiful,* readers are aware that, sooner by far than Herriot would have liked, he would have to leave the work he loved, the animals whose personalities gave him so much pleasure, the Dales whose natural beauty sustained his spirit, and the people, from his adored Helen to the lowliest plowman in the field, he had come to cherish.

Change fell upon Herriot with a vengeance during the period of *All Things Bright and Beautiful.* The early years of the war brought scientific innovations that allowed him to save increasing numbers of animals with new miracle drugs and spend more time with the cats and dogs he preferred, but not all change for Herriot in the early 1940s was so happy. While he was polishing his veterinary skills, the war raged on, no longer limited to the Nazi rape of Europe and the ferocious bombardment of England. A month after Herriot's marriage, the Japanese attack on Pearl Harbor brought the United States into the war, vastly raising the ante of the global conflict. In May 1942, the British began to pay Nazi Germany back with a 1,000-plane bombing raid on Cologne. In the Far East, however, Japan had conquered the Philippines, storming through many other Pacific islands and the Malay Peninsula; the fall of the 70,000-man garrison at Singapore dealt the most crushing blow of the war to British imperial prestige. By autumn of 1942, though, the tide began to turn for the Allies. British field marshal Montgomery decisively defeated Germany's "Desert Fox," field marshal Erwin Rommel, at El Alamein. In the Pacific, Americans won the naval battles of Midway and the Coral Sea and, in their first land offensive of the war, captured the vital base of Guadalcanal. In the winter of 1942–43, the Red Army forced a crucial German surrender at Stalingrad. In Churchill's words, however, even these enormous successes were only "the end of the beginning," and two more years of ferocious fighting still lay ahead.

When Herriot the author looked back to the life he had led in October 1943, the close of *All Things Bright and Beautiful,* he called it "untidy," and he claimed it was in part at least his own fault, as he admitted planning had never been one of his strong suits (*ATBB,* 378). His draft notice had just arrived; he had no money to speak of in the bank; and he and Helen, now pregnant with their first child, were still living on the top floor of Skeldale House and had no home of their own. In one of the most revealing passages of *All Things Bright and Beautiful,* the sober scene in which Herriot and Siegfried talked late into the night before leaving for the RAF, Herriot, whom his family always called "slow on the uptake," introduced a memory that obviously still moved him deeply. That night, Siegfried found a way to give his partner the handsome sum of £50 without injuring the dignity of either one of them, but Herriot said he never realized what his partner was doing, nor thanked him until the author did so in *All Things Bright and Beautiful* (*ATBB,* 380). The two men parted that evening without saying goodbye to each other, and after they left for basic training, Tristan ran the practice briefly until he too joined the war effort. For the next two years, Herriot was separated from everything he had come to love, while the cycle of life in the Dales wheeled onward. At the time, Herriot could not have been sure that one day he and Siegfried Farnon would return and take up their work again, and for the moment, the beauty and brightness of the cherished world he seemed to be losing had dimmed for the young veterinarian from Darrowby.

Chapter Four
All Things Wise and Wonderful

For thy sweet love remember'd such wealth brings . . .
                                        —Shakespeare, Sonnet 29

While *All Things Bright and Beautiful* was selling out its first printing of 100,000 in the fall of 1974, journalist Timothy Green discovered the book's elusive author at 23 Kirkgate, Thirsk, an old Georgian house with its red front door standing wide open:

> A tall, thin man is energetically complaining to anyone listening that with beef prices falling the way they are, the farmers are really being punished. And on the telephone, a short, well-built man with sandy hair just graying at the edges, is saying very firmly that he will come by at 11 o'clock to give the calves their brucellosis shots, and please be waiting . . . That is Herriot, now 57, doing battle on the phone with the farmer, while Siegfried Farnon, still his energetic partner after more than 30 years, is the chap holding forth on the farmers' plight. (Green, 90)

At that time, journalists were still sworn to secrecy about Herriot's real identity and the location of his practice, but Herriot's cover had been blown in the sparsely populated Dales, where folks know much of one another's business. The local library had a two-year waiting list for Herriot's books, and "hardy old farmers, who hadn't read a book since they left school at the age of 12, actually bought copies on market day" (Green, 91). Early on, Herriot himself was delighted at his sudden fame and fortune. " 'I'm on a gorgeous wicket,' he sa[id] cheerfully. 'No one had thought of writing funny books about cows and pigs before. And it's nice to make people laugh' " (Green, 91).

In the first flush of his literary lionhood, Herriot generously allowed Green and photographer Paul Conklin to share his daily rounds. Green's 1974 *Smithsonian* article contains the kind of rare illustrations Herriot hardly ever allowed again, Herriot's wife, trim and attractive in plaid slacks, and their unpretentious town house with Herriot's faithful companions Hector, a Jack Russell terrier, and Dan, a gigantic black Labrador, to both of whom Herriot dedicated his third book, *All Things Wise and Wonderful*. This article also contains Conklin's posed shot of Herriot and Siegfried Farnon "treating" Siegfried's dog in their surgery, and Herriot booted and raincoated in the barnyard, wrestling a sow with mastitis. Herriot told Green that his unexpected success was proving a mixed blessing because of the 83 percent slice the Inland Revenue claimed of his earnings, but Herriot refused to leave his busy practice and go into tax exile. He asked, " 'How could I do that . . . what would happen to my dogs? They'd die if I went away' " (Green, 97).

Herriot had made a brief solo promotional tour of the United States in December 1973, sponsored by his paperback publisher Bantam Books, who to that date had sold about 800,000 copies of *All Creatures Great and Small*. He had appeared on several television shows, but he clearly considered the high points of his trip to be his visits to the American Veterinary Medical Association offices in Chicago[1] and the Michigan State University veterinary school: " 'They treated me like royalty. . . . Deans and professors came round with me, you'd have thought I was the greatest veterinary surgeon in the world" (Green, 97).

Fame was not about to swell Herriot's head. In 1974, he bought himself a good stereo system and "a snappy yellow small sports car for his wife" and was thinking about "a nice new bungalow in the Dales," but his wife told Green, " 'This success has come too late in life to change us; 20 years ago perhaps he might have given up being a vet, but not now.' " Herriot himself reiterated his devotion to his dogs, his vet work, and the Dales, three of the precious things that, after his family, always formed the basis of his life, declaring, " 'I wouldn't give up being a vet if I had a million pounds. I'm too fond of animals . . . [and] driving round the Dales . . . is like a paid holiday' " (Green, 97).

Herriot had also started assembling his next book. He had written the preceding books chiefly from memory and from entries in his diaries, but now he was deliberately taking notes for future projects on a Dictaphone in his car as he went about his daily work. He had plenty of material and knew how to husband it thriftily: " 'Maybe it was cunning in me that made me write only about one year of my life at a time . . . I've got years and years to go yet' " (Green, 96). From 1974 to 1976, Herriot again sandwiched his writing into odd moments between his veterinary calls, producing *Vets Might Fly* and *Vet in a Spin,* published respectively by Michael Joseph in 1976 and 1977 and amalgamated into *All Things Wise and Wonderful,* published by St. Martin's Press in 1977.

Herriot's autobiographical narrative had arrived at the part of his life that was probably hardest for him to relive, the years 1943 to 1945, which he spent in the wartime RAF. *All Things Wise and Wonderful,* like all of Herriot's work, contains some superbly funny episodes, but overall it is far from a funny book. Herriot had abruptly had to leave his wife, pregnant with their first child. Three days later, he was far from his work, the animals he loved, and the Dales where he had been happiest—perhaps forever, because the life expectancy of RAF aircrew in 1943 was notoriously slim. To write this book, 57-year-old James Herriot had to return to his 27-year-old self and show the young Herriot summoning up the inner resources to cope with one of the most severe emotional traumas in his life. By doing so, the author arrived at the sobering theme of *All Things Wise and Wonderful:* real wisdom always comes the hard way, and one copes with present suffering by remembering lessons learned in happier days—even if doing so can be painful.

For a man who loathed change, the ironic uncertainties of Herriot's brief RAF career must have continually galled him. Veterinarian Herriot was shipped at first to St. John's Wood, London, where he alternated basic-training exercises with mucking out pigsties not far from the London Zoo. Fortunately for his hopes of seeing Helen during the latter part of her pregnancy, he then was sent to Scarborough, a resort town on the Yorkshire coast about 50 miles east of Darrowby. The RAF Initial Training Wing was then the toughest conditioning program in the British military, and Herriot and his fellow recruits drilled through the winter and stood guard over such vacation spots as the Grand Hotel. The next May, Herriot found himself in Shropshire for a second "toughening course," followed by Winckfield Flying School at Windsor and then further flying lessons at Heaton Park, Manchester. At Heaton Park, Herriot, older by 10 years than most of his group but suited by his moderate height for fighter aircraft,[2] was the third man to qualify as a pilot. Shortly afterward, he underwent an unavoidable operation that torpedoed his potential as a pilot. This might have been a hernia repair, which in pre–G suit days would have made it impossible for him to fly. He recuperated for two weeks at Puddlestone, near Leominster, and returned to Heaton Park as walking evidence of a bureaucratic dilemma—a pilot-trained veterinarian that the RAF would not allow to fly an airplane. Herriot was then posted as a storekeeper's assistant to the Eastchurch RAF base on the Isle of Sheppy, his last military stop before being mustered out in London. He returned to Helen and Darrowby in late 1945 physically fit but emotionally shaky, wondering what he had forgotten, "whether I was fit to be an animal doctor again."[3]

As he had in *All Things Bright and Beautiful,* Herriot tried in *All Things Wise and Wonderful* to keep the war and its horrors as far away as he could, but the distress it caused him by tearing him away from everything he held dear could not help but darken *All Things Wise and Wonderful.* While in the RAF, Herriot kept himself going with happy memories of his practice and his marriage, but the war cast its shadow over most of those recollections. James Herriot, A2c., knew his situation was precarious at best; he was completely at the mercy of harsh, unavoidable circumstances that were relentlessly disrupting lives all over the world.

When Herriot was called up in October 1943, the tide of the war was changing, but two years of bitter warfare still lay ahead. The Allies had nearly destroyed the Nazi U-boat threat and were preparing to carry the war back into the strongholds of the Axis powers. In the Pacific, Americans under Douglas MacArthur had begun the island-hopping strategy that would eventually bring them to the doorstep of imperial Japan. After the Soviet victory at Stalingrad in February 1943, the Red Army rolled inexorably westward, engulfing Poland, Hungary, and the Balkans by 1944. Italy had surrendered in September 1943, and despite stubborn German resistance, American and British forces moved up the Italian peninsula toward the Fatherland. In the winter of 1943–44, Herriot, like most ordinary recruits, probably heard rumors that Operation Overlord, the D-Day invasion that launched the liberation of Europe, was being planned for the coming June. As Herriot took his flying lessons in the fall of 1944, he would surely have been aware of the Allied campaign in Normandy. During the bitter winter of 1944–45, the fierce Battle of the Bulge ended with a decisive Allied breakthrough, and by the time Herriot was discharged, Soviet troops and British-American forces were close to meeting in the heart of Germany.

Of all the branches of the British military in World War II, the Royal Air Force had the most distinguished reputation—and, Herriot noted, the best food. The servicemen of the RAF did fare better than most people in wartime Britain, but they paid heavily for their elite status. "In too many famous actions, particularly towards the beginning of the war, hardly anybody survived to tell their personal story."[4] At the start of the war, Herriot had volunteered for an old form of combat—one-on-one fighting—that involved totally new, breathtakingly fast-moving technology typified by the lethal aircraft that many felt kept the war from being lost. " 'In the Spitfire,' wrote Richard Hillary, who was the 'type of a new generation' just as the Spitfire was the type of a new breed of fighter aircraft, 'we're back to war as it ought to be. Back to individual combat, to self-reliance, total responsibility for one's fate' " (Briggs, 269).

No one has described early-World War II air combat better than Group Captain "Johnnie" Johnson, a Canadian who became Britain's top World War II ace. Johnson could write as well as he could fly Spitfires:

> The Messerschmidts [sic] come in close for the kill. At this range their camouflage looks dirty and oil-stained, and one brute has a startling black-and-white spinner. In a hot sweat of fear I keep turning and turning, and the fear is mingled with an abject humiliation that these bastards should single me out and chop me at their leisure. The radio is silent . . . far better to fight back and take one with me . . . I fasten on to tail-end Charlie and give him a long burst of fire . . . perhaps my attack has its just reward . . . [once landed] we clamber into our meagre transports, one small van per flight, and drive to Shopwhyke. We sit on the lawn and drink tea served by Waafs. . . . The sweat from the combats of but an hour ago is barely dry on our young bodies.[5]

If Herriot had to fight to defend his home, the RAF's reliance on individual combat between 1939 and 1941 might have appealed to him. Despite his claims of suffering from vertigo, he sought out high, solitary places when at home in Yorkshire, and he proved to have a dependable stomach for flying. But no one, including Herriot himself, knows how he would have reacted to aerial combat, because his operation put an end to his flying career. In 1943, he certainly found most other aspects of life as an RAF airman, second class, disagreeable. His RAF recollections, mostly melancholy, form the "now" of *All Things Wise and Wonderful,* arranged as a chronological succession of small specific episodes in his service career. Herriot the author matched each RAF episode with a memory from his veterinary practice in which an animal and its owner faced a similar situation. This arrangement of his materials was more sophisticated than the straightforward presentation of memoirs he had used earlier. Drawing analogies between his happy prewar past and his dreary RAF present helped the young Herriot understand and cope with his day-to-day unhappiness, and doing so also allowed Herriot the author to offer some lessons in living that greatly enrich *All Things Wise and Wonderful.* Unpleasant as Herriot's wartime separation from his wife, his work, and the Dales was, the experience made him an even more perceptive practitioner than he had been and enhanced the wealth of insight into human and animal behavior that makes his books so effective.

Change he could not control, Herriot's lifelong bugbear, was responsible for much of the pain in the lessons he learned as a serviceman.

Pressures of the war effort were accelerating a nationwide shift toward the centralization and bureaucratization—some might say dehumanization—of British life, changes that on the individual level substantially aggravated Herriot's personal trials. Young Herriot found such changes at best unpleasant and at worst completely unacceptable, but he seems to have constantly tried his best to deal with them, and as his older self recounted the stories, he sometimes managed to hit upon highly amusing solutions.

At the beginning of *All Things Wise and Wonderful,* young Herriot was so homesick that Herriot the author said he had never since been able to use the brand of scented soap Helen had packed in his kit bag for those first achy days of physical training in London (*ATWW,* 3). The flashback story that rescued him from self-pity also demonstrates Herriot's literary ability to tread the dicey tightrope between genuine feeling and soggy sentimentality. On one of his first nights in London, the young Herriot had dreamed about a call he had made to one of his Yorkshire farmers to treat a sick cow. Herriot had watched old Farmer Dakin send Blossom, an elderly milk cow nearly at the end of her usefulness, off to market, but before Herriot left the farm, Blossom had turned around and made her way home, back to the stall where she had spent her days. Moved by the "pathetic dignity" of the patient old animal (*ATWW,* 7), Dakin took her back to live out her days at home, the only place she, like homesick young Herriot, ever wanted to be. Blossom and Mr. Dakin together set the complex tone Herriot chose for *All Things Wise and Wonderful.* This book revolves around not only Herriot's longing for his home but also the sweetness of justice when a hardworking life is rewarded and, above all, respect for an individual's rights, even when that individual, like an old cow, seems of little use any more.

Herriot devoted the first seven chapters of *All Things Wise and Wonderful* to memories that carried him through his basic training in London. Some of these stories are hilarious, such as the gut-busting saga of Cedric the flatulent boxer and his fastidious female owner. Some are triumphant, such as the successful first-aid struggle Herriot waged to remove a ball stuck in the throat of a handsome collie. In both those stories, animals hold center stage, but in another, more poignant story in this group, Herriot—like Dickens—focused on a small human victim of socioeconomic stress. Glimpsing a London street urchin made Herriot think about a local Darrowby "imp of hell" he had known, Wesley Binks, who lost his young dog Duke, the only being that had ever loved the boy, to distemper. Softhearted Herriot would likely have treated the dog for no charge, but Herriot knew that as long as Wesley had to earn a little money to pay for Duke's care, there was hope the boy might be able to make something of himself. However, when the dog died despite all that Herriot could do, Wesley reverted to delinquency. Wesley's tragedy notwithstanding, though, Herriot was able to summon up enough "little triumphs" such as watching Blossom come home and finding the only possible owner for Cedric, one who had no sense of smell. These scenes allowed Herriot to experience again the "old feeling of fulfillment and satisfaction" that made his life worthwhile (*ATWW,* 20) and helped him cope with the gnawing homesickness that gripped him in London.

Once Herriot had been transferred to Scarborough, he was agonizingly near and yet so far from Darrowby and Helen, because Early Training Wing policy prohibited him from taking any leave until after his child was born. Herriot was not only emotionally miserable but also physically hurting. Before he entered the RAF, Helen's good cooking had begun to pad out his midsize physique, but more than the merciless RAF physical training at Scarborough was now at work to slim him down. According to Herriot the author, Yorkshire folk jokingly say that husbands who suffer during their wives' pregnancies are "carrying" their babies, but Herriot was always convinced he actually did share the physical manifestations of Helen's pregnancy. As time passed, his symptoms, like hers, became more severe, culminating with wrenching pains in the lower abdomen. Finally unable to bear the situation any longer, the normally law-abiding Herriot risked penalties, even prison, and went AWOL. It took six hours' traveling for him to spend one hour with Helen, and he said unequivocally, "it was worth it" (*ATWW,* 89).

Herriot executed his temporary escape with the help of an unexpected ally, a corporal who had grown up between the wars on the mean streets of Glasgow, "Stunted, undernourished, but tough and belligerent as a ferret" (*ATWW,* 91), a spiritual brother to the slum-bred Glaswegian noncom who exemplifies the town's terrier personality, always at its most vivid in a scrap, in a traditional Glasgow pub story:

During the First World War, an English officer rode past a Bantam H.L.I. lance-corporal marching some twenty sturdy German prisoners down a country lane.

"You all right there, Lance-Corporal?" the officer asked.

"Fine, sir," the Bantam answered. The officer remained unconvinced.

"Sure you can manage all these men on your own?" he inquired.

"D'ye ken whit's in my hand, sir?" the Bantam asked, opening his palm. The officer found himself peering down at a common type of hand grenade.

"Why yes, of course. A Mills bomb."

"Ay, sir, but whit they ken and I ken but you dinna is that the pin's oot." (Lindsay, 282–83)

Herriot sized up his salty compatriot, couched an appeal in broadest Glaswegian dialect, smothered it in his intimate knowledge of football, and got himself to the bus for Darrowby on time. Amusingly as Herriot recounts the circumstances around his first surreptitious visit home, a note of melancholy intruded on his happiness at seeing Helen again. Two weeks from delivery, she still looked wonderful to him, but Herriot the author said he had never been able to forget the cheap maternity dress she was wearing; it was one of the few occasions in his life James Herriot wished that he was a wealthy man.

Herriot went AWOL again on February 13, 1944. He arrived home just after the birth of his son, Jimmy, whose purplish, misshapen newborn appearance stopped the experienced veterinarian in his tracks and made him rush to inspect another newborn to make sure his own was normal. On the bus back to Scarborough, Herriot then hatched a clever plot to take his "compassionate leave" later, when Helen and Jimmy had returned to her father's farm, so Herriot could spend that time with his family.

From the vantage of 30 years later, Herriot observed that his moral scruples had quickly dissolved (*ATWW*, 117) when he was confronted with a conflict between what he felt were the RAF's senseless regulations and his emotional needs as a new father. His disgust with inhumane bureaucracy probably inspired chapter 15 of *All Things Wise and Wonderful*, an episode that contains not one reference to an animal—a rarity in Herriot's work. Herriot could not help ridiculing the inconsistencies of military life, which put people at the mercy of inane whims sent down impersonally from highly placed VIPs (*ATWW*, 131). In similar circumstances, many people might have exploded with bitterness, but Herriot made his point with an anecdote about aircrew recruits being trained to deliver bloodcurdling shrieks in preparation for hand-to-hand combat. One reluctant screamer eventually produced a war whoop—but unfortunately, too soon. Funny as the story is, Herriot's humor did not completely mask his disdain for mindless bureaucracy and his longing for his veterinary practice, where he could take responsibility for his own decisions with a minimum of governmental interference.

Being sent to Shropshire, south and west of Yorkshire, in the summer of 1944 helped Herriot a little because being there gave him a chance to get back into the countryside. For further toughening, he and his fellow pilot candidates were incomprehensibly assigned to dig a vast, reservoir-like hole out of a hillside, and the callow brassiness of his 18- and 19-year old barracks mates made Herriot feel ancient in their company. He could not help comparing their adolescent profanity with what he considered the preferable, wholesome reticence of rural Yorkshire, for example, poor Mr. Gilby's total inability to describe—even to the veterinarian—an excruciating kick he had received in an indelicate portion of the anatomy.

For Herriot, the one redeeming feature of the hard but meaningless work he had to do in Shropshire was being outdoors again near farming folk, and he gladly volunteered to help out with the harvest. A local farmer exerted immense patience in instructing him in the now-lost art of "stooking" (shocking) grain, stacking sheaves together to cure and dry before threshing: "It's just knowin' how to do it," said Farmer Edwards. When one of the Edwards's massive Red Poll cows needed help calving, and the farmer's best efforts proved useless, Herriot jumped at the chance to throw off his shirt and pitch in. Breech presentations, with the calf's hind legs coming first instead of the head and forelegs, usually baffled untrained farmers, but Herriot loved the procedure. To the amazement of the farmer, Herriot speedily delivered "a grand bull calf" before admitting that he was a qualified veterinarian. Herriot the author couldn't resist rounding off the episode tidily: "It's just knowing how to do it," he told the astounded Mr. Edwards (*ATWW*, 221–26), and the two shared a resounding belly laugh.

This story also allowed Herriot the author to leap ahead to a reflection on postwar rural sociology. In the 1970s and 1980s, British and American academic futurists browsing for dissertation fodder hit upon schemes for turning remote rural areas, in particular Yorkshire and the Dakotas, into recreation areas that U.S. researchers call "buffalo commons," triaging out small, "uneconomic" towns and shifting rural populations to larger cities. Herriot saw the situation in more practical and more compassionate terms that leave no doubt where his own sympathies lay: "The clever economists who tell us that we don't need British agriculture and that our farms should be turned into national parks seem to ignore the rather obvious snag that an unfriendly country could starve us into submission in a week. But to me a greater tragedy still would be the loss of a whole community of people like the Edwardses" (*ATWW,* 222).

Herriot regretfully left Shropshire and the Edwardses for Winckfield Flying School, near Windsor, where he fell into the hands of Flying Officer Woodham. On the ground Woodham was a decent enough veteran of the Battle of Britain, but he was so terrorized by having to teach raw aviation apprentices like Herriot that, once aloft in a rickety wooden Tiger Moth trainer, Woodham turned into a shouting demon. In Woodham's defense, he was trying to cram a great deal of his bitterly won experience into Herriot and his fellow trainees in an agonizingly brief time. Moreover, by 1944, flying tactics were changing rapidly, abandoning individual combat for mass assaults. When Woodham had flown in the Battle of Britain, "air fighting was a high-speed, heavy-gunned continuation of World War I dogfighting," but in "the warfare of 1944 and 1945 . . . air armies of 2,000 bombers escorted by nearly 1,000 fighters fought their Battles of Verdun and the Somme four miles high in the smoky sky" (Parks, 114).

Flying itself—leaving aside the overwrought directives of his instructor—seemed to suit Herriot. He enjoyed the sensation of freedom that flying gave him, and he surprised himself by forgetting the vertigo that had always troubled him elsewhere. When he was airborne in the cramped cockpit of his trainer, Herriot was back in control of his own destiny for the first time in his military career, if only for a little while.

At Windsor, too, Herriot was reminded of the similarity between men and animals (*ATWW,* 240), not because human beings can be all-too beastly, but because, like Herriot's patients, human beings were all individuals to him. In the midst of his torturous flying lessons with Flying Officer Woodham constantly destroying Herriot's self-confidence by finding fault with every move he made, Herriot took refuge in thoughts of farmers he had known who constantly complained about his veterinary work and took matters into their own hands. He ruefully recalled that sometimes their home remedies had proved disconcertingly more successful than the veterinarian's scientific cures. Once, after Herriot's ministrations proved fruitless with an unruly postpartum sow named Gertrude, an aged Dales granddad effectively sedated her with two gallons of "John Smith's best bitter" (*ATWW,* 247).

After one especially rough flight with Woodham and none of John Smith's or anyone else's best bitter in sight after landing, sympathetic noises from his barracks mates also made Herriot recall two of his dog patients who perfectly illustrated the elemental need for companionship that humans and animals share. When Herriot couldn't save Jingo, a three-year-old bullterrier, the veterinarian grieved, as he always did, along with the dog's owners. Herriot the author, veteran of many such losses, observed that such cases were all the harder for him when owners "were nice" because he had been there himself and knew too well how grief stricken they were. After Jingo died, his old corgi friend, Skipper, went into a decline, refusing food and wasting away. Herriot was on the verge of ending the old dog's misery until the desperate owners bought Skipper a new bullterrier puppy and the old corgi found new reason to live. In the trying atmosphere of flying school, this memory of the saving bond between animals helped restore Herriot's emotional balance at a time when he needed it very badly.

While Herriot was grappling with Flying Officer Woodham and the Tiger Moth at 7 shillings 3 pence per day, less an allowance sent to Helen, one of the most unsettling events that Herriot ever experienced in his practice also arose to haunt him. A "pub terrier" he saw one day reminded him of a dog he had put to sleep for Paul Cotterell, an Englishman who lived quietly in Darrowby. At first Herriot thought that Cotterell was taking the loss well, but shortly afterward, Cotterell killed himself, unable to face life without his small best friend. Cotterell's death brought home to Herriot a lesson he was never able to forget— that the world is full of sensitive people like Paul who "are not what they seem" (*ATWW,* 333).

As he had done in his earlier books, Herriot tempered tragedy by following it with a similar case that had turned out for the best. Not long after Paul Cotterell's suicide, Andrew Vine, whose fragile personality almost shattered when he learned his dog was going blind, came out of his depression only after Herriot forcefully reminded Vine that he was his dog's only hope. Herriot himself had had a dog go blind—his Jack Russell terrier Hector, whose death broke Herriot's heart more than the loss of any of his other dogs (Taylor, 72; Nickel, "Revisited," 18). Thus, Herriot the animal lover could easily empathize with Andrew's grief, but at the same time, Herriot the professional insisted that Andrew Vine roll up his sleeves and do something concrete to overcome his blues.

By virtue of his special position between owners and their animal companions, the veterinarian in general practice often finds himself treating the psychological distress of owners as well as the ailments of animals. Herriot's story of Andrew Vine, like many other episodes in his books, shows how well Herriot was intuitively practicing animal therapy, a newly-recognized mode of healing that investigates and utilizes the therapeutic emotional bond between animals and their humans.

For a long time, the lives of handicapped persons have been immeasurably improved by animal assistants such as guide dogs for the blind, hearing dogs for the deaf, and small monkeys to assist the paralyzed. In 1994, over 400 rehabilitation programs in North America utilized hippotherapy, the medical use of horseback riding to normalize muscle tone and mobilize joints wasted by such diseases as multiple sclerosis and muscular dystrophy, a therapy traced to European medical writings in 1735.[6] Only recently, however, have the less tangible benefits of animal association (which every animal lover knows are real) been accepted as important adjuncts to psychological and emotional health.

Since 1945, when Ann Gritt Ashby, an American psychologist, pioneered the use of animals in working with mentally ill veterans, "the healing arts professions have been awakened to the inestimable value of pet-assisted therapy."[7] Dogs are especially able to connect with human psyches. For more than 20 years, New York psychotherapist Joel Gavriele-Gold has followed Sigmund Freud's example by having a dog present during his consultations with patients. Gavriele-Gold observed, "There was something about having a dog in the office that offered a kind of connection and warmth that contributed to the dynamics of therapy and the treatment process." Gavriele-Gold has never trained any of his dogs, all rescued animals, to behave in his office: "Instinctively, they knew how to act with patients."[8] Dogs even have been proved able to predict their epileptic owners' seizures.[9]

Researchers are also pursuing the possibility of a healing energy transfer that seems to occur from dogs to sick people. Veterinarian H. C. Gurney, of Aspen Park, Colorado, has used "Kirlian photography" to document "healthful interaction." Gurney claims that "the dog with which you're bonded can transfer and share its energy in an act of concern over your well-being."[10] Jack Butrick, who worked with Therapy Dogs Inc. for many years, noted in 1993 that therapy dogs often take a day or two to recuperate fully from only a half an hour with seriously ill patients, "as though they had given all their power away and must regenerate it. . . . It appears as though therapy dogs have a special power over patients suffering from depression, which is an emotion we are always dealing with." Butrick, like Herriot and many others who have witnessed the healing effect of animals on sick or maladjusted human beings, saw enormous benefits in the process: "even though the training is difficult, it is that personal satisfaction that you have given someone hope to continue on with life that is the reward."[11]

Many of James Herriot's stories prove how well he earned that kind of satisfaction. In his own difficult RAF period, Herriot's recollections of his successes in helping human beings and their animal companions to maintain mutually restorative relationships helped sustain his spirits. He managed to hang on through the required nine hours' flight instruction and successfully soloed, an accomplishment that flabbergasted him almost as much as it did Flying Officer Woodham. Herriot's pleasure at this achievement did not last long, however. Shortly after being transferred to Heaton Park, near Manchester, where he was graded as a pilot, Herriot learned he had to undergo surgery, which might have been a repair of an earlier hernia operation (*ATWW*, 356). In any case, he was unable to fly after the operation. One of the reasons the Spitfire proved so effective against the Messerschmitt 109, whose Daimler-Benz engine outperformed the Rolls Royce Merlin at high altitudes, was the ability of the British aircraft to make extremely tight turns, "like an eel doubling up on itself to escape a shark," as German ace Werner Molders, who had had plenty of chance to observe, pithily put it.[12] Before the advent of G suits, withstanding the ferocious stresses involved in flying the "Spit" demanded enormous physical stamina, the reason the RAF inflicted such intense conditioning on its aircrew trainees.

The flight of 50 men with whom Herriot had sweated out his training courses shipped out to Europe without him, and he was posted to Creden Hill, near Hereford, for his operation. While in the hospital, Herriot seems to have been one medical man who behaved well as a patient. In *All Things Wise and Wonderful,* he expressed great praise for the hardworking nurses who cared for him, his inspiration for an engaging recollection about Judy, the nurse dog on a Dales farm, who tended her four-legged patients with just as much TLC as her human counterparts had shown Herriot (*ATWW*, 362). His ensuing two-week convalescence at Puddlestone gave him plenty of time to reflect. At this point, Herriot the author included a tale of Tristan's misdeeds in which a romantic rendezvous between that roisterous young man and the luscious Lydia went badly haywire, forcing Herriot and Tristan to chase down an escaped Scottish terrier patient. This story, recalling the lighter-hearted style of *All Creatures Great and Small,* briefly brightened the grim wartime atmosphere of *All Things Wise and Wonderful* with comfortingly familiar humorous characters—Tristan as the thwarted romantic hero, the fearsome retired teacher who was the Scottie's owner, and Siegfried in his role of the perennially disapproving elder brother.

Once Herriot had convalesced, he hoped to be sent overseas and perhaps even rejoin his old flight, but he had unwittingly become entangled in a bureaucratic military dilemma. His operation had made it

impossible for him to function as a pilot, but his veterinary occupation
was reserved, meaning that he could serve only in an aircrew capacity.
The RAF simply did not know what to do with him. This situation
threw Herriot into the unhappiest state he had been in since he joined
the service. Recalling his loneliness, his feeling of uselessness, and probably, as often happens after major surgery, the contemplation of his own
mortality, Herriot gloomily reflected on the waste of his "contribution
to the war effort":

> I hadn't fired a shot in anger. I had peeled mountains of potatoes,
> washed countless dishes, shovelled coke, mucked out pigs, marched for
> miles, drilled interminably, finally and magically learned to fly and now
> it was all for nothing. (*ATWW*, 378)

To show his younger self coping with one of the lowest moments in his
life, Herriot the author paired this episode with the story of a retired
farmer that young Herriot had known in Darrowby, an old man who
had pitifully little to show for a life of hard work, nothing much but his
own memories. Like many retirees, Mr. Potts hungered for a taste of
human companionship that would give him back some of the self-
respect he had lost when the work that had defined him was over, and
he cherished the little conversations he and Herriot would occasionally
share when they met on a walk. The day before Mr. Potts died, the two
men together recalled the memory of a tough Clydesdale foaling they
had had when Herriot had first come to Darrowby. Herriot the author
needed only a few words to sketch a remarkable dialogue that greatly
illuminated two lives. Remembering Mr. Potts's long-ago kindness to a
young vet unsure of his work, Herriot returned the gift by telling Mr.
Potts what a good job Potts had done, restoring some of the old man's
lost dignity. In this story, Herriot the author had the ideal material for
rebuilding young Herriot's confidence in himself as both a competent
professional and a compassionate human being, two roles that for James
Herriot were always inseparable.

Holding tight to the conviction that he still possessed skills that others needed would likely have been hard for Herriot when the RAF was
dithering over what to do with a pilot-trained vet whose wings had been
clipped. Helpless in the grip of the military system, Herriot fell into one
glitch after another. He obediently took aptitude tests that purported to
show he was tailor-made to be a mechanic, while in reality, as he put it,
"if ever there was a mechanical idiot that man is J. Herriot" (*ATWW*,

385). Desperate, the military psychologists then suggested he try mete-
orology, but Herriot wound up as an assistant storekeeper, a mercifully
brief stage of his military career that he described as "bizarre" (*ATWW,*
385). Bureaucracy cast him up against the impenetrable laziness that
the military system fosters in some individuals, like Herriot's last RAF
superior, a quartermaster corporal who refused to exert himself to sort
the servicemen's laundry. Worse yet, the corporal wouldn't allow Herriot to do it, either, and in the resulting melee of enlisted men hell-bent
on clean socks, Herriot says, he was nearly lynched.

As a serviceman, Herriot had only one way out of this quagmire, his
ability to take the edge off his day-to-day frustrations by recalling better
days in Darrowby. The sight one day of a baby carriage on a Manchester
sidewalk brought back to him the tale of Roddy Travers, an enigmatic
odd-job man who contentedly wandered the Dales pushing a pram containing the entire paraphernalia of his life and his only family, Jake, a
handsome lurcher (a large, crossbred hunting dog). After Herriot extri-
cated a pebble that had somehow lodged in the big dog's throat, Roddy
happily went on his way again, living proof of the old Dales axiom that
Herriot himself had adopted: "As long as a man can pay his way, he's got
enough" (*ATWW,* 393). Herriot's own determination to remain in the
Dales despite the crushing income tax he paid on his earnings elo-
quently demonstrates that those words stayed with him all his life.

Near the end of *All Things Wise and Wonderful,* Herriot followed
Roddy Travers's story with the unlikely romance of little Ned Finch, a
hired hand who had patiently plodded through a life of routine farm
chores, waiting for something good to happen to him. Waiting and
waiting—though not quite so patiently—to be released from the RAF,
Herriot's situation paralleled Ned's. As Herriot gently told it, Ned and
Miss Tremayne's housekeeper Elsie fell in love at first sight and settled
into amazing wedded bliss, just what Herriot had so unwillingly left in
1943 and now wanted so badly to regain.

As Herriot described them, both Roddy Travers and Ned Finch are
characters not shaped so much by Herriot the author as by the Dales,
where hardship and trials are accepted conditions of living. Both Roddy
and Ned had succeeded in coming to terms with circumstances most
Americans would describe as poverty stricken; both characters managed
to find happiness, but not without enduring plenty of misery first. Herriot's quick diagnostic eye had spotted an old photograph of a pretty girl
among Roddy's few belongings in the baby carriage—a family picture,
perhaps, or a memento of a love that couldn't be. Herriot also had seen

the wretched loft where Ned Finch had lived for his entire working life before he married, the waste of 30-odd years that never could be replaced. "Aye well. These things happen" (*ATWW*, 404), was the Dalesman's stoic response to life's blows. Learning that lesson was hard for Herriot, who had come to the Dales as a young city man, impatient with bad weather, government regulations, and foolish farmers who didn't call the vet soon enough. Not until his experience in the RAF showed him what really mattered—his wife and baby, his devotion to his work, and his self-respect—could Herriot face personal disappointments with the maturity the Dales required of its people. Ned Finch's unlikely romance might have tempted Herriot to close *All Things Wise and Wonderful* on a "happily ever after" note, but instead Herriot concluded by recounting the loss of Oscar, a cat he and Helen had rescued and had come to love before Oscar was reclaimed by his former owners. "You get over these things in time," Herriot the author claimed (*ATWW*, 436); but animal lovers know that he knew the ache remains. This bittersweet mood pervades the ending of *All Things Wise and Wonderful* as Herriot the RAF veteran sets out from Darrowby's market square on foot, bound for Helen and eventually home.

Most reviewers described *All Things Wise and Wonderful* as "the third of the delightful, autobiographical series"[13] and "another engrossing view of humans and beasts."[14] Writing for *The New York Times Book Review,* however, Richard Lingeman noted that with this book subtle changes had appeared in Herriot's writing: "On the whole, '*All Things Wise and Wonderful*' is as ingratiating as the previous ones: niceness still triumphs, but this time around, it's a near thing." Lingeman sensed "formula creeping into the stories," and "mechanical plot-shifts, as though Herriot were straining to heighten and point up a diminishing store of materials."[15]

Significant differences do exist between *All Things Wise and Wonderful* and Herriot's previous two books. Most important, *All Creatures Great and Small* and *All Things Bright and Beautiful* were blessedly free of the shadow of war that clouds *All Things Wise and Wonderful*. In terms of his autobiographical narrative, too, Herriot was learning his veterinary profession in *All Creatures Great and Small*, settling into the Dales and courting Helen, while in *All Things Bright and Beautiful* he had taken up his rural veterinary routine and was savoring the small happinesses of married life. In both cases, his personal adjustments played an essential but quiet accompaniment to his professional adventures and the colorful characters that he encountered there. As Richard Gardner has pointed out, Herriot's first two books used carefully selected details to depict "situations in relation to clear general observations, without oversimplifying or overcomplicating. The main weakness of this technique is that the reader starts and stops uncomfortably often between anecdotes, as the most important events are left too much in the background to hold his continuing attention" (Gardner 634). So long as Herriot's personal life, despite temporary setbacks, was proceeding in the presumably satisfactory fashion that his traditional 1930s middle-class British upbringing had led him to expect—career, marriage, and children—his books focused on the amusing episodes of his veterinary work in the Dales, an area previously untouched in popular English literature, and readers found them irresistible.

On the other hand, when Herriot came to write *All Things Wise and Wonderful,* he was describing events in his life that were largely beyond his control. To make sense of them, he shifted emphasis to the major adjustments he himself had had to make during his months in the RAF, balancing those experiences against the kind of basically happy recollections that earlier had proved so popular. Furthermore, in this book, Herriot was setting his readers a wonderful example of quiet courage. As Joy K. Roy has pointed out, Herriot's "matter of fact recounting of hardship, study, and practice displays courageous fortitude . . . This unusual vicarious experience helps the reader climb out of his or her private Slough of Despond. The reader will be stunned at the amount of hardship encountered as a matter of course; one's own lot is bound to be better by comparison . . . this reading can patch up the human spirit."[16]

While he was working on *All Things Wise and Wonderful,* Herriot's whole world, even his cherished corner of Yorkshire, was changing rapidly. As time passed, he was losing the old Dales characters from the 1930s that he loved to write about, and his profession was in the process of transforming itself forever. In the decades following World War II, the industrialization of agriculture, its almost total mechanization, and the application of herbicides and pesticides on bigger and bigger fields all were making farm laborers, like draft animals, increasingly obsolete. By 1972, in fact, Herriot's U.S. veterinary colleagues were making more horse calls to pleasure animals than to draft horses (W&W, 14–15). Companion-animal practice had become the mainstay of most American and British veterinarians, whose historians describe the essence of their clinical practice from the early 1970s as being "flexible and sensitive, and thus tun[ing] in to the relationship between a client and his animal" (W&W, 15). This trend could not have suited Herriot's particular medical, emotional, and literary talents more perfectly, but he probably could not help but regret the loss of "the good old days," of old friends, and, most of all, his privacy.

Almost in spite of himself, James Herriot had become an international celebrity. David Susskind produced a full-length movie version of *All Creatures Great and Small* that was televised on the U.S. Hallmark Hall of Fame in February 1975. Soon Herriot had to battle the demands of invading journalists and hordes of tourists to protect the priorities his wife had set down for their life, "family, dogs, veterinary practice and his books and movies—in that order,"[17] and his real identity as Alf Wight, an ordinary veterinarian in a rural practice with his son Jim and his friend Donald Sinclair at Thirsk.

Invited to receive the American Veterinary Medical Association's 1975 Award of Appreciation for "the outstanding contribution his books ha[d] made in enhancing recognition and understanding of the veterinary medical profession" (*JAVMA* 75, 713), Herriot refused to leave his practice, so Dr. Ronald Jackson, then chairman of the American Veterinary Medical Association's executive board, took the award to Herriot in Thirsk. Typically enough, when Dr. and Mrs. Jackson arrived, Herriot was headed out to vaccinate Galloway calves. He loaded Jackson into the cluttered backseat of his car because Hector and Dan as usual occupied the front, but Dr. Jackson understandingly remarked that Herriot's dogs were "more important to him than money" (*JAVMA* 75, 704).

Visitors who met Herriot in person over the years saw exactly what they had already encountered in his books, "what is to Americans the best of what it is to be 'British': dignified, secure in one's history and place, tolerant, fair, reserved, intelligent, modest, humanistically educated, loving the English language, and projecting the empowerment of precise discourse" (Sternlicht, 16). To present the Award of Merit to Herriot, Dr. Jackson arranged a dinner, which happened to fall on Donald Sinclair's 31st wedding anniversary, June 3, 1975, and so the Jacksons also managed to provide a suitable cake. The October 15, 1975, issue of the *Journal of the American Veterinary Medical Association* contains a remarkable photograph of a cozy celebration that looks as if it comes straight out of one of Herriot's chapters. "Siegfried" is shown from the back toasting the group, which included his wife Audrey, "Tristan" and his wife Sheila, "Jimmy" Herriot and his wife Jill, "Granville and Zoe Bennett," Dr. and Mrs. Jackson, and the guests of honor, James Herriot and his wife Joan.

Herriot was enormously affected by the celebration. "I was truly staggered," Herriot wrote to the AVMA, "because I never expected such a superb gift [as his award] . . . if there is one single thing which has touched and rewarded me more than anything else, it is the warm-hearted and generous response of the American veterinary profession to my books. . . . [the plaque] will be my most treasured possession" (*JAVMA* 75, 704).

Chapter Five
The Lord God Made Them All

Damned to everlasting fame . . .
—Pope, An Essay on Man, ep. iii, l. 281

James Herriot's literary popularity peaked between the appearance in 1977 of *All Things Wise and Wonderful* and his fourth book, inevitably titled *The Lord God Made Them All,* published in 1981. *All Things Wise and Wonderful,* his last book to appear as two volumes in British publication, had taken Herriot about 18 months to write, but several factors slowed his work on *The Lord God Made Them All.* Herriot continued to insist that his practice came first, firmly describing himself as "a vet who scribbles in his spare time" (Gonzalez, *M,* 6), and he declared that he had no intention of changing the proportion of his life: "99 percent vet and 1 percent writer."[1] The enormous popularity his books had gained, however, was the biggest reason for his delay in producing *The Lord God Made Them All.*

So far, Herriot had endured his necessary exposures to the literary limelight with good grace, but his discomfiture with the demands fame made upon his time was growing. He had not been very happy doing his first U.S. book-promotion tour by himself, and much to his relief, his wife accompanied him on his second tour after the publication of *All Things Bright and Beautiful,* a crowded three weeks that except for his stint in the RAF marked his longest-ever absence from Yorkshire. Herriot had been booked for so many U.S. television talk shows that he later discovered he couldn't keep their famous hosts straight: "I think I was on Johnny Carson, but it might have been Mike Douglas" (Gonzalez, *M,* 6). He did, however, recall "being on that morning TV show with that lady newscaster—Barbara What's-Her-Name? She had a dog that was nipping at her and she kept yelling over to me between tapings that I was a vet and ought to do something to calm the animal down" (Gonzalez, *M,* 6).

That whole tour experience, Herriot said, almost ruined him (Taylor, 75). It also cured him of doing any more overseas publicity tours, but *All Things Wise and Wonderful* had such strong sales anyhow that it

remained on the *New York Times* best-seller list for 51 weeks. Herriot did
spend his annual winter holiday of 1977 in London talking to journalists
about *Vet in a Spin,* the British version of the last half of *All Things Wise
and Wonderful,* and soon his total sales reached 13 million copies. This
literary success wildly exceeded anything he might have dreamed about
when he began writing a decade earlier, but success was turning out to
be not at all Herriot's cup of strong Yorkshire tea. He told an interviewer in late 1977 that he was not sure his "next book w[ould] even be
about being a vet. I thought about doing a novel and that concept
appeals to me. Sport, too, could be the subject of a possible book. In
time I know I'm going to have to take a crack at something different"
(Gonzalez, *M,* 6).

Herriot's wife did her best to discourage interviewers and head off the
demands his fans were making on his time, and Herriot himself
expressed his distaste for public display in no uncertain terms: "I frankly
don't like fame. It doesn't give me any kick at all. It's nice to meet
glamorous and interesting people in the literary world once in a while,
and also the showbiz world. It's nice to be friendly with them, but not
to go into their world. It's not my world. I wouldn't be happy there."[2]

The uproar over Herriot's books was also disrupting his beloved
Dales, where most of the pragmatic home folks found that the novelty
of having a worldwide celebrity for a vet was quickly wearing off. Many
may have wrongly suspected that Herriot was becoming inordinately
wealthy from his memoirs. A local schoolteacher commented, "At first
we rushed out to buy his books, but now we say, 'Never mind your millions, just look after our Petunia' " (Del Balso, 177). Herriot claimed
with some glee that dour local farmers had even decided that his "books
are about *nowt* [the Dales term for 'nothing']" [italics in original] (Taylor, 75), but outsiders, particularly Americans, were voraciously roaming
the countryside, relentlessly combing the Dales for their favorite author,
insatiably photographing the landscape, interrogating the natives, and
unsettling the sheep. In addition, two movie versions of *All Creatures
Great and Small* were made on location in the Dales shortly before the
first BBC television series based on Herriot's stories aired in early 1978,
using the same title.

All this notoriety brought hordes of tourists and a deluge of mail to
Skeldale House. Several journalists also succeeded in locating Herriot
between 1978 and 1980, the short period when he seems to have been
most accessible to the press. He graciously, if a little wearily, cooperated,
and the resulting handful of interviews and articles remains the most

extensive view of James Herriot at the height of his popularity that currently exists.

David Taylor, who interviewed Herriot for London's *Radio Times* in
the winter of 1977, had the rare opportunity to see him in his natural
habitat. So as not to lose time from his practice, Herriot took the journalist along on his daily rounds. Taylor later described the experience
with some bemusement: "Bumping along in a mud-camouflaged Peu-
geot with a Labrador, Dan, and a stone-deaf terrier, Hector [Hector was
in fact blind, not deaf, and Herriot's dogs always rode in the front seat],
we had discussed mastitis and Bob Hope, laminitis and publishers, the
temperament of sheep, room service at Claridge's, pigs, television in
America, and whether cats get flu."[3] Probably at his wife's ultimatum,
Herriot's home life was now strictly off limits to journalists, but he told
Taylor that he had recently bought a new, smaller home outside of
Thirsk because now that their children were grown he and his wife no
longer needed a large house. The Herriots had also been taking package
vacations to Spain, a place Herriot confessed he was "partial to" (Taylor,
77) because of its sunny climate. What Herriot called the "side-effects"
of his fame, however, were proving to be major obstacles to his veterinary practice, which continued to be just as arduous as it ever had been.
At this time, Herriot did mostly cattle work from 9 A.M. to 7 P.M. daily,
although he now—in his sixties—was able to take every second weekend off.[4]

A few months later, despite the best efforts of Herriot's wife to dis-
suade him, British journalist Arturo Gonzalez Jr. managed to get one
interview with the world's most famous vet and economically milked
three articles out of it.[5] Herriot admitted to Gonzalez that "I'm naturally a quiet sort of chap and it's a bit of a nuisance when people call in
at the surgery just to shake hands . . . I counted two dogs and sixteen
visitors in my surgery the other day" (Gonzalez, *M*, 6). Herriot noted
that the fans—mostly Americans—who turned up uninvited at the
bright red door of Skeldale House were "well-intentioned people, and
they're paying me a compliment. I hate to be uppity, and I can't be
rude, but I have to insist that it's 'hello and goodbye,' and not let it
interfere with work that's got to be done" (Taylor, 76).

By now Herriot's daily mailbag took two men to lift (Taylor, 75).
"The mail is terrible. I just couldn't believe it when the avalanche first
started. I used to answer every one. If I did that now, it would be a full-
time occupation. And I wouldn't have the time to be a vet or to write
any more books" (Gonzalez, *M*, 6). Herriot, in fact, had instructed his

secretary to send out form letters in response to most of his mail, though he attended to quite a few himself.

Many people who have had limited financial success tend to lose their sense of proportion when some great stroke of fortune such as winning a lottery comes along. Nothing could have been further from Herriot's reaction to his literary earnings. Although Herriot struggled financially until *All Creatures Great and Small*, he remained throughout his life the same person he always had been, enjoying relatively few tangible rewards for his literary success. Besides the holiday trips to Spain, he treated himself and his wife to an occasional brief stay at a luxury London hotel like Claridge's, "way out of reach of the ordinary veterinarian." He sensibly commented, "I haven't got rich tastes . . . But it's good to have some security. Country vets make a very modest living" (Del Balso, 80). Herriot was never a spender, but his friends said that he generously saw that everyone around him was taken care of (Del Balso, 80). Herriot's accountant was also pleading with the author to find a less taxing residence, perhaps Ireland or the Isle of Man, but Herriot constantly refused to leave his practice in the Dales (Gonzalez, *M*, 6). All in all, Herriot had not changed because of his success, but he realized that his life certainly had: "I used to be just a poverty-stricken country vet. Now with all the extra pressures the books have produced, life has closed in on me somewhat" (Gonzalez, *M*, 6).

Not surprisingly under these circumstances, Herriot found it difficult to settle down to the next volume of his reminiscences. Although he toyed with the notion of writing a different kind of book, he finally decided that he had a good deal more to say about the Dales. He addressed his feelings about the land and its people directly in *James Herriot's Yorkshire,* a loving tribute to his adopted English county, published in 1979, but he still felt the urge to record more about "the old black-magic era" of veterinary practice in Yorkshire (Gonzalez, *A,* 37).

In late 1978, *Good Housekeeping* interviewer Suzanne Del Balso also spent a day with Herriot, jouncing from farm to farm with him in his "cluttered, not too clean" backseat. She found the famous animal doctor "intensely shy," with a passionate desire to remain anonymous. Herriot allowed Del Balso to observe him at his work, though he gruffly asked her to leave when he had to put a dog down, something he seems never to gotten used to doing. During the visit, Herriot told Del Balso that he was working on his next book, which his fans knew would have to be titled *The Lord God Made Them All,* from the final line of Cecil Frances Alexander's Victorian hymn that had provided the American titles for

Herriot's other books. Just as he had done earlier, Herriot drew this batch of stories out of his own memories, spinning yarns as easily as if he were leaning on the bar of the local pub: "I sometimes can't remember things I did last week, but there's something about conversations which I do remember. I can remember things that were said verbatim from my earliest days as a young vet. I didn't bother keeping a diary then. Now I keep a pad in my car and even a Dictaphone and speak into that when I remember something that will make a particularly good basis for a chapter" (Gonzalez, *A*, 38).

When *The Lord God Made Them All* appeared in 1981, many reviewers agreed with *Time*'s Stefan Kanfer that "All four Herriot books are bolts cut from the same Scottish tweed, carefully interweaving the local patois ('Owt a gurt cow wi' nawbut a stone in t'kidney') and technical jargon ('You can get hypertrophy of the rumenal walls and inhibition of cellulose-digesting bacteria with a low pH'). Each volume has become increasingly formulaic . . . But it is Herriot's original formula, an unfailing blend of exotica . . . and accounts of extraordinary happenings to ordinary people and creatures" (Kanfer, 74). Other reviewers now professed themselves unimpressed with Herriot's latest efforts; Richard Lingeman had already commented that *All Things Wise and Wonderful* showed "signs of wearing thin around the elbows,"[6] and regarding *The Lord God Made Them All*, Philip Johnson observed that Herriot "clearly knows the vein he is working by now, and the vein seems to be playing out. . . . Herriot's readers will be disappointed to discover that the unaffected charm that made his stories popular in the first place has now become a carefully reproduced commodity."[7] A few lampoons of Herriot's unmistakable style, "the tribute that humor pays to celebrity," also surfaced in 1981. "Monty Python kidded the title verse: 'All things gross and gangrenous, / All creatures gross and squat,' [and] Nature Writer [*sic*] Edward Hoagland parodied the books in the *New York Times:* " 'It's time t'awd bitch was up,' I said. I put my arm up her lug end to untwist her uterus . . . 'If tha'll just wipe off the fly that's on my snout, Colonel,' I said. 'I'll kill nowt gurt nor small! They's gentle things!' he roared, and took a bite of his stirk sandwich' " (Kanfer, 75).

Herriot remained as unaffected by literary critiques of his work, good or bad, as he was by one of Britain's highest honors, the OBE (Order of the British Empire), conferred on him by the Prince of Wales in 1979, or the Scottish and English honorary doctorates he received in 1979 and 1983 respectively. Whether his books were formulaic, whether they were "lightweight," as some critics claimed (Gonzalez, *M*, 5), or as superficially simple as basic truths about human behavior often seem, writing was always hard work for Herriot. While he was in active veterinary practice, he said, "I can't understand any writer who says putting a book together is easy. . . . The best days are those when I have the whole day off and can do nothing but work on my next book. I go like a bomb in the morning; it's tremendous how much I can do when I'm fresh. I wonder how many books I could have written if I'd been able to devote every morning to them" (Gonzalez, *M*, 6).

Until he retired from veterinary work, about 10 years later, Herriot never had the leisure to write that way. Still laboriously plugging along in the evenings like Charles Dickens, who also managed to do his writing while his children played noisily around him, Herriot stretched his time frame for *The Lord God Made Them All* over a much wider chronological range than he had ever used before, assembling material from several decades of his practice and "pour[ing] time back and forth like sand in a kitchen hourglass" (Kanfer, 74).

Writing between 1978 and 1980, Herriot principally harked back to his practice in the years immediately after the war. He also included more recollections of his favorite period, his first years in Yorkshire, as well as descriptions of two working-vet trips his friend John Crooks set up for him, a sea voyage to the Soviet Union in 1961 with £20,000 worth of sheep and a chancy 1963 flight to Istanbul with some valuable Jersey cattle breeding stock. *The Lord God Made Them All* thus includes three quite different sets of stories: the familiar Dales veterinary anecdotes that he wrote most often, this time drawn from the late 1930s to the early 1950s; a few proud-parent tales about Jimmy and Rosie as children that reveal some important aspects of Herriot as a parent; and mostly undigested diary entries from his two short trips abroad with farm stock in 1961 and 1963. These diary entries, which Herriot strewed randomly throughout *The Lord God Made Them All* as a kind of autobiographical padding, do not seem to come up to the level of the rest of the book. One reviewer gamely commented, "these travels . . . do not logically fall in with the postwar memories, [but] they add a lively touch to the more mundane, though still intriguing adventures at home."[8]

Because of England's postwar austerity, Herriot's principal historical backdrop for *The Lord God Made Them All* was worse than mundane. In *All Creatures Great and Small* and *All Things Bright and Beautiful,* he had worked with colorful old characters seen against their charming, simple prewar world, and in *All Things Wise and Wonderful,* he had balanced his own wartime miseries against the same healing prewar recollections of his home and work. In the late 1940s, however, Britons were grinding through a drab, dispirited existence because the costs of the war and its aftermath meant they were trying to accomplish the impossible—to eat the nation's economic cake and have it, too. World War II had been "the people's war," and afterwards the British people who had paid such an unprecedented price expected to be paid back. "Warfare and welfare seemed to go together . . . Soldiers, sailors and airmen were as concerned as civilians for their future after the war was over. . . . The prewar experience of the 'bitter society', as Arthur Marwick has called it, was turning people towards the vision of a better society" (Briggs, 273).

Britain's welfare state, initiated by the 1942 Beveridge Report on Social Security, proposed to abolish the " 'five giants' of want, sickness, squalor, ignorance and idleness" through a unified plan of social insurance that the new British Labour government implemented almost immediately at the end of the war.[9] Churchill and the Conservatives, widely blamed for Britain's harrowing prewar unemployment as well as for the war itself, were trounced in the general election of 1945. The victorious Labour Party at once set about nationalizing basic industries, establishing a national health service, and putting into effect the National Insurance Act of 1946, a comprehensive flat-rate plan of individual contributions and taxation that dealt out "benefits covering sickness, old age, unemployment, and industrial injury: it provided 'a shield for every man, woman, and child . . . against the ravages of poverty and adversity' " (Briggs, 284).

Britons soon realized, though, that the cost of bringing this utopian welfare state into being would be enormous, and the entire country suffered from its labor pains. "The clash between ideals and economics was always there after 1945 . . . Financial outlay on the social services . . . quadrupled between 1938 and 1949 . . . [and] The principle of offering to all [italics in original] the optimum social service, not the average, was always difficult to implement" (Briggs, 284). Millionaires as well as the poorest wage earners were to receive the same services, causing costs to increase and complaints to soar when the services thought best could not be offered to everyone. The new social programs had to be financed by both heavy taxes and austerity programs such as the rationing of food and fuels, which continued until 1948 despite some of the most severe winters England had seen in a century. The British "planning movement" attempted to move large numbers of urban poor into rented suburban housing "estates," and one of the promises that helped bring the Conservative Party back into power in 1951 was their pledge to build 300,000 new homes per year for the middle class to buy (Briggs, 289). Most of the estate building and new-housing construction took place at the edges of old villages and swallowed them up completely, a visible symbol of the disappearance of traditional British culture. Family sizes were falling, and domestic service had all but disappeared. The British housewife was demanding leaner cuts of meat in the butcher shop, presaging vast changes in the cattle industry. In the arts and education, famed British elitism and polish were giving way to an ideology of "the best for the most." A general decline in British taste was becoming all too evident: "Chain-store modernism, all veneer and varnish stain, is replacing the old mahogany; multi-coloured plastic and chrome biscuit barrels and bird-cages have come in" (Briggs, 280).

Yorkshire had always had its share of "poverty and adversity," most pervasively between 1931 and 1936, just before Herriot arrived in the Dales, when unemployment levels there had risen as high as 70 percent.[10] In the years just after World War II, even England's most remote areas like the Dales keenly felt the pangs of social change. Working as a rural veterinarian and raising children on a severely limited income—Herriot earned £10 a week in 1948 (*LGMTA*, 195)—might have driven many men to more lucrative pastures, but not James Herriot. Despite his bank manager's continual warnings about overdrafts (*LGMTA*, 164), Herriot was still in love with "the only job I've ever had." The Dales were "the only place I ever loved. I came here 44 years ago and smelled the summer," he stated in 1981; "I never wanted anything else" (Kanfer, 75).

No matter how dreary England's postwar condition was or how hard Herriot had to work to support his growing family, he enveloped *The Lord God Made Them All* in the warm nostalgia for the days that Herriot believed are the happiest time of a father's life, when his children are young. By the time Herriot returned from the RAF to the practice in Yorkshire, Siegfried Farnon had married, and Tristan had left the practice for the Ministry of Agriculture. Herriot and his wife again took up residence, now with their toddler Jimmy, on the top floor of Skeldale House, "with a view of the town and the surrounding hills. It was an ivy clad Georgian house which fronted the street and boasted lawns and a rockery at the back" (*SATA*, 187). Herriot included a lovely description of Skeldale House in *James Herriot's Yorkshire*, in which he praised the wisteria that covered the whole back side of the house and the "lovely room" that at first was the scene of many happy bachelor hours he spent with Siegfried and Tristan. After the war, the same room, open to the garden, became his family's sitting room, and now it is the waiting room for his son's veterinary practice (*SATA,* 187). The Herriot's daughter, Rosemary, was born in May 1947, arriving as had her brother at the Sunnyside Nursing Home on the village green at Thirsk. Herriot suitably commemorated the event at a local pub with good friends, a glowing celebration he made into one of the most satisfying chapters of *The Lord God Made Them All.* During the eight "hard but happy" years he and his family spent in their rummage-sale-furnished quarters above the headquarters of his practice, Herriot declared that he was rich because he had two children that he adored.

In 1949, Herriot was at last able to get his wife out of those charming but woman-killing quarters, which had been designed to be kept up by a squad of now nonexistent domestic servants.[11] The Herriots moved to a more convenient home, but Herriot wrote years later that Skeldale House had given him some of his dearest memories, such as playing "Kids' games [with Jimmy and Rosie] after a long hard slog round the practice . . . [and] even now as I look down the years I know I have never found a better way of living" (*SATA,* 167).

Describing events that took place during his children's youth allowed Herriot to reveal another engaging side of himself, the "big streak of old hen" (*LGMTA,* 47) that paternity brought out in him. Jimmy and Rosie attended the local school at Thirsk, but Herriot was one of those fine fathers—Siegfried was another—who gladly took his children with him on his daily rounds whenever he could, savoring "the intense pleasure of showing his life [to them]" (*LGMTA,* 203). Herriot's son, Jimmy, who grows from infancy to 10 years old in the course of *The Lord God Made Them All,* was evidently destined from the start to become a veterinarian, and his father later claimed that Jimmy turned out "a better vet than I would ever be" (*LGMTA,* 48). As a youngster, though, Jimmy's wall-climbing and piano-recital exploits, the stuff of which sheepishly proud parental anecdotes are made, gave Herriot the author the chance to laugh with his audience at his younger self, entirely at the mercy of his son in moments when Herriot, trying to work on a dog as Jimmy hung by his heels from a precarious wisteria vine, or suffering through Jimmy's interminable piano recital, simply couldn't discipline his son.

Everyone knows that fathers can also be reduced to putty in their daughters' little hands, so Herriot's admission that he talked his daughter Rosemary out of her dream of becoming a veterinarian shows an unexpectedly stubborn side of his personality. As a small child, Rosie unknowingly caused one of Herriot's most harrowing moments by wandering into the path of an enraged cow (*LGMTA,* 207), which inexplicably paused, rather than running her down, when Rosie said "Mama." Herriot's fear for his child, which like most parents he probably never quite got over, may have contributed to his disapproval of Rosie's original choice in careers. In the 1950s, when Rosie was growing up, few women went into veterinary medicine; the field then demanded even more physical strength and stamina, more endurance of unpalatable working conditions, and more risk to life and limb than it does today, and Herriot admitted that he could not bring himself to consider Rosie's doing the work that he performed every day—work that he was proud his son wanted to take up. Herriot evidently succeeded only partially in dissuading Rosie, because she became a physician and now practices near her brother at Thirsk. Also like many parents looking back at their children's youth, Herriot the author wondered whether he had done the right thing, but he took comfort that he and his children had shared a lucky, even blessed, relationship, and he believed that to a great extent his work in the Dales, rough and ill-paid as it was, had made that relationship possible. As Siegfried told Herriot at the close of *The Lord God Made Them All,* "We'll have no regrets, because we have both enjoyed our children and been with them from the beginning" (*LGMTA,* 371). No parent could ask for more.

The veterinary profession that Herriot's son Jimmy had already set his heart upon was entering the greatest period of change the field had ever experienced. In 1978, B. W. Kingrey, reviewing the history of veterinary medicine, observed that

> Several decades ago—almost suddenly in terms of our total history—the pharmaceutical industry began to make available to the practitioner its many "miracles" in bottles, tablets, and syringes. This growth of pharmaceutical manufacturing in the 1940s and 1950s can be attributed mainly to the introduction of the new sulfa drugs and antibiotics. The introduction of mass drug manufacturing resulted in a large increase in productivity, with new methods displacing the individual compounding of tablets and what was virtually a handicraft industry. Drugs became more plentiful and less costly.
>
> Now, then, the practitioner suddenly found himself armed with sulfas, antibiotics, antiparasitic compounds, corticosteroids, growth promotant and growth permittant drugs, commercial viral antigens and a succession of new drugs from which he could pick and choose with relative abandon.

The veterinarian, like his colleagues in human medicine, was quite suddenly highly effective . . . [but] As the practitioner systematically discarded an array of liquids and powders of imaginary value he was also required to understand that the more promising and effective the drug, the greater must be the skill and comprehension of the use. In response, our laboratories were also presenting amazingly prompt and precise diagnostic techniques and helping to direct the logical selection of drugs. There was a falling away of various cloaks that had shrouded our diagnostic ignorance. Large animal practice acquired the mantle of sophistication. (Kingrey, 116)

James Herriot, who was a compassionate working physician, not a sophisticated scientist, was watching his entire working world being reshaped, and he was not sure he approved. Some of the changes, of course, lightened his physical burdens, but change also meant that Herriot had to adapt to new treatments and procedures and governmental policies—and no matter how grueling his working life had been, Herriot had always found innovation difficult to accept.

In the early 1950s, the enormous progress taking place in veterinary medicine was only one aspect of Britain's new agricultural revolution. Major scientific discoveries continued to alleviate the suffering of animals, their owners, and their physicians, and most of the veterinary anecdotes Herriot included in *The Lord God Made Them All* deal with the heartwarming cures that practicing veterinarians now could effect: "Almost each day the large animal practitioner found himself able to cure a disease previously uncurable, or to prevent a disease previously unpreventable" (Kingrey, 116).

In a modest way, Herriot pioneered veterinary advances in Yorkshire, not so much because he wanted to, but because he had to. Since he was a man who frequently stressed his dislike of change, Herriot the author had to show considerable adjustment taking place in the younger Herriot's outlook during the time recorded in *The Lord God Made Them All*.

At the beginning of this book, the older Herriot positioned his younger self on the beautiful green heights of the Dales, facing the disturbing eve of a "world of change" with a stance that his RAF experience had probably intensified: quite simply, Herriot "did not like change" (*LGMTA*, 28). As in his earlier books, the conflict between what Herriot perceived as "a world of change" and the security of the unchanging Dales provides much of the creative tension of *The Lord God Made Them All*. Now young Herriot was confronting the uncomfortable fact that not just the outward, but more important to him, the inward aspects of

the Dales he treasured most—the people's attitudes and their way of
life—had already begun to react to outside pressures, and moreover,
whether he liked it or not, he would have to embrace the approaching
revolution in veterinary medicine. *The Lord God Made Them All* records
Herriot's difficult but graceful decision to come to terms with changing
times.

In both *All Creatures Great and Small* and *All Things Bright and Beautiful,* the elemental Dales world that Herriot had come to love was being
shaken by the dreadful imminence of war, which threatened the kind of
changes that Herriot abhorred most—separation from his family, the
conscription of his friends, the deaths of his countrymen, and the devastation of their land. All of those things came to pass, and Herriot the
author used them as the inescapable backdrop to *All Things Wise and
Wonderful*. In *The Lord God Made Them All,* however, the younger Herriot was back in the unchanging natural beauty of the Dales, with the
people whose consistent traits of character he had come to know well
and respect deeply. The countryside and its people gave Herriot the stability he needed to deal with the unknowns waiting in his future. As *The
Lord God Made Them All* begins, even Siegfried's slapdash, high-speed
driving over the narrow, hair-raising, hairpin Dales roads boosted Herriot's enthusiasm at being home again: "So many things were new and
different, but the Dales hadn't changed, and Siegfried hadn't changed
either" (*LGMTA,* 33).

Ultimately Herriot accepted most of the new and different elements
that were poised to invade his veterinary practice mainly because of his
grief over losing many animal patients to diseases whose treatments had
not yet been discovered. Such frustrating losses have always been and
will always be an unhappy constant in physicians' lives, and Herriot the
author made one such loss the most affecting episode in *The Lord God
Made Them All,* if not in all his work.

No one knows why or how the mysterious bond between a particular
animal and its chosen human being arises, but every animal lover can
testify to that bond's warmth and power. Early in his practice, Herriot
lost his heart to Amber, a beautiful young shepherd cross, but not until
The Lord God Made Them All could he finally bring himself to tell her
tragedy, simply and poignantly, in some of the best writing he was capable of doing.

Like so many companion animals cast out into the world through
their owners' carelessness or rejection, Amber was homeless, and Herriot
happened upon her while he was caring for animals in a public shelter.

Amber was suffering from demodectic mange, an appalling disease for which no effective treatment existed until well into the 1970s. Deep down, Herriot knew that Amber was doomed, but he took her home anyhow and kept her in an outbuilding away from Helen because he did not want his wife, too, to become attached to the suffering dog. Herriot tried every remedy his training and his heart could offer, but finally he had to give Amber a gentle death, the only relief he could bring her, but always one of the hardest acts a veterinarian must perform.

Herriot delayed writing Amber's story until the fourth book of his memoirs, an indication of how painful Amber's memory still was for him 40 years after she died. Losing Amber was a terrible blow for Herriot not only because her death came close upon the heels of Oscar, the "cat-about-town" the Herriots had healed and then had to return to his previous owners at the end of *All Things Wise and Wonderful,* but also because Amber's death increased Herriot's feelings of his inadequacy as a veterinarian. Worse yet, Herriot had allowed himself to become emotionally involved with his patient, a lapse of professional detachment that he admits he had not been able to avoid. Readers who have ached with guilt and grief at the loss of a beloved pet can forgive Herriot much more readily than he seems to have been able to forgive himself, but the same emotional bond with Amber that Herriot simultaneously confessed as a dog lover and deplored as a physician allowed him as a writer to achieve one of his most unforgettable scenes. Amber's memory lives on vividly in the pages of *The Lord God Made Them All* because it always remained clear to Herriot; afterward, every time he saw a healthy dog he had cured, "The picture of Amber [came] back into my mind. It is always dark, and she is always in the headlight's beam" (*LGMTA,* 142). Amber's story unforgettably reminds Herriot's readers that a beloved animal, like everything else we love, remains bright in our memories, silhouetted against the darkness—in our world or in ourselves—that brought about the loss.

The pain Herriot suffered at losing Amber echoed every time he shared the suffering of owners whose companions could not be saved. This probably was his major motivation to experiment with new medicines and procedures in his practice. Taken together, Herriot's accounts of his dealings with veterinary innovations form an important narrative stream in *The Lord God Made Them All,* and most of these episodes illustrate some facet of his younger personality and the changing face of agriculture in the Yorkshire Dales. One more time, Herriot played all of this out against the common denominator of the sturdy values that stubbornly lingered on in the Dales, defying some encroachments of popular culture and technological progress.

Rather in spite of himself, Herriot was the first veterinarian in his part of Yorkshire to go in for innovative large-animal surgery such as cesarean sections (Green, 97). Until just after World War II, tough deliveries of calves or foals meant hours of heavy labor for veterinarians, exemplified by the arresting scene Herriot chose to open *All Creatures Great and Small*. In *The Lord God Made Them All*, Herriot described the traditional solutions to those cases with a postwar vocabulary and a note of weariness: "Sawing up calves with embryotomy wire. Knocking my guts out trying to bring heads around or reach feet. I think I must have shortened my life" (*LGMTA*, 64). Herriot was thus ripe for innovation when Norman Beaumont, a veterinary student interning with Herriot and Siegfried Farnon, glibly claimed he had been trained at college in the new veterinary cesarean procedure, which would make such agonies obsolete. Awash with pioneering zeal "in a moment of decision, of history" (*LGMTA*, 65), Herriot drew out his scalpel and made the crucial incision only to discover that Norman's reach had far exceeded its grasp: as it turned out, Norman had seen only one cesarean section, and that from the rear of the classroom. Describing his surgical point of no return, Herriot squarely hit the right mix of humor and pathos. His maternity case was a wretchedly small cow, totally exhausted from straining for a whole day to deliver an enormous bull calf. Norman's overweening self-confidence was properly deflated; and despite not knowing exactly what he was doing, Herriot himself mustered stoutly onward, only occasionally (and justifiably) growling or shouting at Norman, whose pretentiousness had gotten them into the mess in the first place. In a "sudden wave of illumination" Herriot admitted, "I wished with all my heart and soul I had never started this ghastly job" (*LGMTA*, 65), but to his amazement, cow, calf, Norman, and Herriot all managed to survive the operation. A little later, over a necessary restorative pint, Herriot's innate generosity overcame him, and he apologized to Norman for "shouting and nagging" him in the throes of the struggle (*LGMTA*, 75). This episode clearly defines Herriot's role as reluctant medical innovator. Once he allowed himself to get into a bad situation, he gamely saw it through as best he could, with only a few understandable lapses from gentlemanly conduct.[12]

Whereas Amber's story traced one of Herriot's greatest disappointments, and his first attempt at a C-section remained one of the major miracles of his veterinary career, Herriot's account of his attempt to introduce artificial insemination to the Dales stands as the comic masterpiece of *The Lord God Made Them All*. If, as the French philosopher Henri Bergson put it, humor arises from our perception of incongruity, Herriot managed to capture in sublimely well-chosen words one of the most incongruous of situations: the hapless veterinarian's attempted deception of a bull, a massive animal violently determined to carry out his only excuse for existence, breeding with the first available cow. The bull in Herriot's story is a particularly mean-eyed, rapier-horned specimen of Ayrshire that Herriot had to deceive into making its contribution to the rural economy via a brand-new scientific apparatus wielded by an untrained professional, namely Herriot, whose dubious preparation for the job was a single sketchy reading of a veterinary pamphlet on artificial insemination. When several of Herriot's attempts at scientific innovation proved fruitless, the bull's patience ran out, and with retribution uppermost in his mind, he charged his tormentor. Herriot escaped intact, but after that incident, he said, he often wondered whether he was "the only veterinary surgeon to have used an artificial vagina as a defensive weapon" (*LGMTA,* 238).

As well as the tragedies and comedies inherent in treating animals and dealing with their owners, no Herriot book would be complete without chapters praising the qualities of character he most respected in the farmers of the Dales. At the time when antibiotics were being introduced, many farmers had difficulty with the then-revolutionary notion that one shot of penicillin in the neck could cure an infection in, say, a hoof. One of Herriot's early antibiotic injections went badly wrong, causing the death of a cow from an unexpected blood clot. Though Herriot blamed himself, the cow's owner, Robert Maxwell, accepted the loss with the stoic Dalesman's "Ah well. . . . These things happen in farming." Maxwell never once mentioned Herriot's mistake to the veterinarian again in the 30-odd years of their acquaintance (*LGMTA,* chapter 10). Herriot the author maintained that Maxwell's conduct taught him far more about living than about veterinary practice; Herriot acknowledged that later when he found himself with justifiable grievances against his fellow men, Robert Maxwell's essential decency provided Herriot a noble example of conduct to follow.

From his portrait of Robert Maxwell, Herriot turned to the supernatural lore of the Dales, a subject that had always intrigued him. The local barber Josh Anderson had stranger talents than cutting hair, talents that fit into the old, unhallowed Yorkshire tradition of folk magicians such as the wise man of Sowerby, who could read the future in a crystal the size of a goose egg, or Old Sally Kindreth of Scorton, "active 1800 to 1810," whose divinations, without benefit of equipment, were reputedly just as uncannily accurate (Williams, 22, 53–54). In this episode, Herriot got more than the usual hair-jerking cut from Josh Anderson, who apparently had little talent for barbering, for the victims of his dull implements, including Herriot, tended to emit moans of anguish when Anderson broke out the thinning shears. Anderson had a curious habit of running hair he was to cut thoughtfully through his fingers, a gesture he often used with his little dog, Venus. When a chicken bone became wedged in Venus's throat, Anderson proved too ham-handed and squeamish to help Herriot get the bone out, so after sending Anderson away, Herriot, a self-confessed nervous anesthetist all his working days, had single-handedly to put Venus under. When he got the bone out, Venus did not resume breathing, so Herriot dashed outdoors and resuscitated the dog by whirling her around his head several times, much to the delight of little Jimmy, who had solemnly witnessed the entire performance.

Herriot never told Anderson what he had done, but during Herriot's next haircut, Anderson confessed he had a talent for reading thought—human as well as canine—through the hair, intimating he had "seen" Venus flying through the air. When working, Herriot usually seemed as commonsensical as any hardheaded Dales farmer, but as most physicians do, Herriot encountered phenomena in his practice that apparently could not be explained by hard fact, and Anderson's purported telepathic talents seemed one of these cases. Herriot's observation seems again to have been ahead of his times. Besides scientific experimentation on human-to-human telepathy that has been carried on for many years in the United States and other countries, the U.S. Navy has devoted considerable time and funds to establishing various types of contact, including telepathy, with dolphins, and several reputable current studies seriously discuss the possibility of extrasensory contacts between animals and humans.

Pet owners, especially dog obedience trainers, frequently feel that they and their animal companions communicate in some unspoken way. An intriguing analogue to the implications of Herriot's title *The Lord God Made Them All* appears in the work of Larry Dossey, a medical doctor and author of *Recovering the Soul—A Scientific and Spiritual Search*. Dossey suggests that "millions of pet owners may be convinced that their pets may be 'part human' because of a universal mind that connects human beings, animals, and all other living things. . . . Telepathy would be an easy task to accomplish if the minds of all living creatures were somehow united in a great universal mind pool."[13]

In *The Lord God Made Them All,* besides hinting at such murky matters as the possibility of telepathic communication with animals, Herriot also attempted on-the-spot communications with such foreign species as the Russians and the Turks, unusual departures for a homebody like himself. Besides filling up his fourth book for St. Martin's, Herriot's recollections of his October 28–November 6, 1961, trip to Lithuania, then a part of the former Soviet Union, and to Istanbul, Turkey, August 8–10, 1963, illustrate unusual experiences from the middle of his career. Herriot, who after his discharge from the RAF had declared that he wished never to leave Helen or the Dales again, attributed his suddenly itchy feet to a desire to get out of a rut in which he seemed to find himself in the early 1950s. Through his good friend John Crooks, who had worked with Herriot and Siegfried Farnon for a few years before taking a position with the British Ministry of Agriculture in the mid-1950s, Herriot received these two unexpected opportunities to satisfy a wanderlust he felt he had inherited from generations of seafaring ancestors.

Herriot seems to have chosen most of the episodes of *The Lord God Made Them All* to show how they allowed him to stretch and grow as an individual, and his trips to faraway places certainly gave him spectacular changes of pace—North Sea storms, mountainous cholesterol-laden Danish breakfasts that Herriot seems to have heartily enjoyed despite heavy seas and his distaste for dietary fats, and a harrowing, uninsured flight from Turkey back across the Alps in a rickety war-surplus Globemaster. These experiences seem to have done more for Herriot as a person than as an author, making him give renewed thanks for all he had at home, but as samples of his writing, his diary entries of his ten-day voyage to Soviet Russia and his three-day odyssey to Istanbul lack the careful shaping by which he turned his other experiences, so much less exotic, into literature.

Except for these out-of-sequence diary records, possibly included to swell *The Lord God Made Them All* to contractual proportions, Herriot dwelt vividly on the years that he called the best ones of his life, and story after story, such as the tale of detestable businessman Walt Barnett who weeps over his dead cat and makes Herriot like him better for it, demonstrates Herriot's constant theme: the saving grace animals bring with their companionship not only heals people but also brings out the best in them.

At the end of *The Lord God Made Them All*, Herriot seems to have deliberately chosen to bring his cycle of Yorkshire stories full circle, an implicit declaration that he had completed all the memoirs he was going to write. Just as about 10 years earlier he had opened *All Creatures Great and Small* with a younger Herriot waking up from a nap in the garden of Skeldale House to listen to Siegfried's predictions for their profession, Herriot now closed with himself and Siegfried contemplating the future of their profession on a grassy slope in the western Dales. Both men felt that the recent developments in veterinary medicine had brought them a "high noon" of new achievements and new respect for their work, but they both also knew substantial challenges lay before them as their practice shifted from large farm animals to the companion-animal work that today chiefly occupies the veterinarians at Thirsk. Siegfried, unquenchably optmistic, proclaimed, "I tell you this, James. There are great days ahead!" (*LGMTA,* 373). On the verge of middle age, James Herriot may not have been so sure—and he, like Herriot the author who wrote about him 30 years later, was a tired man.

The period of his life that Herriot covered in *The Lord God Made Them All* took its end points from his children's ages. At the beginning of this stage of Herriot's memoirs, Jimmy was a toddler, and Rosie had just been born. When Herriot closed the book, Jimmy was ten and Rosie six, a time when Herriot's younger self was regretfully watching the precious years of their childhood slip quickly away. As a young father, Herriot always yearned to spend more time than he could with his children, and as he looked back from his sixties, Herriot the author decided *The Lord God Made Them All* would be the last book of his memoirs so that he could be the kind of grandfather he wanted to be.

By now, the Herriot industry was in full swing. For some time, Herriot had employed both a secretary to help handle his fan mail and an accountant to handle his business affairs, because the author claimed he was "no good at all" at handling such matters himself: "I've had all sorts of clever people advising me on this, that and the other with investment and so on, but it's just no good—if I can't understand it, I steer clear of it."[14] Herriot had also acquired a literary agency, the well-known David Highet firm in London, which from that point on stringently limited access to the author and his works.

Herriot's lifelong publishers, Michael Joseph in London and Thomas McCormack of St. Martin's Press in New York, had hoped Herriot would send them a book a year, but after Herriot had said "Enough!", his publishers and his agency found other ways to keep the chronicles of

Darrowby before Herriot's adoring public. After *All Things Wise and Wonderful*, Herriot was persuaded to begin work on his travel book, *James Herriot's Yorkshire*. Various collections of his stories were planned; "James Herriot's Yorkshire Calendar" became an annual holiday staple in bookstores; and self-contained episodes, both new and previously published, appeared occasionally in *Good Housekeeping* and *Reader's Digest*.

Herriot wanted badly to take his life back from the boa constrictor of literary fame that was threatening to engulf him, his family, and the work he loved. In 1981, he forthrightly insisted

> I've got enough ideas written down as chapter headings, to fill another five or six books, but I'll never write them. *The Lord God Made Them All* is my last. . . . I look at the last ten years and realise how much experience has been lost while I tapped away at a typewriter. Not enough time has been devoted to my grandchildren. I'm missing their youth and the fun of doing things with them.
>
> There's so much gardening neglected and so many walks never taken over the fells, when the air was warm and the pale sun fingering the heather. But there's one day to which I still look forward. It's the one when I open my surgery curtains in the morning and there's no one outside pointing a camera at me. (*SATA*, 172–73)

Chapter Six

James Herriot's Yorkshire

There is a pleasure in the pathless woods,
There is a rapture on the lonely shore,
There is society, where none intrudes . . .
—Lord Byron, Childe Harold

In the late 1970s, between finishing *All Things Wise and Wonderful* and starting *The Lord God Made Them All,* James Herriot watched the popularity of his books rocket to undreamed-of heights, not perhaps the fate for his books and himself this quiet man would have chosen. Herriot's real name and whereabouts had become more common knowledge than he liked. Visitors now far outnumbered clients in his Thirsk waiting room, and his fan mail was threatening to overwhelm his postal carriers. This torrent of attention was disrupting Herriot's whole life, interfering with his veterinary practice, diminishing the time he could spend with his family, and upsetting his hope of trying his hand at a completely different kind of literature, perhaps a novel, as a change of pace from the reminiscences that he had been tapping out on his portable typewriter for the past 10 years.

As events proved, though, Herriot could no more leave the Dales in his writing than he could abandon them physically for a tax haven. Many of his letters from abroad contained questions about his beloved Dales, an area then little known outside of England, and before he began *The Lord God Made Them All,* he tackled his only work not directly involving animal anecdotes drawn from veterinary practice, his travel book *James Herriot's Yorkshire,* published by St. Martin's Press in 1979.

The text of *James Herriot's Yorkshire* is actually a long essay divided into 30 short sections—the demands of Herriot's veterinary work evidently solidified his longtime habit of writing in bursts of two or three pages—illustrated delectably by Derry Brabbs' photographs. *James Herriot's Yorkshire* is unique in Herriot's works, too, because in it he presented his recollections and reflections directly, not addressing his readers through third-person accounts of his younger self. Herriot's subject in this book is Yorkshire itself and its "sweet places of memory" (*JHY,* 224), his refuge from the threatening world of the 1970s. The author begins the book with a long retrospective account in which he reveals more of "Herriot the author," his mature life and personality, than he did in his four hymn-titled books.

Herriot still thought of "Yorkshire" in its centuries-old context as England's largest county. For administrative purposes, Yorkshire's 6,091 square miles used to be separated into three ridings that met at York, the traditional county town that belonged not to a riding but to its own small district of Ainsty. Each riding also had its own administrative center. The towns of Beverley in East Yorkshire and Northallerton in Herriot's North Yorkshire headed largely rural areas resembling America's Great Plains. Both the Plains' rural economy and North Yorkshire's were based on livestock (cattle and sheep), grains, and sugar beets. Wakefield, in West Yorkshire, largest of the ridings, was the center of Herriot's "other Yorkshire," containing decaying industrial cities such as Leeds and Sheffield, long famous for wool, coal, and metallurgical production. At the time Herriot began writing, Yorkshire's total population had reached about five million people.

In 1974, the year *All Things Bright and Beautiful* appeared in New York, Parliament divided Yorkshire into four separate counties, North Yorkshire, Cleveland, West Yorkshire, and Humberside. North Yorkshire contains Herriot Country in the largest sense. North Yorkshire is a spacious, squarish area of north-central England bounded by the Pennines to the west and the North Sea on the east. England's northernmost county, Durham, lies on Herriot Country's northern border, and the cities of Harrowgate and York abut it to the south. East and west of Thirsk, Herriot Country has two sets of "Dales," a word the English language borrowed from the Norse to describe austere, scantily populated upland valleys. Herriot was fond of all the Dales and did handsome justice to them all in his writing.

The eastern set of Yorkshire's Dales stretches southeast from the Cleveland and Hambleton Hills in England's North York Moors National Park, an expanse of excellent walking country, moorland, and heath covered in pines, broom, and a large variety of wildflowers, an area famous in English literature as the romantic locale of the Brontës' popular nineteenth-century novels. Herriot first worked in the western set of Dales, though, 680 square miles designated since 1949 as the Yorkshire Dales National Park, still 99 percent privately owned and extending southeastward from the Pennines, England's highest mountains, whose summits approach 2,000 feet. The more remote western valleys seem always to have been closest to Herriot's heart. "Ribblesdale is the most dramatic, with waterfalls and towering crags, interesting caves and large quarries. Swaledale is also wild, with rugged gorges and jagged rocks. Wharfdale, particularly Upper Wharfdale, is a gentler valley of great beauty. Wensleydale is wider, with lush pasturage, but also with waterfalls and areas of heath."[1]

Picturesque as the scenery of the Yorkshire Dales National Park is, farming there has always been marginal, and veterinarians have always had plenty of hard work to do. Agriculturally, the western Dales are

> predominantly an area of permanent grass and rough grazing, only a very small proportion being regularly ploughed. The farming is [today as in Herriot's early career] therefore almost entirely pastoral, devoted to the rearing of sheep and cattle.
>
> About one-third of the farms, particularly those in the valleys where the grazing is richer, concentrate on dairy farming, whilst the higher hill farms, having to contend with the harsher conditions of the fells, are concerned almost entirely with sheep. . . . in a typical summer there are over half a million ewes and lambs within the Park and about 75,000 cattle and calves. These produce sufficient milk, beef and lamb for about a half million people, an output worth more than eleven million pounds annually. (Duerden, 14)

Opening in the rugged western high country, Herriot organized *James Herriot's Yorkshire* in the geographical west-to-east pattern of the Dales, working his way toward England's northeast coast.

Herriot had sentimental reasons, too, for beginning this book in the western Dales. He had started his veterinary work there, spending most of his time 20-odd miles as the crow flies northwest of Thirsk, in the hills west of Leyburn, the "doorstep of the Dales" locally renowned for the longevity of its citizens (*JHY,* 28). Herriot then worked primarily in Wensleydale, Coverdale, and Swaledale with Siegfried Farnon's older partner Frank Bingham, who like Farnon was "a heaven-sent expert" with horses (*JHY,* 21). Herriot said he never met a man he liked better than Frank Bingham, whom he portrayed briefly but movingly as Ewan Ross in *All Things Bright and Beautiful* (*ATBB,* 207–15), a soft-spoken, hardworking vet who would tell Herriot funny stories about his day's work when they relaxed over drinks at night. According to Herriot, Bingham had ridden with the Canadian Mounties and Australian drovers before settling into practice in the Dales just after World War I, and to the horse-shy Herriot, seeing Bingham work horses "was an education in itself" (*JHY,* 21). Bingham and his wife Emmy became two of Herriot's closest friends, and Herriot admitted still feeling "a dull ache" when in later years he thought about Frank, who died "like many good vets, in a cow byre doing a tough job" (*JHY,* 18).

Herriot's literary portrait of Yorkshire moves eastward from the high country, over the Pennine passes through the historic town of Richmond, to the ancient Yorkshire lead mines, then to the area around Thirsk, the market town of a few thousand people that is geographically the center of both Herriot Country and the Farnon-Herriot practice, near some of the most handsome ruined Cistercian abbeys in Great Britain. Near Thirlby, a small village a few miles east of Thirsk, is Herriot's home, Mire Beck, a small bungalow with a large garden and a duck pond, on the way up steep 900-foot Sutton Bank, the gateway to the eastern Dales, which once contained more sheep than people. The sparsely settled eastern valleys, principally Bransdale, Farndale, and Rosedale, lying south of the North York moors, are picturesque areas punctuated by white outcroppings of limestone, clumps of woodland, and avenues of tall trees. To bring more land into agricultural production, the thin covering of poor soil in the eastern Dales has recently been improved, so that the eastern Dales have become a fertile, wheat-producing region. These Dales are dotted with little stone bridges carrying heavy loads of England's history, a field that intrigued Herriot greatly.

Although he vastly preferred to write about rural areas and their people, *James Herriot's Yorkshire* also includes sketches of the largest cities in Herriot Country. Harrowgate, an old spa town he called "Brawton" in his books, was frequently the site of his cherished half-day outings with Helen, and York itself, the ancient capital of England's North, was duly noted in his books as the shopping mecca where his wife purchased her wedding ensemble. Herriot closed his travel book at vacation spots around Whitby and Scarborough on Yorkshire's North Sea coast, where his seafaring heritage made him also feel at home.

Although Herriot could not resist including a few witty observations about animals and their owners in *James Herriot's Yorkshire,* nonveterinary preoccupations dominate this book, which also contains the insights into the local geography, history, and linguistic heritage that he absorbed over more than 40 years in the Dales. *James Herriot's Yorkshire* is uniformly warm and nostalgic, because in order to write it Herriot had to look back to some of his happiest days, among them the infrequent holidays he could take from his veterinary work. At first, he had had very little free time—just a half day off once a week, and later only every other weekend—so the moments he could spend with his family were precious. Like many natives, the Herriots usually took their vacations somewhere in Yorkshire. "Yorkshire folk—who have a well-deserved reputation for hard-headedness and for knowing good things when they see them—have, of course, always visited the Dales in droves; nearly one in three of those taking their holidays there are from Yorkshire. To Yorkshiremen and women home is still best, apparently, whether at work or play" (Duerden, 7).

Aside from being James Herriot's home, Yorkshire's major tourist attraction has always been its singular combination of natural beauty and historical treasures, both of which display an exceptionally broad range of features. Reading *James Herriot's Yorkshire* is like taking a leisurely ramble through the hills and dales and ruins beside the book's middle-aged author, athletically fit from a lifetime of hard physical work and willing to share his favorite spots with outsiders. One of Herriot's favorite pastimes was walking—walking in the old quasi-religious British sense that is little known or practiced today in the automobile- or aerobics-obsessed United States. In the Britain that used to be, the traditional sport of walking was not grim-faced cardiovascular exercise, but rather approached a philosophical way of life. A stout-booted British walking tour of a dozen or so miles a day allowed walkers to linger over sunrises and rainbows, watch birds and animals, and mingle with like-minded strangers at friendly hostels. This kind of walking fostered a comradeship with nature impossible to achieve any other way, shoring up the spirit and sharpening the perceptions just as much as the exercise toned up the physique.

From his boyhood onward, Herriot was a great walker in the classical British sense, and following his introduction to *James Herriot's Yorkshire,* he devoted a substantial chapter to a walking tour he took with his son Jimmy and one of Jimmy's friends in the triangular area of the Pennines bordered by youth hostels in Aysgarth, Grinton, and Keld (*JHY,* 28), where Herriot had worked with Frank Bingham. The first time Herriot saw such bare, sweeping vistas as the view of Wensleydale from the road to Aysgarth, they convinced him to make his home in Yorkshire, and every time he saw them later they thrilled him every bit as much. Herriot treated many a thoroughbred in those broad, high fields, where the underlying limestone, as in Ireland's famous horse-raising Connemara district, gives grazing animals the extra calcium that produces the outstanding bone development of some of England's greatest racehorses and steeplechasers.

Near the twelfth-century Aysgarth church and a steep stretch of road made world famous by Herriot's description of his heart-stopping brakeless descent in *All Creatures Great and Small*, he and the boys also visited 200-foot Aysgarth Falls in one of England's most spectacular gorges, one of those spots that Herriot, with his intense sensitivity to the spirit of Yorkshire places, found magical, "a secret place, a place of wonder" (*JHY*, 40). Both here and throughout his memoirs, Herriot practiced his own magic, his ability to find exactly the right words to convey the awe he felt in the presence of natural beauty to his readers. Walking tours such as the one which opens *James Herriot's Yorkshire* inspired Herriot to link his firsthand experience of Yorkshire's geographical and historical beauties with the wealth of knowledge about his adopted county he had gleaned over the years from his reading and his close association with the men and women of the region.

Besides Yorkshire's rivers and falls and its dignified old gray stone villages such as Swaledale's Askrigg, which the BBC used to represent Darrowby in the television series *All Creatures Great and Small*, Herriot Country seems to possess more than its share of the exceptionally varied geographical features that characterize Yorkshire as a whole. Herriot Country's western section, occupying roughly the northwestern quarter of the old county of Yorkshire, is the Yorkshire Dales National Park, the third largest national park in England, forming a rough oblong a little over 25 miles on each side.

The Yorkshire Dales National Park is "karst" country, a primeval seabed formed during the Carboniferous Period between 350 million and 220 million years ago. The geology of the park is characterized by many horizontal and vertical layers of limestone, the lowest of which is responsible for the enormous "scars," or cliffs. Herriot's favorite, Sutton Bank, lies at the southeast edge of the park. The most common feature of karst country, which Yorkshire shares with the shores of the Adriatic Sea, is the presence of limestone on or near the surface (Duerden, 16). Over the ages, water percolating through joints in such rock and soil formations produces eerie features. Herriot described the forbidding Buttertubs in detail, great fluted rocky holes almost a hundred feet deep near the top of the 1,682-foot pass between Wensleydale and Swaledale, one of the highest passes in England (*JHY*, 63). Dales streams often abruptly disappear underground at a "sink," producing dry creeks and sinkholes 10 to 30 feet deep, and then mysteriously emerge again some distance away, and numerous caves and potholes created by water action run along vertical joints of limestone deposits. Near Ingleborough, in the park, vertical crevices called "grikes" provide a moist, sheltered habitat for plants found nowhere else in England, making the area a treasury for botanists (Duerden, 18).

One of the greatest intangible treasures of Herriot's life in Yorkshire was a view above Crackpot Hall, an old shooting lodge, in the open upland country at the head of Swaledale: "nowhere is the Dales ambience of peace and mountain air so strong" as there, he wrote, a healing place for him: "I could never be unhappy here or plagued by the little worries of the world" (*JHY*, 53).

Many of his world's little worries—and some of Herriot's own— involved the necessity of making a living from a land that possesses some of the most forbidding climatic and geographical features in the British Isles. Because farming was such a chancy occupation in the western Dales, their inhabitants turned to other natural resources, and even before the Romans entered Yorkshire in strength during the first century A.D., Bronze Age peoples had exploited the large deposits of lead found north and east of Swaledale and to the east of Wharfdale (Duerden, 18), areas Herriot gingerly explored on his walks. The Romans began shipping out pigs of Yorkshire lead to Italy in the second century, and as Herriot proudly noted, lead from Yorkshire was subsequently used for the roofs of many great medieval European cathedrals. Because of injections of capital and new mining techniques during England's Renaissance in the sixteenth century, the British lead industry soared to its peak in the 1800s, when the exhaustion of the seams and a cheaper imported supply of lead caused the Yorkshire mines to be abandoned. Centuries of lead mining left their lasting mark on Swaledale and Wharfdale with abandoned buildings, dangerous "levels" (horizontal passages branching off steep vertical shafts), and "hushes" (gullies produced in the search for new veins of ore) (Duerden, 19).

Above ground, the features of Herriot Country he and the television series have made most famous are, of course, the Dales themselves, green in summer and relatively sheltered in winter, anchored by river bottoms banked by trees and nestled between the high, solitary landscape that Herriot liked to call "the wide green roof of England." Coming down from the heights where he often walked his dogs as relief from the pressures of his daily work—and after he became famous, from the smothering hordes of camera-brandishing tourists—Herriot would encounter welcoming woods, placid streams, and such hidden roaring waterfalls as Hardraw Force, another unearthly place where Herriot said he almost expected to see goblins. Narrow hairpin roads crawl back up to breathtaking summits: 900-foot Sutton Bank looms above Herriot's Mire Beck, a height that he claimed gave "the finest view in England." Seen on a clear day from Sutton Bank, the fertile Vale of York stretches 30 miles from the Pennines to the Hambleton Hills and then the sea. Herriot gamely insisted that his urban countrymen deserved the chance to savor that gorgeous vista, too, but he was saddened nonetheless by the glossy visitors' center that took over the grassy spot where he and his children used to play (*JHY,* 142).

Herriot's rapt sense of place may have been all the more intense because he had not grown up in Yorkshire. To a Glasgow Scot justifiably smitten with the considerable natural attractions of the rolling Border country, Yorkshire's beauties struck Herriot with a degree of awe and delight he had never expected. Over the years, Yorkshire's natural charms only deepened for Herriot as he made intellectual excursions into Yorkshire history, drawn by his love of ancient things whose mysterious allure could never be completely explained.

In *James Herriot's Yorkshire,* Herriot engagingly personalized his discoveries of all the major cultures that have inhabited Yorkshire by relating them to his family's outings. Herriot even covered the remnants of Yorkshire's earliest settlers, whose very existence is shrouded by time and the dearth of their written artifacts. When Herriot took young Jimmy and Rosie on the author's favorite walk along the Old Drovers' Road on the way south of Thirsk toward York, he showed them odd slopes in the ground that had turned out to be grass-covered burial mounds of Neolithic Yorkshire hunter-farmers dating from about 2000 B.C. (*JHY,* 146). The name of Herriot's own town of Thirsk is unique in England, he said, probably a derivation from the Celtic *Tre-ussig,* "the place by the water" (*JHY* 116), settled during the great Celtic Iron Age migrations from Europe that began around 600 B.C. A century before the Golden Age of Athens, fiercely individualistic Celtic warriors founded many settlements that are still alive in Yorkshire, such as Topcliffe on the River Swale, a town that Herriot claimed had long been associated with Celtic Druidism.

The Celts in Yorkshire remained relatively undisturbed for several hundred years, until about A.D. 84, when savage fighting by the Roman legions under Julius Agricola subdued all the tribes of Celtic Britain. Herriot often walked with his children along still-usable remnants of soundly engineered Roman roads and buildings. He was especially intrigued by the Roman ruins in and around York, which had been founded in A.D. 71 as Eboracum, the capital of Roman Britain, and later became the headquarters of the renowned Sixth Legion and the birthplace of Constantine, the soldier-emperor who Christianized the Roman world. Herriot delightedly quoted Humbert Wolfe, who with a Northerner's relish compared York's history to London's: "York was a capital city when you were a nameless stew" (*JHY,* 166). To this day, York proudly remains the second most important city in England.

Assailed from without by Gothic barbarians and within by its own metastasizing corruption, the Roman Empire withdrew its legions from Britain in the sixth century, and despite the legendary defensive exploits of King Arthur and his Round Table, Germanic invaders from Saxony and Denmark filled the British power vacuum. Once the Saxon settlers accepted the new religion preached in Britain by Ireland's zealous missionary monks, Yorkshire became the capital of Saxon Northumbria, the religious and intellectual hub from which Christianity spread over the whole north of England. Yorkshire's monastic scholars were so renowned that in the eighth century Charlemagne summoned Abbot Alcuin from York's fine library to France for advice on establishing schools throughout the new Holy Roman Empire. Professionally, Herriot might have been just as intrigued by Yorkshire's earthier contribution to civilization in the Middle Ages. The region's beef and sheep industry met "the challenge of victualling Britain's new towns which emerged from the seventh century onwards" and helped establish a wealthy Anglo-Saxon medieval economy largely based upon the wool trade.[2]

Herriot enjoyed exploring many of the fascinating tangible artifacts that the Anglo-Saxon culture had left in Yorkshire. Pudding Pie Hill, just south of Thirsk, is a flat-topped 17-foot rise convenient for sliding where Herriot's children played as toddlers. The hill has the local reputation of being a "fairy house," but Herriot was fascinated to discover that it was really an ancient tumulus, or burial mound. When excavated in 1855, humble Pudding Pie Hill had yielded the skeleton of a huge Anglian warrior chieftain, his weapons and the remains of his animals, and the bones of two members of his *heorthweard,* warriors sworn under the Germanic code of the *comitatus* to defend their lord unto their own deaths.[3]

Christianity proved no defense for York in 876, when invading Danes burned much of the city and rebuilt it as Jorvik. A subterranean tour of the meticulously reconstructed eighth-century Viking settlement is one of York's major tourist attractions today, enormously important from a historical perspective because Jorvik was the ruling center of the Danelaw, the northern portion of England ruled for over a century by Scandinavians under a treaty signed by King Alfred the Great in 886.

For Herriot, who appreciated history in any form, one of the most fascinating vestiges of Yorkshire's Dano-Norwegian heritage was the Viking linguistic influence that lingers strongly in the area. Yorkshire and its neighbor Lancashire contain most of the 1,400-plus Scandinavian place-names in England. Some Yorkshire districts have as many as 75 percent place-names of Scandinavian origin, marked by suffixes such as -*dale* (valley) and -*by* (town or farm) denoting Viking settlements. In Yorkshire, many last names such as Alderson, the maiden name Herriot gave Helen in his books, end with the characteristic Scandinavian -*son,* recalling that almost three-quarters of the personal names recorded in Yorkshire's medieval records were of Scandinavian origin.[4] The heavy cultural impact the Scandinavians made on Yorkshire still gives rise to humorous anecdotes about traits Yorkshire folk seem to have in common with their distant Scandinavian cousins:

> Old Charley used to claim, when the port had been around a few times, that after the Fall, God decided to have a second shot, learning from the failure of the first. This time he created a man who was hard of head, blunt of speech, knew which side his bread was buttered on, and above all took no notice of women. Then God sent him forth to multiply in Yorkshire.[5]

The Scandinavian claim to major parts of England continued until 1066. Harold Godwinson, last Saxon king of England, defeated his brother Tostig, in league with Harold III of Norway, at Stamford Bridge, a little west of York, that August. Almost immediately thereafter, Harold Godwinson made a forced march south to Hastings and there was slain by the Norwegians' coconspirator William of Normandy. After two centuries of Viking rule in Yorkshire, the Normans arrived with a vengeance, burning York again and strewing the countryside with castles and austerely elegant Cistercian monasteries that grew powerful through farming and sheep raising. Herriot was especially taken with the remnants of the great abbey at Rievaulx, founded in 1131 as the first major monastery built in Britain by the white-clad, black-cowled Cistercian monks, skillful agriculturalists bent on reforming the monastic life and purging all extraneous embellishments, such as architectural ornamentation, from their buildings as rigorously as they shunned meat and eggs in their diet. Herriot found Rievaulx's simple grace the abbey's most powerful attraction, just as he felt strongly drawn to the stunning combination of archaeological and natural beauties at Richmond, where a Norman castle looms over the picturesque River Swale (*JHY,* 170).

Herriot also called the ancient town of Middleham in Coverdale "glamorous," in the word's older sense, which connotes a magical allure. Today, Middleham, in the midst of high, flat country perfect for long, unobstructed gallops, is a training center for some of England's most famous racing stables, but in the Middle Ages, the town played a pivotal role in English history. In the fourteenth century, the black death (bubonic plague) killed a third of England's population and began the demise of the great monastic foundations as well as the downfall of the ruling Plantagenet dynasty, whose two powerful branches, the houses of Lancaster and York, fought one another to the death for England's throne in the fifteenth-century Wars of the Roses. Middleham Castle was the residence of the king-making Earl of Warwick, last of the great feudal barons. The castle was also briefly home to Warwick's Yorkist son-in-law Richard III, the only Northern-born king of England, whose death in battle at the hands of Henry Tudor on Bosworth Field in 1485 ushered in England's Renaissance. Henry's son, the much-married Henry VIII, seeking both a new, fertile wife and a fresh source of revenue, broke with the Church of Rome and dissolved the monasteries between 1538 and 1540. Bent on crushing Roman Catholic resistance to his newly established Church of England, Henry, through his minister Thomas Cromwell, mercilessly demolished most of the Roman Catholic structures in England, devastating the once-wealthy northern Cistercian houses and dispersing or executing their monks. In thrifty Yorkshire, many dressed stones from torn-down abbey buildings were recycled into farm structures; Herriot, for example, was startled to happen upon medieval burial statues near a barnyard trough. As intrigued as he was with Middleham's historical connections, however, Herriot found its site in Coverdale most of all "wonderful because of its austere beauty" (*JHY,* 94), an indication of his need for occasional spells of solitude in the wide-open spaces of the upper Dales.

Despite his need for peace and quiet, Herriot was never a recluse. Whenever his work permitted, he thoroughly enjoyed his holidays on Yorkshire's colorful coast. There he visited resorts such as Robin Hood's Bay; the shipbuilding town of Whitby, home of the explorer Captain

Cook; the resort city of Scarborough, where Herriot spent the chilly winter of 1943 mostly doing scantily clad RAF calisthenics; and an out-of-the-way fishing village where he cheerfully stayed with his family and their old friends the Taylors, with the North Sea waves breaking savagely against the stones just beyond their bedroom walls (*JHY*, 211). The pleasure Herriot took in being near the sea might seem surprising in a self-described homebody, but during the 1961 voyage he made to the Soviet Union and described in *The Lord God Made Them All*, he indicated that his seafaring ancestors had blessed him with a digestive system remarkably resistant to seasickness. They probably had also bequeathed him the penchant for broad empty vistas and solitary places where the spirit can heal itself in quiet, a preference in landscape that seems to prevail throughout *James Herriot's Yorkshire*.

By the time Herriot was working on *James Herriot's Yorkshire* in the late 1970s, he had lived long enough to see and regret that everything he loved in the Dales was changing—except the Dales themselves. During his 40 years as a veterinarian, Herriot witnessed great shifts in modern agriculture and veterinary medicine, and from time to time, he seems to have wondered whether the price of losing the intangibles that had made his life so fascinating might have been too high (*BJH*, intro.). In middle age, Herriot was torn two ways; he had to celebrate the scientific advances of his profession, but his heart remained true to what could never change—the historical and natural beauties of Yorkshire.

In the tumultuous twentieth century, cultural gulfs widened between urban and rural lifestyles, even in Yorkshire. Herriot ruefully described the "other Yorkshire" as "a wilderness of decaying brick buildings bristling with factory chimneys" (*ACGS*, 468), cities that in the 1970s faced growing crime rates, drug problems, and gross unemployment, while small Yorkshire towns struggled for existence as fewer and fewer farmers could afford to work the land.

When he first came to the Dales, Herriot was struck by qualities he found peculiar to the farmers he met there: "The Yorkshire farmer doesn't rush out and kiss you hello, but his careful friendliness and politeness are attributes on which I place the very highest value" (Gonzalez, *SR*, 59). By the late 1970s, when he was writing *James Herriot's Yorkshire*, however, the relentless homogenization television brought was diluting even the stubbornly traditional culture of Yorkshire. The "old farming characters who formed such fertile soil" for Herriot's writing had largely "vanished, leaving behind them another generation of scientific agriculturalists." Herriot praised the new generation's efficiency and industriousness, but, he said, "they are not as much fun as their fathers" (*BJH*, intro.). Inexorably, death was beginning to claim Herriot's old friends, even his beloved Jack Russell terrier Hector, blind since the age of five (*JHY*, 120). "Just Dan and me now," Herriot mused in *James Herriot's Yorkshire*, watching so much that he had loved slip away. All the acclaim that was now descending upon Herriot, the fame he had never wanted, could not give him back what time was stealing from him, "the last remnants of the men I cherished, living by the ancient values, speaking the old Yorkshire dialect that television and radio have swamped" (*LGMTA*, 29).

After completing *James Herriot's Yorkshire*, Herriot went back to his vetting and his writing, fully intending *The Lord God Made Them All* to round off his memoirs so that he could return to a quiet life in the Dales. The Herriot industry, however, guided by Herriot's agency and publishers and fueled rather than sated by Herriot's warm and affectionate tribute to his Yorkshire, rolled inexorably on.

Around the time James Herriot was completing *The Lord God Made Them All*, he was also selecting stories for *The Best of James Herriot*,[6] a handsome collection subtitled "The Favorite Stories of One of the Most Beloved Writers of Our Time," published jointly in 1982 by The Reader's Digest Association, which holds the book's copyright, and St. Martin's Press. This collection of Herriot's best pieces contains nineteen stories about his first days as a Yorkshire veterinarian and thirteen from his second year in the Dales, chosen from *All Creatures Great and Small* and *All Things Bright and Beautiful*. Thirteen more were taken from his wartime recollections in *All Things Wise and Wonderful*, and nine stories about his return to Darrowby were drawn from *The Lord God Made Them All*.

According to the title page of *The Best of James Herriot, Reader's Digest* editors contributed "additional material" to embellish Herriot's stories: an introductory map of Herriot Country; 100 color pages of attractive photographs arranged in groups—landscapes, pubs, castles, and farming scenes—and, on nearly every page, clever sidebar sketches and notes about colorful scraps of Yorkshire life, from specimens of English cattle and sheep to recipes for scones and the infamous piccalilli. Besides choosing his "favourite memories," as the title page of this book indicates, Herriot also contributed a page-and-a-half introduction, one of his rare commentaries on the development of his writing method over the years.

Herriot called this introduction "The Books I Almost Never Wrote," referring to his difficulties in getting started with his memoirs of the

early days of his practice. In this introduction, as he did in several interviews made in the 1970s, Herriot recounted the unlikely genesis of his
phenomenal literary success, stressing that after 25 years of listening to
Herriot's anecdotes about his daily work, his practical-minded wife Joan
had spurred him into action. Humor, Herriot said, was his first criterion
for including stories in a collection of his best, because after all he
seemed always to agree with the *Reader's Digest* that laughter was the
best medicine. But Herriot also indicated that in putting this collection
together he took his readers' preferences into account. For balance, he
included sad, touching tales—the story of Darrowby's juvenile delinquent, Wesley Binks, who despite Herriot's best efforts lost his dog, his
only friend, to distemper. Of course, highlights of this collection are the
comic masterpieces of Cedric the flatulent boxer and Herriot's use of an
artificial bovine vagina to defend himself against a bull who considered
himself not only cheated but outraged by modern medicine.

Herriot remarked in his introduction to his best stories that that kind
of fun had long since vanished from his life, his work, and his writing.
As he often commented, the years had robbed him of the colorful Dales
people whose personalities he had originally wanted so badly to capture
for posterity, as well as the old "magical" veterinary remedies pushed out
of his practice by new techniques and antibiotics. Those inevitable
changes in Herriot's world seemed to shift his writing perspective, possibly accounting somewhat for the small but apparently growing critical
opinion that his tweedy recollections might be wearing a little thin.
Herriot said that in the beginning he had used his personal life merely as
the skeleton for his writing, which he fleshed out with sketches of Dickensian characters, accounts of Siegfried Farnon's brilliant Holmesian
deductions and Tristan's pranks, and anecdotes about animals. As the
years passed, however, his diminishing stock of suitably vivid raw material as well as his readers' insatiable interest in his private life made Harriot turn stories about his marriage, his RAF service, and his children
into the backbone of his books, a progression that is mirrored in brief by
the four sections of *The Best of James Herriot*.

In the first section, "Early Days in Darrowby," cleverly drawn, eccentric characters dominate Herriot's initial experiences in the Dales,
beginning with his familiar portraits of the volatile Siegfried Farnon and
his rapscallion brother, Tristan. Mrs. Pumphrey and Tricki Woo; Old
John and his two pampered plow horse pensioners; and poor dying Miss
Stubbs, who wonders if her aged animal friends will be able to join her
in heaven, all balance against Herriot's courtship of his wife and his awe

at attending the eternal miracle of birth with his animal patients. Rein-
forcing the motif, the two sets of photographs that accompany this section complement each other. One comprises long shots of the Dales and
moors; the other, close-range portraits of towns where Herriot worked
and vacationed.

As the second section of Herriot's best stories, "The Vet Finds a Wife"
plays Herriot's text against the backdrop of castles and houses and
abbeys and little churches pictured in two handsome sections of photographs, many of which were originally shot by Derry Brabbs for *James
Herriot's Yorkshire*. Herriot again chose instances where he as the scientific animal-medicine authority takes a willing backseat in healing to
amateurs such as crusty Mrs. Donovan, who nursed an abused golden
retriever back to health with the greatest of all home remedies, unadul-
terated love. Herriot never hesitated to poke fun at his younger self, as
he did in the episodes of his near-disastrous wine tasting with Mr.
Crump and his encounter with the midnight vocalist Harold Ingledew,
but this portion of *The Best of James Herriot* begins and ends on two
choice examples of Herriot as a practitioner who was equally successful
at dealing both with animals and their owners' sensibilities. In this section's leadoff story, "A Tactful Remedy," for example, Herriot straight-
facedly coped with Mr. Pickersgill's home remedies and his hilarious
Dickensian malapropisms. Herriot rounded the section off with an
episode that blends the bad news of those times with the good. Herriot
set the painful irony of his RAF call-up papers arriving on his birthday
cheek by jowl with his successful repair of Benjamin the sheepdog's dis-
located shoulder. Benjamin's reclusive owner, Mr. Summergill, takes the
"effortless miracle" for granted, a reaction Herriot recognized as the
ultimate Yorkshire compliment, one of those "little triumphs" out on a
remote farm that made it so hard for him to leave the Dales.

For "Memories of a Wartime Vet," the third section of this collection,
Herriot chose the stories that seem to have consoled him most during
his months in the RAF, tales about animals, farmers, and craftsmen he
might have told—and probably did—in one of the vintage country
pubs featured in this section in exterior and interior photographs. As
Herriot's self-prescribed antidote for his wartime misery, the unselfcon-
scious wisdom that animals display in dealing with the humans in their
world still figures strongly here: Blossom the cow comes home, Cedric
the boxer adopts the perfect owner, ill-tempered Georgina the cat and
parsimonious Mrs. Beck do Herriot out of his well-earned fee, and free-
spirited Roddy and Jake, his big lurcher, show Herriot how well they

have come to terms with their less-than-perfect environments. Against these stories about animals, Herriot juxtaposed episodes from his private life: the riotous account of his son Jimmy's birth, Herriot's frustrating encounter with veterinary bureaucracy, and a rare, funny vignette out of his RAF training days. In the most telling anecdote in this group, however, Herriot and Siegfried Farnon forgo the Hunt Club Ball to operate on a stray dog badly hurt by a car without hesitating or thinking about a fee. Their unequivocal act of kindness illustrates in a nutshell the heart and the soul of the veterinary profession.

Continuing the shift in emphasis Herriot began with *All Things Wise and Wonderful,* about half the episodes of "Back to Darrowby," the last section of *The Best of James Herriot,* recount some of Herriot's happiest days, those involving his young children, including the stories of Rosie's birth and her narrow escape as a toddler from a rampaging cow, Jimmy's pursuit of a pair of proper farm boots, and the inimitable piano-recital episode dead certain to make every piano student's parents writhe in sympathy. The proper close for *The Best of James Herriot,* as it was for *The Lord God Made Them All,* is Siegfried's joyfully optimistic declaration of "great days ahead" for the veterinarians of Darrowby. This conclusion is strengthened by appealingly annotated Dales wildlife illustrations and photographs that celebrate traditional Yorkshire styles of "work and play," including spreads on cricket, one of Herriot's passions, and on the Great Yorkshire Show, one of England's premier agricultural exhibitions. A handsome photograph of a sheepdog trial near the end of *The Best of James Herriot* sums up one of Herriot's major messages, the perfection of loving interdependence between man and animal when work has changed from a necessary evil to daily fulfillment for them both.

When *The Best of James Herriot* appeared, James Herriot was in his late sixties, still practicing in Thirsk, cheerfully doing the hard work that had always made him happiest. His children had grown up, gone away to study medicine, and returned to the Dales to practice near him, and with grandchildren in the offing, Herriot seemed content to mark time as far as his writing was concerned. While *The Best of James Herriot* contains no new story material, the book does offer many clever illustrations to enhance the reading experience of rural Yorkshire life in a past that Herriot himself prized as "a sweet, safe place to be." As changes in the world beyond the Dales proliferated and accelerated into the 1980s, the vastly successful *The Best of James Herriot* offered the precious stability of traditional values anchored by the stunning backdrop of the

Dales, without which none of Herriot's literary work would have been possible. Like the "James Herriot's Yorkshire Calendar" that has appeared yearly since 1983, *The Best of James Herriot* brings home to every reader the Yorkshire people, the old-fashioned moral code they live by, and the stunning landscape where Herriot always found solace and inspiration.

Chapter Seven

Tapering Off

Animals are such agreeable friends—they ask no questions, they pass no criticisms.

—George Eliot

From 1972 to 1982, while James Herriot was working six days a week as a veterinarian, writing his first four books, and coping with hordes of tourists, an enormous societal change was sweeping Britain: "The great Victorian engine of Britain's prosperity had finally run out of steam."[1] The permissive 1960s had driven chinks into the foundations of traditional British life, and as Christian worship declined, "it was left to humanists to promote reforms of the [British] moral code" (Shaw and Shaw, 24). The do-gooding efforts of the welfare state, however, proved disastrous to Britain's political and economic well-being, contributing materially to the collapse of most of the institutions that had anchored the British Empire—and even to the decline of such staples of English culture as T. S. Eliot lovingly enumerated in *Notes Towards the Definition of Culture* (1948): dog races, Wimbledon, the dartboard, the music of Elgar, beetroot in vinegar and boiled cabbage cut into sections, and Wensleydale cheese (Briggs, 294).

Britain's old norms of family life and the nation's famed elitist educational system had changed forever. By 1969, 50 percent of British housing was owner owned, but the goings-on within Englishmen's castles had become decidedly untraditional. In that year, Parliament enacted measures permitting abortion and private homosexual acts between consenting adults, and the Divorce Reform Act of 1970, denounced by one woman Labour politician as "a Casanova's Charter" (Briggs, 306), treated men and women equally. So did the Equal Pay Act and the Matrimonial Property Act, which established that "a wife's work as either a housewife or wage-earner should be considered as an equal contribution towards the creation of the family home" (Briggs, 306). Although these measures were not enforced until some years later, they eventually helped create a British "feminist left" (Shaw and Shaw, 37).

Educational changes were no less startling. In 1971, about a third of Britain's children studied in comprehensive schools, and "open universities" that did not require enrollees to live on university premises were flourishing across the land. California's hippie culture, largely imported through transplanted American studies programs, infected even the sacred quads of Oxford and Cambridge, and as in the United States, British educational permissiveness soon fostered student rebellion that washed over into the arts, moving them, too, to the left. In British academia, the solid and demanding Arnold-Leavis scholarly tradition that had celebrated the great achievements of Western literature was now denounced in Whitmanesque barbaric yawps as the work of "yesterday's men." Popular entertainment, such as the televised soccer games Herriot loved to watch while he wrote, became highly organized, with a dismaying concurrent trend toward hooliganism.

As the old proverb goes, the devil finds work for idle hands, and British hooligans now had plenty of discontent and plenty of time to express it in. Between 1965 and 1973, industrial employment in Britain had fallen by 12 percent while prices trebled. British domestic investment rose only about 30 percent, in contrast to West Germany's miraculous 90 percent gain. The 1970 discovery of North Sea oil did not produce the expected economic boom immediately, and in that year, the British gross domestic product was 27 percent lower than that of the six-nation European Common Market (ECM). Just when *All Creatures Great and Small* became a runaway U.S. best-seller in 1973, Britain unwillingly joined the European Economic Community (EEC), embarking on what many British citizens considered "a journey to an unknown destination" (Briggs, 296). Halfway through the 1970s, when the North Sea oil finally began to flow, prices in Britain were rising more rapidly than at any time since the war, unemployment had reached one million, and the value of Britain's money, converted to the decimal system in 1971, was about a fifth of what it had been in 1945. All of these unhappy statistics boiled down to one simple statement: "We survived: that was all that could be said economically of the 1970s" (Briggs, 295).

In the face of such widespread changes at home and abroad, readers who longed for the good old days found that they could vicariously experience them again through James Herriot's books. Just when his popularity was peaking at home and abroad in the late 1970s and early 1980s, a "moral majority" cultural reaction to Britain's "permissive sex-mad society" (Shaw and Shaw, 24) was also setting in, a symptom of the all-encompassing malaise the Annan Committee on the Future of Broadcasting described in 1974: the increasing difficulty in holding British society and culture together, because all the elements of national

life seemed to be flying farther and farther apart—social classes, generations and sexes, North and South, London and the provinces, and prag-
matism and ideology (Briggs, 308). The polarization of British society as
regarding the entertainment industry became particularly evident when
in 1979 Margaret Thatcher's victorious Conservatives reduced funding
for the arts by a million pounds, shifting responsibility for artistic pro-
gramming largely from public to business sources, while large popular
audiences entertained themselves with spectator sports, chiefly soccer
and racing.

The British masses badly needed their bread and circuses because life
in the welfare state was becoming more, not less, uncomfortable. By
1980, comprehensive schools educated 80 percent of Britain's children,
but shockingly little opportunity greeted most of them when they left
the classroom at age 16. "The country faced the prospect of a high-wage,
high-tech future for the few, and for the rest, a low-wage future for some
in service industries, and unemployment for many" (Shaw and Shaw, 41).
With unprecedented unemployment rates and 17 percent of the population over age 65 and clamoring for government assistance, three million
Britons—more than ever before—were "on the dole" in 1982, and
strange new extremist groups—Technicolor-spiked-hair punks, dread-
locked Rastafarians, and neo-Nazi skinheads—prowled the streets of
once-quiet British towns. In the 1960s and 1970s, the popular BBC
series *Coronation Street* had evoked enormous nostalgia for the cozy British
working-class life that would never be seen again, but by the 1980s, the
gritty *East Enders* typified the sour urban mood of the country.

A torrent of documentary television programs also publicized the
enormous shift in Britain's agriculture that was afoot around 1970
(Shaw and Shaw, 38). Cultural historian Asa Briggs painted a dismal
portrait of the new "agricultural revolution," which he compared with
nothing less than the "neolithic breakthrough"; not industrialists or
land speculators but the heavily subsidized British farmer, supported by
EEC policies made in Brussels, now threatened the very life of the
British countryside:

> Modes of farming—and with them the appearance of the farm landscape
> and buildings—have changed more during the last quarter of a century
> than they did in the eighteenth century. . . . Thousands of acres of down
> and heath have already disappeared with the spread of battery farming
> . . . barbed wire has supplanted hawthorn and pylons stretch across the
> plains, corrugated iron barns and silos have appeared in well-drained

farmyards, and everywhere there are chemical fertilizers and pesticides (Briggs, 312–13).

Spurred on by BBC documentaries, animal-rights groups became inflamed at the sorry lot of Britain's factory chickens, calves, and pigs, lending credence and support to antivivisectionists and vegetarians. Environmentalists, already appalled at the loss of England's ancient woodlands, ponds, meadows, and marshes and the accompanying endangerment of wildlife since 1945, swelled the ranks of such groups as The Friends of the Earth, part of the Green movement that in the 1980s was beginning to stretch its political and economic muscles. Their sworn enemy, mechanization, was already taking its toll. An "even more important species, the farm worker, was becoming increasingly obsolete as mechanisation progressed, and alarm grew that with his disappearance there was a possibility of the loss of parts of rural England and its villages" (Shaw and Shaw, 38). In 1945, after six years of war, Britain had had 563,000 regular full-time farmworkers, whereas in 1980 only 133,000 remained (Briggs, 313).

In response to the perceived evils of mechanization, "alternative" became the English watchword in the 1980s. "The growth of organic farming, the development of small craft industries, the campaign for real beer, the interest in alternative medicine, the return to natural fibres for clothing, the anxiety about chemical additives in food, even the move to do-it-yourself and the upsurge of interest in cooking, were all part of the search for alternatives" (Shaw and Shaw, 38). In literature as well as in documentary television, popular taste swung toward environmental concern and nostalgia for the long-gone days when mankind lived more harmoniously with nature, positions that James Herriot's stories of his country practice in the 1930s and 1940s could not have suited more effectively.

Herriot's veterinary profession had also changed enormously since he began writing. As far as he was concerned, considerable losses accompanied the advantages of modern medicine. In the late 1970s, Herriot regretfully observed that virtually no small farmers remained in the Yorkshire Dales (*LGMTA,* 263), areas as remote as can be found in England. British draft horses, too, were almost extinct. In 1950, 300,000 horses still worked on British farms, but in 1979, only 3,575 were left (Briggs, 313). Rural veterinarians like Herriot had to turn to small-animal care, though not all vets were as well suited for such work as Herriot proved to be.

A lifetime earlier, when Herriot was a youngster dreaming of spending his life taking care of dogs, the Glasgow Veterinary College had needed students so badly that its officials went out on the road begging for recruits. When Herriot published *All Creatures Great and Small,* though, the demand for small-animal doctors was on the upswing. In the late 1960s, "the dog took the veterinarian out of the stable and put him into the living room," according to a distinguished American veterinarian, Leon F. Whitney, whose 1973 book *Animal Doctor* chronicled the history and practice of veterinary medicine, warts and all, for prospective entrants (W&W, 28). The field was then wide open in the United States because in 1973, 5,758 U.S. veterinarians were struggling to care for 70 million companion animals. Whitney noted that each graduating American veterinarian could choose from 5.6 jobs, mostly in mixed large- and small-animal practice, "one of the brightest futures of any profession" at that time (W&W, 101, 231).

Most rural British vets like Herriot were just as embroiled as every other ordinary Britisher in their country's economic woes. British veterinarians could not expect the kind of financial returns that their transatlantic colleagues enjoyed, one reason for Herriot's decision to take up writing in the first place. However, British and American veterinarians whose practices had become mixed like Herriot's shared the same physical burdens and intangible rewards of their singularly demanding profession.

Whitney confronted his idealistic, dog-loving veterinary hopefuls with a blunt, "Have you got what it takes?" In his opinion, what it took for the veterinary profession was a demanding combination of strength, endurance, mental ability, and, most of all, moral courage. Throughout his books, Herriot tended to downplay his own talents, but he clearly had all those tough prerequisites Whitney posed for veterinary success. Herriot gladly juggled his tough, exacting physical and mental labors in the service of a profession that has a unique moral dimension. As Whitney succinctly put it, "there are many kinds of values. Money is one. Friendship is another, and to us it is of much higher value" (W&W, 6).

Friendship and family ties seem to have had the highest value for Herriot. By the time he was in his late sixties, his books had made him very comfortable financially, if not as enormously wealthy as the envious might imagine, and making extra money was no longer one of his major preoccupations. In the Yorkshire idiom, he had enough to pay his way— and to provide generously for his family and friends—and that was enough for him, since the Inland Revenue was absorbing most of what he made anyhow. Even now, Herriot was working very hard, insisting that "when animals are ailing I still have to pack up and go." In a 1986 interview, Herriot could not recall a Christmas Day when he hadn't had to work, but he waxed philosophical about it, claiming his treks to the chilly hillsides helped him work up a better appetite for his Christmas turkey than his more sedentary friends could produce (Gonzalez, *SR,* 59). Herriot also acknowledged that he was tiring and that the demands of his work were taxing his aging physique: the work "keeps you fit all right . . . The difficult thing . . . is that first you have to catch your patient. I can remember rounding up a litter of sixteen piglets not long ago. [And] Take the prolapsed uterus in a pig. . . . Most of the time not succeeding, with the result that the pig eventually becomes pork pies. You have no idea how tough it is, lying on cold concrete, fighting to get that uterus back into the animal until your breath gives out, your feet braced against the wall and shoving, gasping, shoving, gasping, until you're completely exhausted" (Gonzalez, *SR,* 89).

At his age, Herriot realized he could not continue to do everything—the practice, the tourists, and more writing. With several successful books behind him and about "500 people a day swarming through the Yorkshire Dales looking for James Herriot" (Daniel, 32), Herriot decided to slacken off his writing, but he stubbornly stuck with his veterinary work because of his strong "sense of fulfillment and satisfaction that emerges from the triumph of life over death." He readily admitted that, for all his efforts, an animal sometimes might have gotten well anyhow, "But there is a satisfaction which lingers, flowing like balm over the discomforts and frustrations of veterinary practice and making everything right when you know that, without a shadow of doubt, you've pulled an animal back from the brink of death into the living, breathing world" (Gonzalez, *SR,* 59).

Children's Books (1984–1991)

"Is it true?" is the great question children ask.

—Andrew Lang

After writing so hard for so long, James Herriot might not have wanted to abandon his typewriter completely, but he probably needed a change of pace, and he badly wanted to spend more time with his grandchildren. His next project meshed those two desires neatly. Herriot published a popular series of eight children's picture books, about one a year between 1984 and 1991. Herriot economically took these narratives mainly from stories in his earlier books, shaping his material cleverly to the tastes of his younger readers.

Like his adult books, Herriot's children's books became enormously successful. In much the same fashion that he taught himself to write in the first place, Herriot seemed to rely on his literary and grandfatherly instincts rather than starting off with some weighty psychological or pedagogical ax to grind. In doing so, he ran counter to the twentieth-century phenomenon of the children's literature industry.

Long ago, children either had to read "edifying" books purposely produced to instruct youngsters in manners or morals, or greedily read (usually under the covers) adult books as exciting forbidden fruit. Today, children's books have burgeoned into an industry of their own, and "an amazing variety" of books is being deliberately and scientifically developed for children: "picture books, some without text, and some designed to clarify concepts or give information, some to tell a story; easy-to-read books, invaluable for the beginning reader and the poor reader; pop-up books and choose-your-own-adventure books; books written with a simple vocabulary but a sophisticated subject or plot, the so-called 'high-low' books for the older reluctant reader" (Sutherland and Arbuthnot, 6). Seemingly without undue effort, James Herriot made his attractive and edifying books for children accomplish almost all of those purposes.

In another sense, however, Herriot's children's books run counter to prevailing norms in the children's literature industry, which presently attempts to "reflect much of the conflict and controversy in our society regarding moral standards and life-styles. Many of the enduring values of the past are reflected in books for children, but so are the values of a contemporary society that is less secure and more mobile than earlier generations knew" (Sutherland and Arbuthnot, 8). Herriot's children's books, like his adult works, concentrate upon traditional values that evidently are more widely accepted by ordinary readers than by professional literary theorists. Children's literature textbooks used in the education departments of U.S. teacher-training institutions tend to ignore Herriot's books for younger readers, although whopping sales figures indicate that both children and their parents agree with reviewers who praise Herriot's traditional "tugs at the heartstrings."[2]

According to children's author Rosemary Wells, "Writing for very young children is the most difficult discipline I know." The challenge in creating this kind of literature, she believes, is that "Kids will believe almost anything you tell them—provided you make it truthful."[3] Telling what his readers accepted as the truth in his books, of course, was always one of Herriot's strong suits. In reshaping stories originally intended for adults to appeal to children as young as four or five,[4] Herriot gently affirmed the old values, primarily truth, that he felt were well worth preserving. He adjusted his material to his audience by simplifying the vocabulary, personalizing the characterizations, and modulating some of the actions, especially the veterinary procedures, but he never watered down his message or compromised his beliefs. Herriot's great charm as a children's author is that he never condescended to his youthful audience, any more than he would have patronized an anxious child whose dog or cat he was treating.

After watching much of Britain's traditional culture disintegrating in the 1960s and 1970s, Herriot seems to have deliberately selected his children's stories with a paternal eye toward old-fashioned virtues, perhaps hoping to help reverse the popular-media trend toward mindless brutality that he saw springing up all over the world.

Children's books, as Leon Garfield has indicated, offer an ideal medium for civilizing the newest generation:

> The reading of books is not a natural activity for human beings; and even less, the reading of good books. But then, the natural proclivities of a human being are precisely what the civilizer hopes to subdue. A human being, by and large, is not the most likable of nature's productions. He has not the grace of the cat, the strength of the tiger, the dignity of the elephant, nor the honesty of the dog. He steals the fur he lacks and kills for sport; and his contributions to the well-being of the planet have been to destroy the ozone layer, poison the oceans, and invent the battery hen. But he has one saving grace. Unlike any other creature, he knows the depths of his own infamy, and, here and there, makes efforts to undo the harm he has done.
>
> It is largely through books that he knows these things. It is through books that he discovers himself, and so discovers others. He is not born with self-knowledge, only with self-awareness. Self-knowledge may be acquired through experience, but that is a very chancy business. It is the rare soul who actually profits by experience. Most of us just keep up with the installments.[5]

Children's books that involve animals are especially well suited to teach civilized values because, as Garfield suggests, each animal in its own way can illustrate its primary virtue, for example, the dog's noble honesty. To accomplish this, the writer with an animal story in mind generally chooses among three methods of presentation: sentimentally portraying animals behaving like human beings; taking the fantasy route, as Tolkien did, with talking animals who still behave like animals; and simply showing animals as themselves (Sutherland and Arbuthnot, 381). Herriot, whose personality combined the scientist's and the animal lover's insights into animal behavior, created convincing animal characters whose thoughts and feelings are entirely their own.

Moreover, animal stories are tailor-made for allowing children to discover themselves, because "Animals can live in a world that children seem to grow right into. It's a world of the past, with clothing from other times. Things aren't modern in the world of animals . . . [and] no one minds" (Zinsser, 135). Relationships with animals involve precious few of the other barriers, such as wealth or status, that society erects between individuals. The children's books Herriot wrote, set in the happy past of his early practice, help youngsters discover the goodness in themselves by recognizing it when animals bring out the best in even the most unlikely characters.

For his first venture into the children's literature market, Herriot chose *Moses the Kitten,* a story he had originally written for *All Things Bright and Beautiful,* and molded it into a children's version that was published in 1984 with appealing illustrations by Peter Barrett. Herriot gave "A hint of religion" to the title of this "brief, sweetly illustrated story of a kitten saved from the cold and nurtured by a sow" (Brower, 91). The heart and soul of traditional British religious observance is just what Moses is all about. In Herriot's quiet way, he endowed this book with sterling examples of kindly do-unto-other-ness: his own compassion in rescuing the newborn kitten from certain death in a frigid marsh, the farm wife's generosity in warming the kitten in her oven, the kitten's resourcefulness in finding a surrogate mother, and the sow's unselfishness in allowing Moses, a non-piggy alien being, to nurse. Herriot described the book as " 'true, every word of it,' " and readers immediately agreed. *Moses,* "a seven-minute read that s[old] for $9.95," immediately hit the best-seller lists and remained there for weeks, but Herriot declared in a 1985 interview the book would "probably be his last literary labor" (Brower, 91–92).

Fortunately for his readers, however, Herriot went back on his word, and all eight of his children's books, most of which had appeared both in his previous books and singly in adult versions for magazine publication, followed *Moses the Kitten* to long stays on the best-seller charts. *Only One*

Woof (1985) told the tale of Mr. Wilkins' silent, lop-eared sheepdog Gyp who unselfishly greeted his brother Sweep's trial victory with the only bark Gyp ever gave. This story, like four others among Herriot's children's books, came from *All Things Wise and Wonderful,* the record of Herriot's homesick RAF years when memories of his work in the Dales comforted him so well. *Only One Woof* illustrates the strength of the bond between animals and the delight in someone else's triumph that most humans, selfish by nature, should learn to emulate. The story also reveals a kind heart beneath the crusty exterior of Gyp's owner, a famous sheepdog trainer who finds himself inexplicably selling Gyp's brother, the flashy high-in-trial prospect, and keeping Gyp, who lacks his brother's talent. The adult version of the story opens with the onset of Gyp's epilepsy, which Herriot did not use in the children's book, perhaps making it easier for him to concentrate on a paradox of behavior he learned from the farm people of the Dales and often explored in his stories: the outwardly hard owner who can show love only to an animal.

In 1986, Herriot brought out *The Christmas Day Kitten,* illustrated by Ruth Brown, who worked with all the rest of Herriot's children's books. This episode from *All Things Wise and Wonderful* retold the story of Debbie, a homeless cat who as she was dying brought her one kitten to the only safe place she knew, a home where she had been welcome to spend a little while out of the cold. Herriot's compassionate but realistic treatment of Debbie's death and the survival of her memory in her kitten helps children begin to understand mortality, the inevitable tragedy that makes companionship with short-lived pets so poignant.

Herriot returned to the mysterious workings of love in *Bonny's Big Day* (1987) and *Blossom Comes Home* (1988). In *All Creatures Great and Small,* adults had encountered Farmer Skipton, a self-made man who had begun as an uneducated farm laborer and became a wealthy landowner, a monumental achievement he had made by sacrificing all the intangibles of human relationships—mutual respect, companionship, affection, and love—that usually make life worth living. At the end of his life, old Skipton had no one to cherish but the ancient pair of plow horses he tended day in and day out, his only family, who had slaved along with him to build a fortune that now in his old age seemed meaningless. Herriot had to rework this story substantially because children might not be able to grasp the adult obsession of ambition. As a sensitive father and grandfather, Herriot knew that what really matters to children is their black-and-white view of morality, or as J. R. R. Tolkien put it: "Is he good? Is he wicked?"[6] "In the world of the young, "good and evil are clearly stamped . . . the young have what the rest of us can only envy, and that is a belief in goodness and perpetual hope" (Zinsser, 143).

Herriot rewrote Skipton's story into the tale of Bonny the horse, giving names to Skipton's old plow horses and giving Skipton the human affection he had never sought but always needed, letting Bonny win the Darrowby Fair Pet Show and proving to the little world of the Dales that Farmer Skipton had a heart. *Blossom Comes Home,* originally the first consoling memory that Herriot called up at the beginning of his RAF basic training in *All Things Wise and Wonderful,* also deals with another aged and apparently useless creature. The cow's owner, Mr. Dakin, tried to do the practical and efficient thing—send the cow off to market—but Blossom returned to the only place she had ever known, and Mr. Dakin kept her after all. Herriot de-emphasized the financial necessity that drove Mr. Dakin to sell Blossom in the first place and spared young readers (though older ones might suspect) the butcher-shop destination Dakin had originally intended for Blossom, but Herriot also introduced a truth about love that resembles Robert Frost's famous rural definition of home—"where when you go there they have to take you in."[7]

Finding homes for stray animals can consume precious time in the lives of busy veterinarians, and over the years, Herriot devoted considerable time and effort to charity work, both private and on behalf of animal shelters. In *The Market Square Dog* (1989), another episode from *All Things Wise and Wonderful* in which an animal finds its way home into a human heart, Herriot blurred for his younger readers the clinical details of the operation he and Siegfried performed gratis on a little stray struck by a hit-and-run driver. Herriot also heightened the drama by showing prospective owner after owner choosing dogs from the pound while the little brown stray watches unwanted. Unfortunately, today more than ever, children and their parents need to learn the important lesson about status-symbol animal ownership that *The Market Square Dog* teaches: animals are conscious beings, not throwaway possessions. In the United States alone, over 12 million homeless dogs and cats are killed each year. According to the American Humane Association in 1995, 20 percent of those dogs in shelters are purebreds; "Most are less than 18 months old, and about 90 percent are healthy and adoptable."[8] Herriot particularized this appalling situation into one little sad-eyed puppy: "Maybe it was because he was only a mongrel and the people who visited the kennels wanted a more elegant dog—yet I knew that he would make a perfect pet for anybody."[9] Herriot succeeded so well with this book that one reviewer claimed, "In all fairness, [it] should probably carry a warning label for parents who have steadfastly resisted their child's pleas for a pet."[10]

Herriot's later children's stories involved animals other than horses and dogs. The little sheep hero of *Smudge, the Little Lost Lamb* (1991), a "new" story not taken from one of Herriot's earlier books, becomes bored and slips under his fence, only to be chased by a dog, frightened by a bull, and lost in a snowstorm before a young girl rescues the sheep and takes him back to his mother and sister, a "reassuring tale . . . especially because Smudge is rescued by a child" (Hutt, 951). This story is one of the few that Herriot told from the animal's point of view, and the effect trembles on the brink of Disneyesque sentimentality, but Herriot returned to his earlier style in *Oscar, Cat-About-Town,* also published in 1991, originally the closing animal episode of *All Things Wise and Wonderful*. After Herriot patched up a badly injured cat and took it into his home, his wife fell in love with "Oscar" and suffered agonies when the cat's former owner took Oscar back. This story is an example of the emotional risk of becoming too involved with a patient that not only the vet but his whole family always runs. In the children's version, however, after Oscar's former family repossessed the cat, Herriot de-emphasized Helen's grief at losing Oscar and stressed the notion of shared emotional ownership (" 'He belongs to all of us now,' says Mr. Gibbons")[11] in order to soften the loss and build a sense of generosity in his younger readers.

Nonetheless, in *Oscar* as in all of his children's books, Herriot told the truth, honestly admitting the potential for heartache inherent in pet ownership as well as the enormous benefits that animal companionship can offer. In 1992, Herriot's collected children's stories were published in England by Michael Joseph as *James Herriot's Animal Storybook* and in New York by St. Martin's Press as *James Herriot's Treasury for Children,* appealing "to every age, from older toddler to mature adult"[12]—a notable achievement for any author.

For fiction involving animals to convince its readers, especially the demanding audience of small persons who see the world in black-and-white terms, animals need to be portrayed both objectively and perceptively. Because tragedy usually comes sooner rather than later in these creatures' lives, animal stories are often dramatic or melancholy, possibly even soggily sentimental or offensively melodramatic (Sutherland and Arbuthnot, 381). Herriot successfully avoided those literary pitfalls because for decades he had been coping daily with the suffering and death of animals, even his own. His children's books appeal to an enormous audience because, in an increasingly fragmented society, young readers find themselves yearning for the stability of truth. Herriot unsentimentally portrayed the kind of world in which human beings want to believe, a realistic but reassuring place where animals and people age and probably soon will die, but where old cows with names and little lost lambs can come home again, stray cats and dogs find loving families, old plow horses retire in comfort and enjoy their own moments of glory, and, as caring veterinarians like Herriot assure us when we grieve over our lost friends, animals do have souls and will be with us in our heaven.

In their abstract view of the universe, physicists define beauty "as having three properties: simplicity, harmony and brilliance," exactly the properties that author Katherine Paterson claims are integral to a good book, "the sum of what is best in us . . . For the stories that have endured, the stories to which we turn as we seek to shape our own lives, are all beautiful in this sense" (Zinsser, 18–19). James Herriot made his children's books as simple as the difference between "good" and "wicked" we all used to know. He celebrated the harmonious bond between human beings and their animals that the child in all of us instinctively recognizes; and he achieved the flashes of insight that children, often wiser than their elders, recognize as truth, shining bright as gold. Although Herriot spent much of his career working with large farm animals, he always seemed to prefer working with pets, whom he came to know as individuals. This was work he could "linger over and enjoy" (*ATBB,* 415), a different dimension, and one he cherished deeply, of the "mutually depending, trusting, and loving association which I feel exists between man and animals" (Gonzalez, *SR,* 86). That bond he understood so well allowed him to create the eight bright and beautiful fables that continue to shape children's lives around the world.

James Herriot's Dog Stories (1986)

God give to me by your grace what you give to dogs by nature.

—Mechtilda of Magdeberg, thirteenth-century hermitess

As he approached his 70th birthday, James Herriot increasingly found his literary fame more a burden than a blessing. According to Monty Brower, who interviewed Herriot in early 1985 for *People Weekly,* "After nearly 15 years of making alternate rounds as vet on the farms of Yorkshire and as a celebrity author on the [British] talk show circuit, Herriot/Wight ha[d] tired of being all things to all people. 'I want to slip back and go do all the things that everybody else at my age does,' says Wight . . . 'It's horrible when you see the sands of time running out, and you have four nice grandchildren. What's the use of me hammering a typewriter when they are there?' " (Brower, 92).

Herriot never considered giving up his practice. "When I'm walking out in a farmyard, out in all the dust and all the old smells and sensations, I think, 'I'd hate to stop doing this' " (Brower, 93). Instead of continuing his memoirs, he had begun tapering off his literary efforts with children's books inspired by the fun he was having being a grandfather, but he did tell Brower that "inspiration might one day call him back to the typewriter. 'I might get what they call a rush of blood . . . Besides, I'm not so good at pushing the horses and cows about as I used to be' " (Brower, 93).

Around Christmas of 1985, *Publishers Weekly* caught up with Herriot playing "push ha-penny" with one of his granddaughters, and Herriot reluctantly described his new project, an intriguing hybrid of old and new: "Well, well . . . My British publisher has asked me to gather a collection of my dog stories. I've written a 10,000-word introduction for it, which is really quite lengthy, and I'm annotating each story with comments, re-reading the stories and including my second thoughts about them, you see. I'm really still digesting them a bit."[13]

The result of Herriot's literary digestion became *James Herriot's Dog Stories,* printed in England and America in 1986 and reissued in a new edition by St. Martin's Press in late 1996, a rich assortment of 50 previously published stories about Herriot's favorite animals and the idiosyncrasies of their owners. All but three of the stories had originally appeared in his four hymn-titled books, and "Abandoned," "Mr. Pinkerton's Problem," and "The Stolen Car" had been published earlier in various popular magazines such as *Good Housekeeping* and *Reader's Digest.*

As the first animals willingly to join their fate to man's, dogs have always occupied a special place in human hearts. Cavemen, veterinary historians claim, would trade their wives but never their dogs,[14] and a bumper sticker seen at American dog shows proclaims, "Husband and dog missing. Reward for dog." Herriot would likely have chuckled over both statements—and he would have understood the sentiments behind them.

Rereading Herriot's stories reminds many readers of a visit with a dear old friend, but the introduction and comments Herriot added to this collection in 1986 also provide a wealth of insights into his choice of career, the psychology of dogs, the benefits and responsibilities of pet ownership, and the challenges for a veterinarian in treating animals for whom he has a special affection.

Herriot devoted the first section of his introduction to descriptions of his veterinary vocation and training. His desire to become a vet had begun when he was a child growing up on the western outskirts of Glasgow, where he says he always had dogs and a "burning ambition" to treat their ailments (*DS,* xi). Everything about dogs fascinated him— their infinite pleasure in human companionship, their unconditional fidelity, and their immense variety of physical characteristics. Herriot entered Glasgow Veterinary College in 1930, the first year of the Great Depression, and beside the disheartening fact that no one wanted vets then, Herriot soon learned that most of his professional training would involve the horse, an animal Herriot was always skittish about handling. Nonetheless, he never abandoned his early devotion to dogs, and when he entered practice in Yorkshire and saw that his partners Siegfried Farnon and Frank Bingham preferred horse work, Herriot happily built up his own small animal clientele, which he called "a bright thread running through the stern fabric of my daily round" (*DS,* xxiv).

Herriot unabashedly described himself "as soppy over my dogs as any old lady" (*DS,* xxv), and he felt he had enjoyed stronger bonds with his dogs over the years than other people might have done because he took them everywhere (Nickel, "Revisited," 18). Beginning with Don, the Irish Setter who rambled the Glasgow hills beside him, Herriot mused over the dogs he had owned: a delightful little white mongrel; then his beloved beagles Sam, an early gift from his wife, and Dinah, who accompanied him for 10 years; Hector the Jack Russell terrier and Dan the black Labrador, to whom Herriot dedicated *All Things Wise and Wonderful;* and, last of all, Bodie the Border terrier and Polly, his daughter Rosie's yellow Labrador who became Bodie's best friend, bearing out Herriot's contention that animals need friendship every bit as much as people do.

Herriot's attitudes toward the different breeds that have shared his life reveal a good deal about his own personality. Herriot always valued intelligence, personality, a sense of humor, and the capacity for loyal friendship in a dog, qualities that stand out just as distinctively in Herriot's writing. One of the most touching passages in *All Things Bright and Beautiful* is the author's tribute to Sam, Herriot's constant companion in those early days when he was discovering how much Yorkshire and his practice meant to him—a happiness that was significantly deep-ened by Sam's presence and what Herriot called "the abiding satisfac-tion that comes from giving pleasure to a loved animal" (*ATBB*, 294–95).

Herriot certainly found nobility of spirit in the Labrador retriever, a breed justifiably famous for its unique combination of devotion, inde-pendence, and humor: "Coming to the [field test] line, a golden [retriever] says, 'Show me what you want, explain why, and I will do it,' " the gentle willingness to please that makes Herriot's story about Roy, the abused golden retriever rescued by the testy Mrs. Donovan, so touching. On the other hand, "A Lab says, 'Show me what you want, forget why, and get out of my way,' "[15] exactly the kind of robust self-confidence bred into the Yorkshire Dales people Herriot enjoyed so much.

Owning a rambunctious terrier is not for everyone, either; a terrier's scrappy determination and defiance of convention can be a downright nuisance if allowed to get out of hand, as Herriot showed in his tale of two spoiled cairn terriers who eventually pushed their doting owner too far. When asked whether he had a favorite among his dogs, Herriot told journalist Ken Nickel, "Oh—I feel very disloyal to all the others, I've loved them all—but a little Jack Russell Terrier called Hector. Oh aye, they'll all break your heart but he did it more than any other when he died. He was full of character, was Hector' " (Nickel, "Revisited," 18). Herriot may have been especially close to Hector because Hector went blind at age five (*JHY*, 120). Perhaps Herriot's story of how the owner of Digger, a dog who was losing his sight, pulled himself out of depres-sion on the end of his dog's leash may have contained reverberations from Herriot's own life; certainly one of Herriot's recurrent themes is the "cheering and soothing effect" (*DS*, 383) that a dog's mere presence can bring, as the work of therapy dogs around the world now abun-dantly testifies.

"Vets are animal lovers," Herriot insists, or they wouldn't have entered such a "caring profession" (*DS*, xxv). Their affection for ani-mals—in Herriot's case, especially for dogs—poises many veterinarians on a slippery emotional tightrope between sharing pet owners' anxiety and grief and maintaining the professional detachment necessary to carry out their work. In *James Herriot's Dog Stories*, no question exists about where Herriot and Siegfried Farnon stand, whether they are working desperately to save a stray dog with no hope of a fee or seized with righteous indignation at cruelty to animals. Herriot was outraged by people who abandon dogs or, worse yet, torture or poison them. In a 1986 interview, he revealed a rare bitterness when he described one of the horrors of human cruelty that veterinarians are routinely forced to witness:

> Something happened once which really put me in a bad mood. A man came in who wanted his dog put down. The gent owned him for ten years, but then he got married for the second time and the new wife wouldn't accept the dog. The man was heartbroken. I had to put his pet down even though I didn't want to. It's better to do it that way. If you refuse, some people will go right out to the chemist around the corner and buy prussic acid and give it to the dog, or even hang the animal at home. I've known that to happen.
>
> So, if a pet has to be put down, it's best for me to put it painlessly to sleep. But if I were that man I'd watch out. The wife may decide to have him put down next. (Gonzalez, *SR*, 89)

Like most veterinarians, Herriot did everything he could to prevent mindless cruelty. Once he had become famous, Herriot always saw to it that visitors received not only his autograph but the chance to contribute to the Jerry Greene Dog Sanctuary just outside of Thirsk, a charity that he enthusiastically supported: "every penny goes to help the dogs," Herriot proudly maintained (*DS*, 153), one of his quiet ways of helping animals cast out by human beings who betrayed them.

All people who love dogs know how tragically short their lives always are, and that heartbreaking grief lies inescapably at the end of every relationship with a dog in spite of—or because of—"the strength of the spiritual ties with which he has bound himself to man" (Lorenz, 68). Many vets, Herriot included, recommend that bereaved owners get another dog immediately, but after Hector and Dan went, Herriot said he found it hard to take his own advice. When he finally acquired Bodie, though, the quirky little Border terrier of Herriot's old age, he discovered and shared the only solace dog owners can expect, a wise and wonderful truth from a dog-loving vet who had often been there himself: "The thing which warms and fills me with gratitude is that he has completely taken the place of the loved animals which have gone before him. It is a reaffirmation of the truth which must console all dog owners; that those short lives do not mean unending emptiness; that the void can be filled while the good memories remain" (*DS*, xxvi). In his last published piece of writing, his introduction to *James Herriot's Favorite Dog Stories,* posthumously published in 1996, Herriot noted, "I don't think any of my other dogs would be too upset if I said that no dog has ever given me so much joy as Bodie" (*FDS*, 6).

Reviewing the 1989 audio version of *James Herriot's Dog Stories* read by actor Christopher Timothy, *Publishers Weekly* commented, "Herriot is so devoted to the canine species that each parable is intended as an object lesson in how dogs can unite us all and make human life complete."[16] Scrappy little Bodie, whose life and Herriot's drew to the close together, like all his predecessors, helped inspire Herriot's *Dog Stories,* especially the warm introductions to both editions, where Herriot shares his second thoughts about some of the most cherished stories he ever wrote, occasioned by dogs he had known, singularly touching animals who for many centuries have taught the language of a love that brings human beings closer together.

Chapter Eight
Every Living Thing

And yet for all that, Nature is never spent . . .

—Gerard Manley Hopkins

While James Herriot was trying to taper off his writing, his Yankee visitors and a few fortunate journalists still managed to find "Skeldale House," 23 Kirkgate, Thirsk, the redbrick, vine-covered Georgian structure where Herriot had settled into practice with Siegfried Farnon over 40 years earlier. Herriot good-naturedly claimed that he was usually "all too pleased to see American visitors down at the surgery and to sign the books, because they bought baby new shoes" (Brower, 97). Herriot was always courteous, but American journalist Kenneth Nickel did not doubt that no matter how famous Herriot had become, his patients continued to come first. Nickel said that locating Herriot on his home turf for the first time took "a lot of luck," the fortification of a pint or two in Thirsk's Three Tuns pub, and hours of cooling his heels in the Skeldale waiting room before Herriot finally appeared.[1]

After every patient in the clinic had been called to an examining room, Nickel's veterinary quarry appeared, wearing a rumpled white lab coat and an endearing grin and "looking about 45 at most; he is still trim and his face is cherubic and unlined." Herriot politely refused to allow Nickel to photograph him treating animals, because his son was just starting in the practice and Herriot wanted "to keep good customer relations, as it were, for the son's future" (Nickel, "Trek," 51). During the visit, though, Herriot said that he had cut traveling out of his life because jet lag detracted from his practice. He also told Nickel that Americans understand his attempt to record the pioneering spirit of early twentieth-century British vets better than his countrymen do, "Americans being pioneers themselves" (Nickel, "Trek," 50).

Arturo Gonzalez Jr., who had interviewed Herriot in 1978, went back to Yorkshire eight years later and found Herriot in a reflective mood, still grateful "for the clean, green land where I live and work," still praising the "careful friendliness and politeness" of the Yorkshire farmers, still compelled "to capture an age that has gone forever," and more than ever humbled by his ability to touch his readers so deeply by restating "the old values, hard work and integrity" (Gonzalez, *SR,* 85). Even though Herriot had recently declared that *Moses the Kitten* would be his last literary work (Brower, 92), he changed his mind and kept on with his children's books, a hint that Herriot's spectacular writing career had not yet come to an end.

In the early lambing season of 1988, *Life* reporters also trekked to Thirsk, population 4,100, the center of Herriot Country, where tourism had brought in more than $8 million over the last decade (*Life,* 66). More than ever, Herriot wanted to live quietly with his family. He was also dealing with the physical problems that accompany increasing age, so his son and four other younger vets had taken over most of the practice. Herriot, whom the *Life* reporters found as always "a very private man who would prefer to suppress his whereabouts," now considered himself mostly retired, though he still wrote a bit and vetted a bit, "shoulder[ing] the burden of being a folk hero as manfully as he has assumed the responsibility for generations of sheep, horses, cattle, pigs and pets" (*Life,* 66). The *Life* article contains some rare and wonderful photos by Barry Lewis showing Herriot in his various Yorkshire roles, stethoscoping a lamb, working at his word processor, and lifting a pint with old friends at the Three Tuns, as well as a view of Herriot's home on five pretty acres in the countryside near Thirsk. The fans were still thronging his waiting room, too. Herriot let them in "with a mixture of reluctance, amazement and embarrassment" and gave each fan a book-plate—"sometimes as many as 150 a day"—that he had signed earlier at home with painful effort: " 'After years of all this, my hand has run up the white flag and surrendered. I say it's arthritis, but I don't know what it is.' He endure[d] the cameras, ask[ed] for donations to the Jerry Greene Animal Shelter and listen[ed] to the shy speeches about why he is so important to these people that they travel[ed] thousands of miles to meet him" (*Life,* 60).

At this stage in his life, Herriot declared that he didn't want to be "pushed" by his fame, preferring to spend time with his grandchildren and live a life as simple and wholesome as Yorkshire pudding. "He rambles the fields with his dog every morning, lunches with his wife and goes on long walks every afternoon with his physician daughter Rosie, 40, and her Labrador retriever. . . . He reads histories and biographies and listens to music. His new six-room house is modest but has a beautiful view. Aside from gadgets like a sunlamp, a computer and a microwave oven, there are few luxuries. Herriot has set aside most of his earnings for his children" (*Life*, 68–69). Herriot's writing career, like his veterinary work, seemed to be quietly slipping into the past.

Throughout his life, Herriot had never been a man to sit idle and watch the television. What was there, both news and entertainment, would have shown him that in the mid-1980s "hard work and integrity," the traditional British values he had always celebrated, were disintegrating more rapidly than ever. By 1985, the Englishman's home had become his "entertainment centre" (Shaw and Shaw, 43); most British homes had a television set, watched an average of 3 hours a day (Shaw and Shaw, 4), and most of what television had to offer was as bleak as the society it reflected. Cultural historians Roy and Gwen Shaw observe that, for all the grand hopes of the visionaries who back in the 1940s had framed the British welfare state, it was not working:

> It seemed, in the mid-80s, that a spiritual vacuum waited to be filled. For more than three decades secular humanism had been the prevailing outlook. At its best it had produced a more tolerant and caring society, and brought about far-reaching and beneficial changes in relationships between the sexes and within the family. But by the 80s the caring society was being blamed for sapping the energies of the people and undermining the individual's will to create wealth, on which, it was held, the future well-being of society depended (Shaw and Shaw, 43).

Despite Prime Minister Margaret Thatcher's trumpet call for a return to Victorian values, officially implemented by such policies as having M15, the government intelligence service, investigate senior appointments to the BBC (Shaw and Shaw, 35), the British public was being bombarded by ominous concerns. Uppermost was the question of moral responsibility for the atomic bomb. Looking outward, the British now distrusted the motives of its World War II allies the United States and the Soviet Union about equally; inwardly, the British seemed to feel even more insecure about the nuclear problem. Novelist Martin Amis declared that the nuclear question "resists frontal assault. . . . The present feels narrower, the present feels straitened, discrepant as the planet lives from day to day. . . . it is ruining everything." Consequently, speculation grew in Britain that the "nuclear neurosis" might be contributing to an unprecedented increase in violence among British youth (Shaw and Shaw, 40).

Along with nuclear anxieties, a crisis in British literacy was looming in the mid-1980s. The working class enjoyed a rise in affluence under the Thatcher government, but the low-paid and the unemployed—some three million Britons—faced significant hardships. Their resentment often erupted into riots against nonwhites who under the postwar open-immigration policy had been pouring into low-paying British jobs. Nonwhite immigrants also boosted school enrollments, while the Tories continued to underfund education. Nearly half of 16-year-old British children left school in the 1980s "barely literate or numerate" (Shaw and Shaw, 32) without passing one O-level examination.

Since 1945, total consumption of British newspapers had fallen by 30 percent. By the 1980s, a cultural crisis was looming in Britain because an increasing proportion of the British population was unable to read, let alone deal coolly with sophisticated abstract concepts such as the morality of nuclear testing. A Tory arts minister declared that he was satisfied simply because "we hadn't had to watch opera performed in Texaco T-shirts" (Shaw and Shaw, 29). In 1986, the gulf between England's decaying industrial areas and small towns like Thirsk, where "both the continuities and changes of English social history are most faithfully recorded today," seemed to be widening so dramatically that despite the preoccupation of British public debate with "yesterday's world," historian Asa Briggs flatly stated, "It is not likely that this [today's] world will survive for long" (Briggs, 313).

The simpler, comforting rural world of the past that Herriot had portrayed so effectively continued to attract an enormous worldwide readership who still wanted to know more about Thirsk's most famous citizen and his life in Yorkshire. On a gray late-October day in 1991, journalist Kenneth Nickel returned to Skeldale House to interview Herriot again for *Dog World*. Though both original partners had now been retired for some time, the brass doorplate still read, "J. D. Sinclair and J. A. Wight, Veterinary Surgery," but "Another more recent notice in the window said James Herriot no longer saw visitors" (Nickel, "Revisited," 19). Nickel observed that Herriot, now a trim 13 stone (180 pounds) at age 75, still did not look his age, except for his gnarled fingers, "certainly aggravated to the point of surgery." Herriot admitted, "My hand had given up . . . the most terrific case of writer's cramp; I must have signed hundreds of thousands of books" (Nickel, "Revisited," 18).

Herriot spent a half hour with Nickel, joking a little about the effect his fame had had on Thirsk and its environs: "Herriot pubs, Herriot wine bars, Herriot this, Herriot that." Herriot also said that he had "more or less slid out" of his practice around 1990, the period when he lost some of his oldest friends. The huge-hearted animal surgeon Denton Petty (Granville Bennett) had died some years earlier, and Brian Sinclair (Tristan) succumbed in 1990 to surgical complications within a few weeks of Calum Buchanan, who was killed in a car accident. Herriot said that Donald Sinclair, however, was well at 81, living near Herriot in the hills around Thirsk, and Herriot's wife was "going strong" as their 50th anniversary approached. For *Dog World* readers, Herriot reminisced a little wistfully about the series of dogs he had taken everywhere with him throughout his veterinary career: "Y'know, you're never lonely if you have a dog. And I'm a great believer in the therapeutic effects of a dog's company" (Nickel, "Revisited," 18).

Herriot also revealed that he had been "quietly pottering on, in my own time, with another of the grown-up books," this one dealing with his practice in the 1950s. " 'I'd given up writing irrevocably, completely, until they asked me if I'd restart the television series because it ended just after the war and I thought that was a lovely ending, on a nice high. But I relented. . . . after I started again I found I quite enjoyed it and that started me writing again.' Herriot grinned and chuckled. 'And now that I'm retired I am very grateful that I've got something to do; I wouldn't like to be just tripping over the vacuum cleaner at home. So it gives me something to do—but in my own time!' " (Nickel, "Revisited," 19).

Besides wanting to keep busy in retirement, James Herriot still intended to preserve that part of "yesterday's world" that meant so much to him, but the new project took "his own time" to appear. The fifth book of his memoirs finally appeared in 1992, dedicated "to my revered and elderly friends Polly [his daughter's yellow Labrador] and Bodie [his feisty little Border terrier]." This time, as he told Nickel, Herriot chose the biblical title *Every Living Thing* himself: "I thought about it for the old book, before we started the *All Creatures*," and he added with typical modesty, "Aye, but it's a provisional title; somebody might come up with one more inspiring" (Nickel, "Revisited," 19). No one did; and *Every Living Thing* joined its predecessors as a long-running Herriot best-seller.

Every Living Thing recounts Herriot's experiences in the early 1950s, a difficult time in England and an equally difficult period in Herriot's life. Britain was struggling to pay for its share of World War II through a spartan austerity program just when the government's Labour pains were thrusting the welfare state into squalling life, and both agriculture and veterinary medicine were undergoing revolutionary changes unsettling to both Herriot and the farming communities he served. By the

1950s, the old farmers Herriot had admired were mostly gone, leaving him without one of his richest sources for his stories. Miraculous medical and surgical cures that Herriot had to learn on his own as he approached middle age had supplanted the old veterinary "black magic" that had so intrigued him and readers of his earlier books. Money was short in the 1950s, and costs were rising. Herriot was growing older, and when he looked back some four decades later to write about all of this, a longer interval than he had handled before, Herriot the author was in his mid-seventies, coping with the emotional fallout from retirement after a life of intense activity. All in all, *Every Living Thing* is Herriot's midlife-crisis book, a crisis he resolved with his trademark self-deprecating humor and his unquenchable warmth toward man and beast alike.

For the epigraph to *Every Living Thing,* Herriot used the same keynote from the King James Bible that gave him his title: "Be fruitful and multiply, and replenish the earth and subdue it; and have dominion over the fish of the sea and the fowl of the air, and over every living thing that moveth upon the earth." As he was writing, Herriot could not avoid the devastating results of selfish human dominion over nature. That unhappy reality seems to have inspired the theme that undergirds every episode of *Every Living Thing:* if mankind's domain, the natural world, is to continue to exist, human beings will have to do the hard work necessary to preserve it.

In the abstract, responsibility is a fine and noble thing; but in the down-to-earth terms of everyday life, responsibility usually demands an uncomfortably concrete price. During the period covered in *Every Living Thing,* the younger Herriot was facing considerable strain in most of the priorities his wife had laid down for their life: "family, dogs, veterinary practice, and his books and movies—in that order" (*JAVMA* 75, 704).

In 1954, Herriot was 37, an age at which to take stock of one's prospects. Whatever ambitions he might have had at the outset of his career, the years had brought him a humbler assessment of himself: "a run-of-the-mill vet, hardworking and conscientious, but that's about all."[2] Even though Herriot the author jokingly described himself now as an "ageing colleague, elder statesman, quaint old fossil," the James Herriot of *Every Living Thing* recognized the sobering truth that no matter how hard he worked, he was no longer a young man; much of the vigor and the optimism of his youth had flown.

However hard Herriot was working, he could also see that, for all its charm and its pervasive atmosphere of good humor, his home, drafty old Skeldale House, was a "woman-killer," wearing his wife out with unending housework and chilling the whole family to the bone during the bitter Yorkshire winters. Herriot watched Jimmy and Rosie fast outgrowing childhood with university fees looming not far down the road, and he clearly recognized his own limitations: "I seldom had any ideas and was constantly opposed to change" (*ELT,* 75).

Like most of his countrymen in the mid-1950s, Herriot found his finances at their "lowest ebb" (*ELT,* 25). During the early days of his practice, he had not had much opportunity to learn to manage money because he had made so little, and as he said after he had become a famous author, he had never had any head for finance anyway. By the 1950s, Siegfried and Herriot had built up a large enough practice to hire John Crooks as their first assistant, but although Herriot worked every day of the week and most nights "getting kicked, crushed, trodden on and sprayed with muck," he found himself "perpetually hard up," physically aching and exhausted with "only a niggling and immovable overdraft of £1,000 to show for it" (*ELT,* 25)—a situation that would have depressed any husband and father.

Herriot, however, was blessed with a singular talent for psychic survival: his memoirs prove that he could see past his problems, make the most of his chances to laugh at his own failings, come out on the other side of self-pity with his self-respect intact, and, as it turned out, set it all down years later in irresistible stories. After opening *Every Living Thing* in his customary manner, square in the midst of a tough vet case—a horse, at that—a case that threatened disaster but came out right in the end, Herriot temporarily doused his financial woes with a visit, cunningly timed for lunchtime, to the marvelous Mrs. Pumphrey, the most colorful of the "harem" of elderly ladies Siegfried often playfully accused Herriot of maintaining.

Herriot never begrudged putting his children's needs before his own, but that morning, after a miserable call to disgruntled clients, he had found his knees coming through his work corduroys, inspiring him to bemoan his perpetual lack of cash. Herriot based the character of Mrs. Pumphrey on Marjorie Warner of Sowerby, a wealthy Yorkshire brewer's widow who in 1983 bequeathed £90,000 for the relief of the area's elderly poor (*SATA,* 173). In her earlier appearances, Herriot had drawn Mrs. Pumphrey as one of his most beguilingly dotty Dickensian characters, chivying her dour gardener into waiting on her pampered Pekingese, Tricki Woo. When Herriot reprised her in *Every Living Thing,* he made her a far more likable, three-dimensional human being. Having wordlessly taken in Herriot's worn-out trousers and frayed shirt cuffs,

Mrs. Pumphrey insisted on giving him an impeccably tailored Lovat tweed suit her late husband had never worn. A little later, that heavy suit, hastily altered for Herriot's smaller frame, turned a threadbare country vet into "Lord Herriot of Darrowby." It won the day for Herriot when he testified at a hearing for a farmer friend—and nearly killed him with heatstroke. The episode of Mrs. Pumphrey's gift set the newly complex tone Herriot struck in *Every Living Thing,* a combination of familiar nostalgia for a simpler life; crushing physical fatigue, which at this point in Herriot's life was not quite obliterated by the intangible satisfactions and humor in veterinary practice and small-town life; and a heightened appreciation for the wisdom of ordinary folk, which daily helped Herriot accept his demanding lifestyle as not only bearable but so worthwhile he would never consider living any other way.

In *Every Living Thing,* Herriot readily admitted his own shortcomings in business and mechanical affairs and managed to make them hilarious reading. Every hapless husband who, despite the best intentions, has fallen victim to a fit of impulse buying can sympathize with Herriot's confessions of his inept rummage-sale bargains. Every wife who has yielded to the blandishments of a flashy door-to-door salesman can identify with Helen's purchase of an exotic but tatty Kasbah carpet—and every married couple could learn from the Herriots' ability to get by with laughing at each other's mistakes because both of them could also laugh at their own.

In *Every Living Thing,* besides showing his younger self doing his level best to provide his family with essentials such as a set of outdated encyclopedias and a concertina (*ELT,* 160), Herriot the author accomplished a notable autobiographical feat by depicting himself convincingly and entirely without unseemly pride as one of the most appealing fathers in print. Because Helen shared Herriot's "besotted" love of animals, their children were almost inevitable candidates for the veterinary profession, another mixed blessing because of the prospect of considerable educational expenses. Herriot said that Jimmy, who at age ten loved to help with night calls, was halfway there already, and Rosie had gone along with her father on his rounds since she was two. Although Herriot, like Siegfried Farnon, was always delighted to have both his son and daughter with him as he worked, he had his generation's full-blown bias against women taking up veterinary medicine. Today's feminists might militate against Herriot's position, but under the circumstances, he was probably justified. Herriot was certain that "tough little Jimmy" could cope with the disagreeable and dangerous conditions of 1950s veterinary work, but Herriot simply could not face exposing his Rosie to them. Herriot admitting using "every wile" he could, "unfairly at times," to deflect Rosie from healing animals to doctoring humans, but like most parents who take well-meant hands in their children's choice of career, he later admitted that he often wondered whether he had done the right thing (*ELT,* 49).

The Herriots were also facing housing troubles. By all accounts, Helen was a fine cook and a meticulous housekeeper who never complained about the numerous hardships of Skeldale House, but getting his family out of there became an obsession for Herriot. A house worth between £50,000 and £60,000 in the 1990s had sold 40 years earlier for about £2,000, and in *Every Living Thing,* Herriot described his attempt to bid on a small duplex that was up for auction. The bidding soared more than £1,000 over his limit, and fortunately for his financial condition, Herriot lost. After he recovered from that narrow escape, the Herriots launched into building a house on a narrow lot at the edge of Thirsk. Herriot the author typically made light of the tribulations he suffered during the construction period (perhaps, as is fairly usual, his wife's were worse), but even his sunny disposition took a hard hit when the half-finished house blew down in a violent windstorm. The place was rebuilt immediately (Herriot did not specify the costs), and the family moved into more convenient but tighter quarters where Jimmy's collection of Elvis Presley's rock music blasted Herriot, a lifelong lover of the classics, awake daily.

As the story goes in *Every Living Thing,* the Herriots lived at Rowan Garth for about a year, until Siegfried suggested that they look into High Field House, Herriot's fictional name for a nearby place in the country that a retiring physician was selling, the kind of home Herriot and Helen had always wanted. Herriot, always reluctant to embrace change, hesitated at first, but he admitted that as usual, he needed a good prod from Siegfried. Once Herriot and his wife saw this "secret corner of Yorkshire" close to the tiny village of Thirlby "on the edge of the wild," they agreed that living there would be "heaven" (*ELT,* 269). High Field House, described in *Every Living Thing* in some of Herriot's loveliest prose, seems to identify with Herriot's home Mire Beck, which he acquired after he began to publish, and it remained his home until he died.

Besides having to deal with finances and housing difficulties, Herriot was struggling with a serious physical ailment. The highly unsanitary conditions of rural veterinary practice at the time he came to Yorkshire had forced Herriot and his veterinary contemporaries to "wallow almost daily" in a horrible infection (*ELT,* 63)—brucellosis, known variously in the United States as Bang's disease and undulant fever. Herriot graphically described the disease and its grave implications in chapter 38 of *All Things Bright and Beautiful,* in which, despite his best efforts, brucellosis wiped out the dream that farmer Frank Metcalfe had sweated into being—a little dairy herd and a new barn he had built with his own hands. Although Herriot treated his own case of brucellosis lightly in *Every Living Thing,* the disease was then and remains today nothing to joke about. Like stockyard workers, veterinarians are still frequently exposed to brucellosis, and although antibiotics have greatly improved treatment for both animals and humans, the standard medical treatment, a combination of tetracycline and streptomycin, still fails to prevent relapse in 10 percent of cases.[3] In *Every Living Thing,* Herriot called his relapses "funny turns," but they were really not funny at all.

Brucellosis is a highly contagious disease with four varieties affecting goats and sheep, cattle and camels, swine, and dogs. Each variety is easily transmitted to humans. Testing cattle, slaughtering infected animals, and vaccinating uninfected herds have now greatly diminished animal brucellosis cases in most industrialized nations—the United States has vaccinated cattle against brucellosis since the 1920s—but it remains hyperendemic in the Middle East, India, China, and the Arctic, areas where the consumption of unpasteurized milk helps to spread the disease. In the early years of Herriot's practice, before Britain had implemented widespread preventive programs, brucellosis took a fearful toll among veterinarians, who had to work closely with animals when they were most infectious, during and after giving birth or being treated for spontaneous abortion, which the disease often causes. Even with U.S. vaccination programs well in place by 1951, the beginning of the period Herriot covered in *Every Living Thing,* 25.6 percent of 203 veterinarians attending meetings of the American Veterinary Medical Association tested positive for brucellosis.[4]

Brucellosis has consistently proved tricky to diagnose, because it resembles many other febrile diseases, like typhoid fever. Brucellosis may take weeks or even months to develop, or it may have a rapid onset five to twenty-one days after exposure, with varying combinations of chills, 104° or 105° fevers, extreme exhaustion, anorexia, diarrhea (later followed by severe constipation), arthritic swellings, headaches, profuse night sweats, abdominal pain, and almost constant weakness. As the disease progresses, patients may feel reasonably comfortable while rest-ing, "but even the slightest physical exertion may induce extreme fatigue and exhaustion. . . . Nights are marked by discomforting sweats and insomnia. . . . Persistent anorexia causes weight loss. . . . Nervousness is a constant feature. . . . The patients become irritable and mentally depressed." Brucellosis may also lead to life-threatening complications such as encephalitis and meningitis. The most frequent complication is "a destructive suppurative arthritis, usually attacking but a single joint," but brucellosis can contribute to heart and lung infections and even cirrhosis of the liver. Brucellosis itself "may remain active for many years with either an intermittent or continuous state of debility."[5] During an attack, the intermittent fever persists for one to five weeks, followed by a two-day to two-week remission. This may happen to a patient only once, or as in Herriot's case, chronic brucellosis ensues, characterized by repeated waves of fever (undulations) and remissions that recur over months or even years.[6]

In chapter 9 of *Every Living Thing*, Herriot vividly described the effects of brucellosis on his fellow veterinarians—anorexia, arthritis, and psychiatric problems—and on himself when he "joined the club"— chills, raging fevers, delirious outbursts of singing, and on at least one occasion some genteelly unprofessional conduct toward the imperious Mrs. Featherstone when she brought her poodle Rollo in for treatment: "I had laughed, even jeered at her, possibly even pawed at her person" (*ELT,* 68), a scene that seems more to be pitied than censured—or laughed at as Herriot had intended. Herriot claimed that his "funny turns" disappeared from his life in the 1960s, but the indisputably painful condition of his right hand as he grew older, his lack of weight gain, and perhaps the tinge of melancholy discernible in his later writing may all have been long-term effects of brucellosis, a constant threat that many veterinarians continue to face today.

The "funny turns" that accompanied Herriot's case of brucellosis would of course have enormously exacerbated the physical stresses of his practice, and his constant, inescapable fatigue must have contributed to the shadow of depression that seems to have crept even into his beloved veterinary work in the early 1950s. Long before, at the start of their association, Siegfried had promised Herriot that their profession offered unparalleled opportunities for making "a chump of yourself" (*ELT,* 183). Throughout *Every Living Thing,* far more often than in his earlier books, Herriot frequently showed himself doing precisely that, botching up cases and having an unprecedented number of difficulties with clients, trying to convince his readers that he was indeed "a run-of-the-mill vet"

(*ELT,* 94) and feeling a strong empathy with cart horses who "plodded patiently" (*ELT,* 115) through their hard, monotonous lives.

By the mid-1950s, the strains of Herriot's work and his life were beginning to tell on him. Another man might have become bitter over the hardships his family had to face and the loss not only of his old friends but of cherished institutions such as the quiet country pub, where Herriot's sensitive eardrums were now continually assaulted by crashing rock-and-roll guitars. Other animal doctors, too, might have been embittered over the cases of human cruelty toward animals Herriot was increasingly forced to patch up.

Other novels about veterinarians, such as Joyce Stranger's widely praised 1972 young-adult novel *Lakeland Vet,*[7] dwell on the tough times a veterinarian and his family grimly endure in quaint but inconvenient rural settings. Stranger's hero trudges doggedly through his cases with occasional outbursts of Welsh temper overmastering the few sunny satisfactions of his job, and his family's besottedness over animals seems more masochistic than inspiring.

When Herriot the author, on the other hand, took the most wretched situations, like the heartless abandonment of a puppy on a busy highway, an act that left him feeling uncontrollable "rage and pity that almost choked me" (*ELT,* 314), he showed his younger self not only doing the morally right thing by finding the dog a home but—and here is the blessed Herriot touch—putting the right dog together with the right master, and then wrote the story with the saving grace of humor. Titch, the crippled little throwaway mongrel Herriot found by the road, and Rupe Nellist, a crippled grocer, took to each other at once. After Herriot repaired the dog's leg, using a new operation he'd had to teach himself, Titch unforgettably commemorated Herriot's skill during a television appearance by balancing on his once-bad leg and cocking his good one on a flowerpot—making himself famous all over Britain.

Humor continually rescued Herriot the author, as it had Herriot the man, from the destructive clutches of self-pity. Lacking his old-time Dickensian characters, for *Every Living Thing* Herriot mined a wealth of funny situations centered on Calum Buchanan, the second assistant hired by the Sinclair-Wight practice. Calum arrived fresh from school in Edinburgh in 1954 following the departure of their talented first assistant, John Crooks, who had left to branch out on his own. In *The Lord God Made Them All,* which contains the account of Crooks's role in involving Herriot in trips to Russia and Turkey, Herriot noted that John Crooks, 10 years the author's junior, deserved a book on his own, but

Herriot never got around to writing it. Instead, in *Every Living Thing*, he dwelt briefly and generously on the good times he and Sinclair and Crooks had for three years at Skeldale House. The admiration Herriot felt for Crooks, whom Herriot saw as a young man certain to succeed, was decidedly mutual. In 1983, when Crooks became president of the British Veterinary Association, the acme of his profession, he chose Herriot to give his induction speech. There, as in his books, Herriot praised Crooks highly for his ability to get along with all kinds of people, his power of instant decision, and his devotion to his wife Heather, whom Crooks had met when he was working in Yorkshire.

However much Herriot admired John Crooks, the younger man's drive and talent probably did make Herriot, intermittently sick, frequently perplexed over his financial problems, and at the threshold of middle age, feel like an "ageing colleague" (*ELT*, 82). Calum Buchanan's effect, however, was quite different, a blast of bracing Northern air that both invigorated and exhausted Herriot and everyone else involved with the practice at Darrowby. Buchanan, who had been born in Yorkshire but favored his Scottish ancestry, did not appear in Herriot's first four books. Herriot introduced Calum when the author began working on the continuation of the television series *All Creatures Great and Small*. In 1991, Herriot told Ken Nickel, "This book, if it ever sees the light of day, will be mainly about Calum because he was such a wonderful character. They couldn't very well bring this out in the television series; he was a larger-than-life character" (Nickel, "Revisited," 33).

From the moment Calum arrived in Darrowby, Siegfried Farnon sensed larger-than-life trouble: "An assistant with a blasted badger round his neck! And a dog as big as a donkey!" (*ELT*, 106). Herriot did his best to calm the troubled waters, but Calum's veterinary skill, demonstrated in an exquisitely executed cesarean section he performed immediately upon his arrival, did little to dispel Siegfried's suspicions of disasters to come, such as being held hostage in his garden privy by Calum's voracious Dobermans.

Calum, however, became the antidote Herriot needed for his midlife crisis, a constant stimulant for Herriot's imagination, both professionally and personally. Herriot insisted that Calum "was determined to drag me into the modern world of small animal practice" (*ELT*, 318). Calum not only introduced cesarean sections but also pioneered the new era of routine spaying at Skeldale House, helping change the Farnon-Herriot practice over to small-animal work as the number of large animal patients decreased. Calum also had an uncanny ability to identify with wild animals, and could even tickle fish out of the water, which made Herriot realize how precious a native intimacy with one's natural environment can be.

Calum's private zoo, a constant source of disruptions at the veterinary headquarters, began with his original badger Marilyn and his mammoth lurcher and soon included a brace of menacing Dobermans, two additional badgers, an owl, some tortoises, and a heron, all of which provoked delicious tension between their master and Siegfried, a horseman who had his own decided views on animal ownership. However, even Siegfried had to admit that although Calum tended to lose track of things others considered important, such as his motorbike and his daily meals, the colorful assistant vet did seem to get life's most important things right, especially marrying Dierdre, whose outdoor interests complemented Calum's own perfectly. Herriot's most haunting memory of Calum was the way he played "Shenandoah" on the concertina, a lovely, nostalgic folk song about American eighteenth-century pioneering life "across the wide Missouri"—followed closely by the discovery that the unattended Marilyn had wreaked devastation upon the rest of Skeldale House during the performance. With Calum, beautiful gestures and dismaying results seemed always to go hand in hand, a combination that frequently helped boost Herriot out of the dumps of early middle age.

Two years after he and Marilyn arrived in Darrowby, Calum and Dierdre and their menagerie left for Nova Scotia. They subsequently moved on to New Guinea, where they happily maintained an enormous collection of animals for many years. Herriot had felt John Crooks's departure keenly, "the loss not only of a great assistant but a friend" (*ELT,* 82), and when Calum left, Herriot quietly mourned: "The silence in the absence of the menagerie was almost palpable" (*ELT,* 332). Over the years, the Darrowby practice saw many young assistants come and go. Herriot probably followed their careers with as much unselfish pleasure as he did John Crooks's and Calum Buchanan's, but each of these men played an especially important role at a tough time in Herriot's life. John Crooks and Calum Buchanan in their different ways raised Herriot's spirits and gave him not just the raw material for entertaining stories but the comradely warmth that helps a person surmount life's disappointments.

Herriot closed *Every Living Thing* with two bittersweet accounts of friendships that commemorated his coming through the difficult passage into middle age. At a time when everything seemed to be going wrong for him and a client even heartlessly claimed, "it's always fatal when Herriot comes" (*ELT,* 300), he lost one of his many charity cases, an aged dog belonging to an archetypal elderly Yorkshirewoman—"self-contained and unfussy but with eternal quiet humour" (*ELT,* 295). Old Molly died shortly after her Robbie went, and among her things, Helen found a picture frame she gave her husband, just what he most needed with his spirits at a low ebb. It contained pictures of Molly's three favorite men: the adored physician who attended her, her film hero John Wayne—and James Herriot.

For some time during these trying years, Herriot had also taken on the ethical responsibility of caring for two feral cats who lived in the brush just beyond his yard. When they were very young, Herriot had managed to capture them in a net and sedate them in order to vaccinate and neuter them, giving them a chance to remain healthy in their chancy wild existence. Helen named them Olly and Ginny and managed with infinite patience to stroke them a little as they shyly fed, but they would not allow Herriot, who had always prided himself on his way with cats, to touch them. That rejection got under Herriot's skin, especially when he had to trap Olly again so that he could clip his unhealthily matted fur. Helen, whose practical ability to cut to the core of a tender issue Herriot constantly praised, declared that if he wanted to become friendly with the cats, Herriot would have to stay at home more and patiently feed them as she did—making him realize suddenly that his life was half over, consumed by the ceaseless demands of his work. Herriot's feeling of responsibility for the cats who shared the margin of his existence made him make time for them. But just as he was succeeding in making friends with Olly, the cat died, leaving Herriot and his wife doubly bereft—not only was Olly gone, but they had to witness little Ginny's grief as she searched hopelessly for the brother from whom she had never before been separated. Faced with the uncomprehending animal misery that he had always found intolerable, Herriot redoubled his efforts at taming Ginny, and at last, he could claim that her acceptance of him was one of his "greatest triumphs" (*ELT,* 342). A little cat's need had done what nothing else could accomplish at this stressful period in Herriot's life—make him take time out for himself.

More than a decade after *The Lord God Made Them All, Every Living Thing* earned Herriot generous praise from most reviewers, who found the book "nonfiction at its most entertaining best . . . easy to read—perfect for the unmotivated reader"[8] with "no surprises . . . just the expected mix of gentle humor and compassion for animals and people alike."[9] The more somber tone of *Every Living Thing,* however, caused at least one critic to remark,

> An older and perhaps more tired Herriot struggles with bad-tempered farmers, difficult diagnoses, an assistant who travels with a live badger, and his own pet cats, who will have nothing to do with him. While the stories and settings hark back to his previous works, the humor and spark are missing. The older Herriot struggles to maintain the wonder and merriment of his youth but gets bogged down in the mundane aspects of shopping for a house and seems numbed rather than heart-broken by the death of some of his patients.[10]

Maeve Binchy, writing for *The New York Times Book Review,* looked more deeply into Herriot's achievement in *Every Living Thing:*

> In this bustling world where people have too often let us down, is it any wonder that we flee to be with Dr. Herriot in his world of soft-eyed dogs, badgers called Marilyn and deer grazing in the nearby woods? . . . James Herriot must now know exactly why we love his world and want to be a part of it, but he has been very careful not to let us take a sentimental journey through the narrow, winding roads of Yorkshire . . . Life is hard for these farmers . . . And life is lonely for those who exist without much human companionship . . . Dr. Herriot moves among them all, never the know-it-all, never playing God . . . to most of the people he served he was just a safe, trustworthy, reliable man. He wanted no more then, and he paints himself as no more now.[11]

Binchy's point is well taken. As a conscientious veterinarian, Herriot could not ignore the implications in the title he chose for what proved to be the last book of his memoirs: every thing that lives must eventually grow old and die. In this book, which he "crafted with foxy intelligence and angelic compassion,"[12] James Herriot came to terms with both his own limitations and the mortality he shared with all his patients and their masters, fulfilling that poignant human responsibility as he had all the others that faced him, with compassion, warmth, and gentle humor, opening the door one last time to the "sweet, safe places" of his past.

Chapter Nine

All Creatures on Film and Tape

If we open our eyes, if we open our minds, if we open our hearts, we will find that this world is a magical place.

—Chogyam Trungpa

Almost immediately after St. Martin's Press published *All Creatures Great and Small* in November 1972, filmmakers began to consider bringing James Herriot's gentle stories of the Yorkshire Dales to the screen.[1] Beginning in 1975, three movies made from Herriot's books have appeared, Herriot's BBC television series has been running since 1978, and all his adult books have been recorded on audiocassettes, some of them read by Herriot himself. Aside from his readings, Herriot did not seem to have played an active role in most of the early adaptations of his books, but he was impressed by the cinematizing process, and though he generally kept his distance, he seems to have approved of the various filming projects on his Yorkshire doorstep.

The first Herriot work adapted for the screen was *All Creatures Great and Small*. David Susskind's British movie version came out in 1974. Hugh Whitemore wrote the screenplay; Simon Ward starred as Herriot; Lisa Harrow as Helen; and Brian Sterner as Tristan. Siegfried Farnon was played by Anthony Hopkins, who ironically would win notoriety and an Academy Award in 1991 as a cannibalistic maniac in the grisly American thriller *Silence of the Lambs.*

In *James Herriot's Yorkshire,* the vet who had never expected to become a famous author described a drive he and his wife took toward Scarborough one summer day in 1974 to watch Ward and Hopkins at work with the EMI production crew at Farndale, south of the North York moors, "so like a Pennine dale with its walls creeping up to the untamed moorland" (*SATA,* 173). Neither Herriot nor Helen had ever met an actor, and both Ward and Hopkins were already famous in Britain. Herriot, with his keen appreciation for language, was enthralled:

[T]hey were filming the episode of the Clydesdale horse . . . [from *All Creatures Great and Small* and] . . . I was snatched back to that first day when I went to Darrowby and met Siegfried.

147

Anthony Hopkins and Simon Ward [drove] . . . up to the farm in a marvelous old car of the thirties. Their clothes, when they alighted, were of that great period, too, and I watched entranced as the farmer led out the horse and Simon Ward lifted the hoof and seated over it as I had done so many years ago.

People have always asked me if I felt a thrill at seeing my past life enacted then, but strangely, the thing which gave me the deepest satisfaction was to hear the words I had written spoken by those fine actors. Both of them have magnificent voices, and every word came up to me and pierced me in a way I find hard to describe. (*SATA,* 173)

Herriot's natural modesty made him shy at first about meeting the actors:

I have always been puzzled by the fact that Simon Ward, who was playing me, told me later that he was absolutely petrified at the prospect of meeting me. For a man who had just made a great name for himself playing Winston Churchill, it seemed odd. An obscure country vet was surely insignificant by contrast. (*SATA,* 173)

Herriot and Ward soon enjoyed a natural rapport. That summer, Herriot, Siegfried, and Tristan and their wives often dined with the actors at the Forest and Dale House in Pickering, the building that was the first cinematic stand-in for the fictional Skeldale House, and the veterinarians from Darrowby also frequently visited the film locations. Herriot was particularly fascinated by the moviemakers' nomadic lifestyle, so contrary to his own preference for stability. Simon Ward, on the other hand, fell in love with Lastingham, a lovely village just south of Rosedale Abbey, where he and his wife Alexandra stayed during the filming. Herriot recalled that Ward often told him "that he would like to give up acting and be a vet in Yorkshire," and Herriot thought he really meant it (*JHY,* 190).

Ward's sensitive characterization of young James Herriot became the centerpiece for the widely praised first film version of *All Creatures Great and Small.* Presently unavailable in either a movie or video version, the film was televised on the NBC-TV Hallmark Hall of Fame on February 4, 1975. Crankily dismissed by film critic Leslie Hallowell as "simpleminded popular entertainment of a long-forgotten kind"[2] but enthusiastically accepted by most other reviewers as "a rich period piece,"[3] this presentation enormously broadened Herriot's already huge American audience.

In early 1978, David Susskind produced a U.S. movie version of *All Things Bright and Beautiful.* The film, in Britain called *It Shouldn't Happen to a Vet,* was adapted from Herriot's second book by Alan Plater for the Reader's Digest Association, directed by Eric Gill, and starred John Alderton as Herriot, Colin Blakely as Siegfried, and Lisa Harrow as Helen. This film is also currently unobtainable. While it inexplicably never enjoyed wide success, an anonymous contemporary reviewer believed it struck the bull's-eye of Herriot's appeal:

> [A] charmer for all ages . . . filled with vitality, warmth, and the truth that genuine people offer. Perhaps more important, it has none of the cutesy-poo Disneyesque aspects of most animal films—and none of the stilted idealization of adults (or low-comedy characterizations as well) that mark too many films suitable for the young. . . . the hardy country folk are individualized and appealing. John Alderton's young vet is a not-infallible delight, and his domestic life as charming as his professional life is fascinating. There is even a remarkable scene involving the birth of a calf that youngsters will find miraculous—and, I hope, adults will have the good sense to share with them.[4]

BBC Television also quickly capitalized on the popularity of Herriot's work. The weekly serial titled *All Creatures Great and Small* initially aired in 1978, and its most recent series with Herriot's stories adapted by Johnny Byrne is rerunning with wide popularity on the U.S. Public Broadcasting System. Carol Drinkwater, who originally played Helen, has been replaced by Lynda Bellingham, but the stars who provided the winning interplay of the first series remained with the show. The brilliant Robert Hardy continued as the aristocratic, irascible Siegfried, and Christopher Timothy, in 1978 a relatively unknown classically trained Welsh actor, was delightedly declared by Herriot himself to have gotten "right inside the part [of the 'young vit'nery'] . . . he was terrific. It's an odd feeling watching someone playing your life. Christopher Timothy became the James Herriot I wrote about" (*SATA,* 173).

Any librarian or schoolteacher can testify that today television reaches a far wider audience than the written word can. Because the televised Timothy-Hardy *All Creatures Great and Small* is the only version of Herriot's work known to a large number of viewers unfamiliar with his books, Timothy's longtime participation in the program and his insights into it contribute valuable sidelights to the video popularity of the rural world Herriot immortalized.

In the summer of 1979, shortly before the first appearance of *All Creatures Great and Small* on U.S. television, the *Journal of the American Veterinary Medical Association* interviewed Timothy via transatlantic phone.[5]

Timothy was then 38 and had had 15 years of stage and film experience. At London's Central School of Speech and Drama, where he had received the Sir John Gielgud Scholarship, Timothy had also won the Laurence Olivier Award for the best character performance.[6] He subsequently spent three years with the Old Vic, three more years with the New Vic, and did several tours abroad before being cast as the young James Herriot. Playing Herriot immediately made Timothy's name a household word with British viewers, who apparently agreed with Herriot about Timothy's capacity for convincingly sloshing around frigid Yorkshire cow byres and thawing out in antique Yorkshire pubs with Siegfried and Tristan. Soon some 17 million Britons, Herriot included, rushed to their sets weekly to savor *All Creatures Great and Small*. It was "one of the largest drama audiences ever in the history of British television . . . so popular among British viewers that in some areas townspeople changed the time of church services so that the congregation could get home in time to watch it" (*JAVMA* 79, 253).

Timothy told his *JAVMA* interviewer that before the series he had had virtually no experience with animals. He did not even have a particular affection for them. He had enjoyed pet cats and dogs as a child, but as he grew up, he claimed, "I didn't become an animal lover. I don't dote on animals, never did," and he had had absolutely no desire to become a veterinarian. He also had "a built-in fear of large animals" that he had to overcome to play Herriot, which Timothy managed to accomplish well enough to become "totally unafraid of cows and bulls." However, like Herriot, Timothy continued to be careful around horses, following the advice of expert horseman Robert Hardy, who early in the filming told Timothy, "You stay wary, you stay alive" (*JAVMA* 79, 254).

Timothy came to play Herriot almost by chance. In 1977, while he was acting in the BBC-TV series *Murder Most English,* its producer died in a car accident. Bill Sellars, the new producer, was also involved in the Herriot project and backed Timothy over "pressure from higher up to cast a star" for the role of his lifetime (*JAVMA* 79, 254).

Until he heard about the possibility of playing Herriot, Timothy had not only avoided reading Herriot's books but also ignored their earlier film versions. He rushed out, bought the books, read them, he said, in "about a day and a half," auditioned, and got the part. Timothy then spent a week at the Yorkshire home of Jack Watkinson, the rural Leyburn veterinarian who remained the technical advisor for the show. To get into the proper veterinary spirit, Timothy "went out on all his

[Watkinson's] calls, watched him in surgery, and learned how to put my hand up a cow's rear end" (*JAVMA* 79, 254).

In spite of an extremely tight shooting schedule, the production crew of *All Creatures Great and Small* diligently strove for authenticity. Timothy recalled that when producer Bill Sellars protested that a makeup girl's simulated cow dung did not look quite appropriate, she conscientiously slathered the freezing Timothy with "the real stuff" (Timothy, 144). All the interior shots for *All Creatures Great and Small* were made on the BBC's Birmingham studio sets, but because the marketplace at Thirsk had become more modernized than Herriot's 1930s milieu demanded, the smaller main square of Richmond was substituted. Most of the outdoor filming was done about 20 miles west of Thirsk, at and around Askrigg (Timothy, 118), a ancient gray stone village in the hilly area where Herriot had worked when he first came to Yorkshire.

As a matter of policy, the animals appearing in *All Creatures Great and Small* were usually amateur performers. According to Timothy, Robert Hardy's whippet Christy became his master's fellow actor and most severe critic (Timothy, 92), and in several episodes, Bill Sellars's two Labradors ably proved the contention of Herriot, who knew the breed firsthand, that there is nothing quite like the innocence of a Lab doing something he knows he shouldn't (*LGMTA*, 327). Nearly all the cows, sheep, pigs, and cats used in the series belonged to private local owners, the animals being chosen not because of their training but because they fit the parts required, as were the real Yorkshire farmers and their wives who often pitched in as extras. Eddie Straiton, the famous British veterinarian-author to whom Herriot dedicated the book *All Creatures Great and Small* "with gratitude and affection," was the first Birmingham studio advisor for the series, and Timothy attributed the show's remarkable veterinary veracity to Straiton's patience:

> He's the little guy who would stand in the studio during rehearsal and I would be saying, "Yes, I can feel his heart," and he would lean over the camera and say, "The heart of a dog, Chris, is on the other side!" I was always making mistakes like that. (*JAVMA* 79, 256)

The 13 episodes of the first BBC television series of *All Creatures Great and Small,* based on Herriot's book of the same title, were filmed in a few months between August 1977 and the winter of 1978. The second series of 14 episodes, which at the time Timothy expected to be the last, used material from *All Things Bright and Beautiful* and *All Things*

Wise and Wonderful and began filming in the fall of 1979, followed quickly by the third series of the program. Herriot himself wrote some new story lines, principally involving his eccentric badger-fancying assistant Calum Buchanan, for later episodes of the series, and these as well as earlier sequences were adapted for the series by writer Johnny Byrne.

To play the role of James Herriot, Timothy had to overcome more serious obstacles than his fear of large animals. Because Sellars wanted "universality," Timothy did not have to reproduce Herriot's soft Scots burr, but halfway through the filming of the first series, the actor was struck by a car that smashed one leg, both his arms, his collarbone, and his head. He was expected to be out for six months, but he told his *JAVMA* interviewer that he was back at work in nine weeks because he had no choice (*JAVMA* 79, 255). Timothy recuperated literally on the set of *All Creatures Great and Small.* During the scenes depicting Herriot's honeymoon with attractive actress Carol Drinkwater playing Helen, Timothy said he looked at least 100 and probably felt worse (Timothy, 152), but he was "motivated by the terrible guilt I felt at messing everyone about, as well as a horrible fear that I would be dispensed with and a new James Herriot found." (Timothy, 149). He discussed this trying period, which coincided with the amicable breakup of his marriage, in *Vet Behind the Ears* (1979), a miniautobiography whose title indicates that, at least in groan-worthy punning titles, Timothy and Herriot had quite a bit in common.

From the outset, Timothy knew he had the role of an actor's dreams, and he proved well equipped to carry it off. Timothy might not have known much about animals, but he certainly knew about children, and he felt "the experiences were not all that different" (Timothy, 16). When he began portraying Herriot, Timothy's household was swarming with six children, two of them adopted, from teenagers down to a toddler, "presided over by Sue, a mother par excellence" (Timothy, 16). Timothy himself suggested the hatless costume that he wears as the television James Herriot, the V-necked sleeveless sweater, shapeless trousers, and well-worn tweed jacket (Timothy, 138). Drawing upon the wholesome boy-next-door appearance that he said had always won him the approval of "mums," if not their daughters (Timothy, 81), Timothy created such a successful image of Herriot that he became the "housewives' heartthrob" and critics faulted him only for being "too charming" (Timothy, 152).

Like Herriot, Timothy also found himself fortunate in the excellent relationship he shared with his coworkers. His costar Robert Hardy, a seasoned veteran of both stage and film, kept the younger actors in stitches to help them relax and graciously handed over to his less-experienced colleagues many of those prized acting moments that make an actor's career. According to the grateful Timothy, "He [Hardy] always allows you to take the scene giving you centre-stage, when an actor of his distinction and experience could easily carry on regardless." Hardy also had a phenomenal knowledge of Herriot's texts and often called out, "Back to the book," which he had neatly cross-referenced and indexed, to make jarring lines ring true or correct the mood of a scene (Timothy, 25).

Timothy also observed that the 1970s decline in British moviemaking propelled highly talented cameramen into television work. Commenting on the importance of the skilled eyes behind the camera, Timothy wrote: "However well an actor might get on with the director, it is the cameraman who is actually filming him. It is his advice on what movement or facial expression looks good through the camera that makes all the difference to how your performance comes over on television" (Timothy, 120). After a shakedown period, Timothy's first cameramen on *All Creatures Great and Small,* Ken Morgan and John Kenway, contributed constant constructive advice and award-winning landscape photography to the program.

By 1979, the fickle British television audience was demanding greater variety of action in *All Creatures Great and Small.* The *Radio Times* was "full of letters that ask[ed], 'Why oh why, must we see Christopher Timothy going up a cow's rear quarters again and again? Don't vets do anything else?' " (Timothy, viii). Timothy said that he wrote his own book in part to show that in the course of filming the series, he, as Herriot had done in his actual practice, frequently ran into amusing, hair-raising, and purely awful situations with animals. During his breaking-in week with veterinarian Watkinson, for instance, Timothy had to decline the local farmers' courteous offer of the glistening by-products of a horse gelding, reputedly a great delicacy. Later during production, Timothy and the rest of the cast had to endure the tribulations inherent in working with animals, such as a terrier painstakingly chosen for his obnoxious temper who turned out to adore Timothy and refused to behave with the requisite aggressiveness. The human actors even risked physical damage for their art; during the filming of the "Boris the Cat" episode, the feline star went berserk and clawed his way through an actress's blouse while the unlucky lady carried on with traditional British aplomb.

When asked about the reason for the series's great success, Timothy once glibly replied, "No sex, no violence, no bad language." Later, however, he did admit that "there was a lot more to it than that" (Timothy, 126–27). Producer Bill Sellars firmly intended to faithfully portray a historical period notably more reticent in vocabulary than our own, and the BBC also refused to offend its enormous post-Sunday-service audience. Sellars strictly maintained a degree of propriety approaching the Victorian for *All Creatures Great and Small,* and although locals in bit parts were allowed to record the occasional heartfelt "bugger" or "arse," off-color responses from the show's lead actors to outrages such as Boris's were strictly forbidden. In the late 1970s, British public opinion, especially in Scotland, also sternly advocated sobriety on the screen. Despite the reputation and economic importance of some of Scotland's most famous exports, Timothy was taken severely to task by the Scottish press over such episodes as those with Granville Bennett that involved characters getting hilariously drunk. Though Timothy maintains that he himself was virtually abstemious and "Only the briefest glance at an episode is needed to see clearly drink is not a good thing," Scottish public outcry "blamed the programme as having an irresponsible and thoughtless influence on drinking patterns." Timothy insisted that the Scots claimed that "I, Christopher Timothy, was personally responsible for the rise in alcoholism" (Timothy, 127), and with a forgivable retaliatory relish he recounted one filming session when prop men waggishly substituted a real glass of potent 1 percent flat shandy for the usual trick glass designed to keep actors sober. Timothy struggled through the scene before losing control of his stomach, but when the director demanded a retake, Timothy threw up—all over the actor who played Granville Bennett (Timothy, 129).

Timothy did not meet Herriot until filming of the first series had been underway for some time. At first, Mrs. Herriot had reacted adversely to the casting of Timothy, whose naturally brown hair had been dyed blond for several previous parts, in the role of her husband: "Not that boy with the awful-coloured hair!" (Timothy, 86), but the "intensely human" Herriot immediately accepted the actor as his "alter ego" (Timothy, 93). As he became better acquainted with the Herriots, Timothy discovered some remarkable coincidences; to his astonishment, Carol Drinkwater strongly resembled Mrs. Herriot in youthful pictures of herself Mrs. Herriot had brought to show the actors, and Robert Hardy's voice was so close to the real Siegfried Farnon's that even Timothy, with his trained ear, found it difficult to tell them apart (Timothy, 87, 89).

As for Timothy's impression of "the man himself," Herriot's enthusiasm for all living things impressed Timothy most.[7] The actor could see only one small flaw in Herriot:

> [T]he measure of whisky he pours you is too generous! At a quiet dinner that James Herriot, Carol Drinkwater, Peter Davison and I had at his home, the whisky and soda he gave me was so strong I had to go and help his wife in the kitchen for fear of being given another and falling in a stupor on the floor (Timothy, 88).

In his book, Timothy also described the attitude he brought to the role of his lifetime, a humility that helped him play the part well enough to satisfy Herriot himself. According to Timothy, the actor's strength is to remember that "However much you immerse yourself in another's work, however much you forget yourself, at the end of the day you are only an actor" (Timothy, 51). Timothy said he learned that principle of his profession the hard way. Shortly before he played Herriot, he had worked in Singapore on a film about young draftees caught up in the atrocities of the 1950s Malayan war, and while "larking around" one evening, still in costume, Timothy and his coworkers came upon a young GI on leave from Vietnam. Timothy never forgot the shock: "His eyes were middle-aged" (Timothy, 51–52).

During his work on the first episodes of *All Creatures Great and Small,* Timothy realized that both good actors and good veterinarians have to deal with the vital difference between appearance and reality. To play Herriot convincingly, Timothy had to be able to submerge his own preferences and understand, if not assume, the values his subject held uppermost. Timothy also perceived the essential paradox of the veterinary profession well enough to turn it into the heart of his performance. When the *Journal of the American Veterinary Medical Association* asked him to define "a veterinarian," Timothy replied that he believed firmly that a vet "cares for animals, and at the same time is able to put people before animals." All of the veterinarians he had met, Timothy said, agreed with Jack Watkinson "that it is a non-emotive job, that he doesn't get involved." Yet, with an actor's perception, Timothy said he "swallowed this until I saw him at a calving and I took a look at that guy's face, and don't ever tell me that vets don't get involved" (*JAVMA* 79, 256). Although he says he never doted on animals as much as Herriot admitted to doing, Timothy was consistently able to display the required emotional involvement in such scenes as the death of Amber, the doomed stray dog who tragically captured Herriot's heart in one of the most touching episodes of *All Creatures Great and Small*.

While Timothy was preparing for his role by shadowing Jack Watkinson, Watkinson also told Timothy that a vet more often than not had to deal with "the psychology of the owner whose loving but misguided care had resulted in their pet's misfortune" (*JAVMA* 79, 256). After playing Herriot for some time, Timothy later estimated that "at least 40 percent of a vet's work, of his problems, is not dealing with the animals, but dealing with the owners" (Timothy, 256). Some of Herriot's most affecting passages deal with the painful lessons about human psychology he learned in his practice. They taught him to look beneath the surface appearances of characters such as Paul Cotterell, who seemed stoical enough when Herriot had to put his beloved pub terrier down but then took his own life a few days later. Like the twinges to the heartstrings both Herriot's books and the television series often provoke, much of the humor and the pathos in Timothy's re-creations derive from just such situations, where the veterinarian treads the slippery middle ground between treating his patient appropriately and gingerly handling a touchy owner.

When he began to work in Yorkshire, Timothy found himself "engrossed by a whole new way of life" (Timothy, 78). In his week with Watkinson, Timothy soon discovered that the values of farming folk did not seem to have changed since Herriot's day. They trusted people about money and were honest to a fault themselves; one day, Timothy saw a farmer stop Watkinson on the road to have him remove stitches from his dog's paw, then traded him a jar of homemade beer for his work (Timothy, 77). As generous as Herriot himself, the farmers who gladly loaned filmmakers their animals and barnyards even welcomed a shivering, muck-covered Timothy into their homes:

> I didn't dare go further than the kitchen. Standing in my underpants, the family set to with scrubbing brushes. More used to dirt than we were, every farm we worked on was as hospitable. Always we were invited to use the houses as our own. The general concensus of opinion seemed to be, "By heck, it takes you back." (Timothy, 145)

Filmmakers evidently did not care to tackle Herriot's RAF experience, which he had integrated into *All Things Wise and Wonderful*, or the overseas trips he chronicled in *The Lord God Made Them All*. Instead, the 1986 film *All Creatures Great and Small*, starring Christopher Timothy, Robert Hardy, Carol Drinkwater, and Peter Davison as Tristan carried on Herriot's reminiscences of his practice just after his return from RAF service in 1945. As dramatized by Brian Finch, this movie does exactly what Herriot said his first books had done, stringing engaging vignettes of the Darrowby veterinary practice on the framework of Herriot's life. In addition, however, Finch unified the film by suggesting a mild conflict to be resolved in Herriot's life, a difficulty in readjusting to civilian life after four years (in Herriot's book, as in real life, only two) of depressing military service in fields very far removed in every sense from the veterinary work he loved.

As an extended version of one of the highly successful episodes of the television series *All Creatures Great and Small,* the 1986 made-for-British-television movie reprised some of Herriot's most appealing characters, including the incorrigibly stingy Farmer Biggins, lavish Mrs. Pumphrey and obese Tricki Woo, and Mr. Mulligan's dreaded Shetland pony–sized dog that none of the Darrowby vets wanted to treat. The film also added some new elements, primarily the aristocratic Caroline, the love of Siegfried Farnon's life (in reality, Siegfried married in the 1940s and raised a son and daughter in a beautiful home near Herriot's in the hills just outside of Thirsk); Herriot's son Jimmy, portrayed as a vine-climbing holy terror; and Mrs. Hubbard, a cook who memorably cremated one of the few chunks of prime roast beef available to the Farnon-Herriot ménage in the postwar period of rationing. The film closes with champagne flowing in Skeldale's drawing room to celebrate Tristan's new job with the Ministry of Agriculture, Siegfried's engagement to Caroline, and Helen's announcement of her second pregnancy, a fitting close, Herriot thought, not only to the series but to his writing as a whole. However, the tourists kept pouring into Thirsk, and audiences proved unable to let Herriot retire in peace. In the late 1980s, he finally agreed to provide new material for one more series of the television program *All Creatures Great and Small,* episodes that formed the backbone of Herriot's last book of memoirs, *Every Living Thing.*

Even though the traditional values of prewar Britain lingered longer in the Yorkshire Dales than elsewhere in the British Isles, as the televised *All Creatures Great and Small* progressed, it had to take its viewers back to more and more recent times. Just as had happened with Herriot's books, the television program gradually phased out wonderful old characters and attempted to find colorful replacements. To enhance the unity of the series, film writers often regrouped episodes and even switched the actions of minor characters to major ones, as in the televised version of chapter 8 of *The Lord God Made Them All,* Herriot's first attempt at a cesarean section, in which Tristan, not the overconfident vet student

assistant Norman Beaumont that Herriot described in his book, pro-
motes the operation neither he nor Herriot really knew how to perform.

For later episodes, Herriot added the eccentric figure of Calum
Buchanan, a complex character who opened the series up to modern elements intruding on the Dales from outside, such as environmental concerns, ethnic festivals, and Herriot's problems with home ownership. In
"When Dreams Come True," episode 5 of the 1992 series, writer Johnny
Byrne showed a city friend of Herriot's visiting him in 1951. Helen,
played by Lynda Bellingham, suffered from back trouble that intermittently kept her in bed rest and out of the series action. Tristan was no
longer in residence, so for comic relief, Siegfried—in his usual dramatic
fashion—coped with the vagaries of Calum and his assorted animals.
Herriot, played by Timothy as slightly older, somewhat more careworn,
and mostly accompanied by an obliging black Labrador, was buying
Rowan Garth, a home in the countryside, and fretting over the financ-
ing involved. From the moment Herriot's city visitor arrived, he
dreamed of taking up idyllic country living, while Herriot longed for the
higher income and the comforts of urban practice, illustrating the familiar "grass is always greener" theme of this episode. After several scenes
illustrating the amusing differences between city and country lifestyles,
each man finally concurred with the homey rural-Kansas wisdom that
there's no place like home.

Herriot read—and liked—all of the scripts for the early series of the
televised *All Creatures Great and Small;* he never missed watching the
Sunday evening programs if he could help it (Gonzalez, *M,* 6), and he
also approved of Johnny Byrne's later scripts. Herriot's stories are also
available in audio versions. For one audio taping, Herriot read works
from his first two books in a grandfatherly tale-telling style and "a deep
musical Scottish burr [that] sounds more like he's reminiscing than
reading."[8] All other audio performances available, issued as tie-ins with
publication of his various books, have been read by Christopher Timothy, whose work in this area has usually been praised as "outstanding."[9]
Regarding Timothy's recordings of selections from Herriot's last book of
memoirs, *Every Living Thing,* reviewers observed that "Timothy reads
expressively in a variety of voices, though he does little with accents,"[10]
and "Timothy's reading captures something of Herriot's character, a
man of honest virtue, whose pleasures come from the surprises that each
day's events can offer."[11]

Around 1988, Timothy and David Nicholas Wilkinson, a young
Yorkshire actor and director, decided to coproduce a video version of

James Herriot's Yorkshire, a travelogue-documentary that was narrated by Timothy and incorporated the only appearance Timothy and Herriot ever made together, a short chat in the garden of Herriot's surgery at Thirsk. Timothy and Wilkinson also added some colorful Yorkshire personalities, personal anecdotes, historical background, and a musical score composed by Rod Bowkett to Herriot's text. In newspaper interviews when the video premiered in 1993, Timothy made no bones about the financial returns he hoped the project would bring, but in *Yorkshire on Sunday* for June 13, 1993, he also colorfully declared his love affair with Yorkshire and its people: "There is a quality of life up there that people down south ought to envy. Yorkshire has gentleness, honesty, and no b—— s——. Apart from the real b—— s——, that is." Evidently the feelings were mutual, because both Welshman Timothy and Scotsman Herriot were made honorary Yorkshiremen by the lord mayor of Leeds on October 31, 1993.

James Herriot's Yorkshire—the Film was released November 15, 1993, and distributed by Big Life Pictures in a 16 mm wide-screen format, but the film never seems to have achieved the success that Timothy had expected. In the film's early stages, many British production companies had rejected the project, and to maintain the excellence Timothy and Wilkinson wanted, they chose to invest heavily in the film rather than take the cheap way out or accept the backing of a pet-food company, which they believed would violate the ethical position that Herriot had always maintained. Actors and crew opted to work without salaries, instead contracting for percentages of any profits the video might make, and in extremis, British veterinarian Tony Lewis, father of the video's film editor, mortgaged his home to invest £50,000 so that the project could be completed.

Even these heroic measures, however, could not affect the change in the British public's viewing tastes. Early on in the project, a Leyburn grocer told Timothy, "For God's sake, make another bloody series quick, or we'll go out of business," but in 1993, even small Yorkshire towns that had been profiting handsomely since the late 1970s from the Herriot craze were debating whether to adopt more up-to-date advertising images, and all Herriot himself wanted was to be left alone with his family and his dogs in the twilight of his life. Timothy, who after 13 years with the Herriot television series found himself too closely identified with the role to be hired for any others, went so far as to brandish a castrator as he hopefully signed copies of the video in remote Yorkshire bookshops, but sales—22,000 copies in the first five weeks of release—

were disappointing. As of 1996, *James Herriot's Yorkshire—the Film* has not been released in the United States, though following Herriot's death, Timothy was reworking the film with additional material, presumably including excerpts of Herriot's memorial service, to which Timothy and Robert Hardy contributed in October 1995 at York.

On the other hand, significant as the success of audio and film versions of Herriot's work had been in Britain in the 1980s, it was and remains far greater in America. As he told Arturo Gonzalez in 1978, Herriot generously attributed his fame to America and to the president of St. Martin's Press, Tom McCormack:

> He spotted something in my books that would appeal to Americans. I frankly couldn't see it myself. Why should sophisticated Americans be interested in the doings of an elderly Yorkshire vet before World War II? I still really can't conceive of why I'm such a success over there. When I try to analyze it, I come up with the conclusion that Americans are even bigger animal-lovers than the British.
>
> Also, you Americans like to laugh. And I think your readers are getting a bit sick and tired of the pornography that's being published there as well. I think the success of my books may be a backlash against some writers who are trying so hard to be sexy. I don't think my books would ever have taken off in England were it not for the American success first. (Gonzalez, "Interview," 44)

Whetted by skillful hands at St. Martin's Press and the David Higham Agency—Christmas 1995 saw a children's pop-up version of one of Herriot's stories—the American thirst for all things involved with Herriot still causes floods of tourists to invade the Yorkshire Dales. In view of the amazing popularity that the various versions of his stories have maintained, the humility that was the chief feature of Herriot's personality seems all the more endearing. After 17 years of overwhelming adulation he never sought or wanted, Herriot, in the words of his friend John Crooks, remained at the close of his life "such a great man and yet such a humble man, and you realized from him what the important things are" (Daniel, 32).

Chapter Ten

"Ninety-nine Percent Vet and One Percent Writer"

The good doctor simply awakens the physician within.
—Albert Schweitzer

Some time around the publication of *Every Living Thing* in 1992, James Herriot learned that he had cancer of the prostate, but the world at large did not know of his illness until Herriot died on February 23, 1995. In the last three years of his life, according to his granddaughter Emma Page, Herriot bore his illness "very patiently and bravely."[1] He seemed to carry on with quiet dignity much as he had always done, though he no longer saw uninvited visitors.

As a man who had been active all his life, Herriot stayed busy as long as he could. He was seriously injured in early July 1994 while defending his garden from marauding black-faced sheep, an accident that returned him to the public eye he was trying hard to avoid. The incident also provoked reporters into attempting parodies of his popular style. According to the Associated Press, "there came the sheep, the rogue sheep, and they got the 77-year-old, savaged him they did. . . . Butted and trampled him, they did." Mrs. Herriot acknowledged, "Yes, they had been having a spot of problems with sheep getting onto their lawn. . . . 'It appears he's broken his leg round the hip. . . . It's most unfortunate.' "[2] British reporter Martin Wainwright took a peevish tack in an oddly titled *Manchester Guardian Weekly* item appearing a few days after Herriot's release from the Friarage Hospital at Northallerton, "Sheep Take Revenge on James Herriot," insisting that Herriot had made a "literary goldmine" from "cat fleas and bovine flatulence." Because Herriot had always particularly enjoyed delivering lambs, and no record whatsoever exists of his abusing any animal, "revenge" seems a strange term to use in this context. Moreover, Wainwright also seemed to begrudge the signs reading "Welcome to Thirsk, the town of James Herriot" being put up on the A19 highway by the U.K. Department of Transportation.[3]

162 JAMES HERRIOT

On July 5, shortly after Herriot's accident, U.S. National Public Radio host Robert Siegel interviewed Wainwright about the perils of dealing with Yorkshire black-faced sheep. Wainwright explained that these sheep are fiercely independent, rather stupid, and have a tendency to gang up on anyone who gets in their way. Tossing British understatement to the winds, Wainwright compared the sheep's attack on Herriot to the buffalo stampede sequence in Kevin Costner's film *Dances with Wolves*.[4] Wainwright declared that the continuing sheep problem represented a conflict between the British agricultural and village lifestyles; because farmers graze their sheep on the hills above the unfenced towns, woolly economic necessity clashes directly with the traditional British passion for gardening. Wainwright also recounted an incident that he claimed proved Herriot's heated defense of his garden was standard British operating procedure: a Yorkshire teacher took matters literally into his own hands, seizing a flock of 10 black-faced sheep that were munching his flowers and holding the sheep hostage in his garage until their owners paid for the damage the sheep had done. In other cases, when farmers stubbornly refused to pay up, similarly kidnapped sheep were sold by enraged gardeners, who kept the cash value of their ruined gardens and in honest Yorkshire fashion returned the rest to the farmers, who presumably were sufficiently impressed to prevent any such depredations from happening again (*ATC*, 14–15).

This conversation between Siegel and Wainwright also illustrates the difference between American adulation of Herriot and his work and a negative British reaction that appears, at the least, ungracious in the light of Herriot's devotion to his veterinary profession, his formidable contributions to the Inland Revenue, and the fact of his injury at the time of this conversation, even if Wainwright was unaware of Herriot's cancer. Siegel felt that, in the town Herriot had made famous, the sheep attack that resulted in the vet's broken leg was a major event that would have fit neatly into one of his books. Wainwright, however, ignored the physical perils of veterinary work that Herriot had endured for over 50 years and disregarded the published accounts of Herriot's tax bills, his abstemious lifestyle, and his generosity toward his family and friends. Wainwright's sour grapes probably resulted from the economic malaise in England's North, still smarting from large-scale unemployment and high taxation. According to Wainwright,

> There's obviously tremendous sympathy for anybody age seventy-seven who suffers a broken leg. But I think there's also kind of a wry feeling

that he made a living, a very good living, out of describing exactly this sort of incident in fiction. I don't think that anything like this has happened to him before. But now it has and so people's natural sympathy is slightly mixed with the feeling that, well, you know, as soon as he is better and writing again this will appear in the next best-selling book. (*ATC*, 25)

After his accident, Herriot was never again up to writing an entirely new best-seller. His *Cat Stories* appeared in October 1994, just in time for the Christmas market. This book contained 10 popular feline fables drawn from Herriot's earlier books, sweetly illustrated by Lesley Holmes and prefaced by a short introduction roughly parallel to the lengthy one Herriot had written for *Dog Stories* in 1986.

In celebrating these enigmatic animals, whose ailments until relatively recently tended to be ignored in veterinary training, Herriot's introduction to *Cat Stories* also commented upon retirement and aging, the bittersweet "end of all created things."[5] Since he was a boy, Herriot said, he had always had cats around him, both his own pets and the farm cats who kept him company on his rural calls.[6] Among the few veterinary techniques he praised himself for mastering were his ability to wrap a cat for treatment and his knack for communicating with his feline patients, including the feral cats Ginny and Olly that Herriot and his wife had eventually tamed in the quietly satisfying conclusion to *Every Living Thing*.

As when he described his relationship to Olly and Ginny, Herriot's joy in his animal friends was tempered in the *Cat Stories* introduction by a melancholy note held as ever in check by his natural restraint and his graceful acceptance of changes in the profession he loved: "now, when I am retired and it is all over, I often look back and think of the [veterinary] changes which took place during my era. The recognition of cats was, of course only a small part of the almost explosive revolution which transformed my profession" (*CS*, x–xi).

Herriot consciously and conscientiously followed the "sensible axiom that, once retired, one should not continue to haunt one's former place of business," but his heart could never allow him to leave Skeldale House completely: "it is a place of a thousand memories, where I shared the bachelor days with Siegfried and Tristan, where I started my married life, saw my children grow up from babyhood and went through a half century of the triumphs and disasters or veterinary practice." Now he seemed to be saying his gradual good-byes: "Today, though, I go there only to pick up my mail and, in the process, to have a quick peep at how things are going." As Herriot the author had always done, he saved the moment from sentimentality by moving quickly from those intimations of mortality to the specifics of a busy animal doctor's practice, allowing his son Jimmy the last word—that "the cats [were] edging ahead" in the surgery where cat-loving James Herriot had spent his life (*CS*, xi–xiii).

James Herriot's Cat Stories proved just as successful with American readers as his earlier books had been, warmly recommended by reviewers as "an ideal gift for cat lovers."[7] On *Cat Stories*'s debut in October 1994, *Publishers Weekly* greeted the book as "The Cat's Meow," noting that the book immediately claimed number 10 on their best-seller list and had outdone any other Herriot title in wholesale sales and independent reorders. Herriot, of course, did not do any publicity for *Cat Stories,* "so the publishers mounted a $300,000 TV ad campaign September 21–27 during the daytime soaps." The results sound like fodder for one of Herriot's episodes: "The commercial, of course, starred cats, and filming was anything but calm. One feline fell in love with the book and kept rubbing against it, repeatedly knocking it off the set's mantelpiece."[8] *New York Times* reviewer Michele Slung commented, "one person's 'slight' is another's 'light,' and producing such an unpretentiously winsome collection is a lot harder than it looks . . . James Herriot is still an expert dispenser of 'light.' "[9]

During the dark Yorkshire winter that followed, though, Herriot's beloved 13-year-old, partly deaf Border terrier, Bodie, whose proclivity for chasing cats prevented the Herriots from keeping an indoor cat of their own, was sleeping out the twilight of his life, just as his master's condition was deteriorating. Herriot's old friend John Crooks saw Herriot "only a month or two before he died. 'His spirit was tremendous. He was frail, he was obviously dying, but he behaved as if absolutely everything was normal. And when I left, he insisted on walking to the garden gate with me' " (Daniel, 32).

On February 23, 1995, not long before the lambing season he had always loved, James Herriot died peacefully at his home with all his family at his side, to the very end exemplifying the hard work and integrity that he had celebrated in both his demanding professions. Gordon Wilkins, one of Herriot's neighbors, declared that Herriot's office had become a shrine, constantly attracting busloads of reverent American tourists.[10]

In 25 years, the 1 percent of James Herriot that he devoted to his writing had produced eighteen books, nine for his adult readers and nine for his audience of children. To date, Herriot's books have sold more than 60 million copies worldwide and inspired three films and a wildly popular television series, all based on his recollections of ordinary veterinary work in an obscure rural area of northern England. Herriot's contribution to the literature of the twentieth century is undeniably "popular," seemingly old-fashioned, and, to some observers, of minimal literary importance, but the reasons behind Herriot's enormous appeal contain some vital truths about the values he incorporated into both literature and living.

Throughout his life and work, Herriot deplored the kind of change that eminent Victorian Matthew Arnold had called "This strange disease of modern life with its sick hurry, its divided aims."[11] Herriot lived through wrenching cataclysms of history that even Arnold could not have envisioned: two world wars, the nuclear age, the decline of the British Empire, and the rise and fall of Communism. Throughout this century, most of civilized humanity has been caught up in the tide of history, dangerously proud of the world it is creating by inflicting on itself exactly the vicious, meaningless changes that make the modern industrialized world so unforgiving. Such changes unnerved Herriot, as they do most of his readers. In the words of Matthew Arnold's most famous poem, "Dover Beach," Herriot had discovered that the "land of dreams" he had envisioned in his youth outside the Dales had precious little joy, peace, love, hope, certitude, or help for pain. In the face of the "terror of history,"[12] Herriot wanted to preserve the values of the way of life that he had found in the Yorkshire Dales, close to the eternal cyclical rhythms of nature. To do so, he drew short memoirs from actual events in his practice and couched them in graceful but economical language, celebrating the values of "hard work and integrity" that had given meaning to his life. Despite the seriousness of his purpose, one of Herriot's most pleasing literary trademarks was the care he took with the words he chose. Despite a dignified sense of propriety, he never flinched from the right word for the right situation, calling a Yorkshire spade full of muck just that.

Because Herriot's appealing sense of humor depended on both his clever way with words and his vivid sense of the incongruous, the vehicle he was best suited to use was storytelling, spinning tales he himself would have enjoyed in the local pub. A good pub story, the kind Herriot heard as a young man in Glasgow, needs to be short, packing plenty of punch between pints. Like the tale of the Glaswegian football fan who had to answer the call of nature, the good pub story also must be authentic in idiom and dialect. It has to evoke strong emotion bordering on sentiment, force the audience to pay attention to catch the point, and illustrate some human foible that is both old and new—old because human nature never changes, and new because of the story's twist that makes its listeners perceive the subject in a way they had never seen before. Whether told from a pulpit or in a Yorkshire pub, a story such as that both teaches and delights, to use Elizabethan theorist Sir Philip Sidney's tried-and-true recipe for great literature—though Herriot, of course, operated closer to the soil than Sir Philip would have.

Circumstances forced Herriot to write in short bursts, producing stories that averaged only a few pages, though he did string some of these together in longer narrative lines, as he did with the stages of his courtship of Helen in *All Creatures Great and Small*. Each of Herriot's stories illustrates some single truth of human nature, told with a convincing colloquial Yorkshire turn of phrase, and the best of them produce good belly laughs no matter how often they are reread.

Herriot's work is often described both positively and negatively as "simple." As Herriot himself knew, honing a story into the apparent simplicity of a Yorkshire brook is grindingly hard work, the kind that many writers today shun and few readers adequately appreciate. Herriot himself would have likely appreciated the observations of British composer John Tavener, who has returned for inspiration to the elemental chants of the early Eastern churches: "There is nothing easy about achieving simplicity. A famous British music critic once said to my mentor and librettist, Mother Thekla, the Abbess of the Orthodox Monastery of the Assumption, Normanby, 'You see, we as critics have great difficulty with John's simplicity', whereupon she cried, 'He gives his life's blood for that simplicity', and hurled the goat's bucket at him!"[13]

Debts to various other writers do appear in Herriot's writing. He derived the early Siegfried-Herriot relationship from Arthur Conan Doyle's Holmes and Watson and learned his economy of form and content from a careful study of Salinger and Hemingway. Besides the spectrum of ironies he valued highly in George Bernard Shaw's work, Herriot probably owed his most substantial literary debt to the Victorian novelist Charles Dickens, whose portraits of eccentric characters such as Ebenezer Scrooge and mistreated children such as Little Nell underlie such Herriot staples as the parsimonious Mr. Biggins and the ill-used delinquent Wesley Binks. Herriot, however, forced by his profession to deal realistically every day with suffering and death, seemed incapable of the depths of sentimentality in which Dickens tended to wallow.

No literary characters sprung from their creator's imagination can ever be completely identified with the actual persons who inspired them; Dickens never "was" either Scrooge or Bob Cratchitt, any more than Richard III or Macbeth ever "was" Shakespeare. As with all fictionalized portraits, no one can completely determine the degree to which the major characters of Herriot's books, Helen, Tristan, and above all Siegfried, coincide with their originals, Joan Danbury Wight and Brian and Donald Sinclair; but as literary creations, each evolves into a more and more convincing three-dimensional figure as Herriot's sequence of narratives progresses. Tristan perhaps is the most one-sided of Herriot's major figures, because a good deal of Herriot's broadest humor relies on Tristan's rapscallion antics and his baiting of his mercurial older brother, Siegfried. As a literary character, Siegfried himself becomes increasingly complex throughout Herriot's first four books. Siegfried first appeared as Herriot's aristocratic employer, a veterinary practitioner enraptured with all the intricacies of his field, from medieval remedies to the latest in medicines and procedures. At the same time, Siegfried had to be the bedeviled older brother standing in loco parentis to a younger brother who seemed to be having all the fun he could scrape up in Darrowby. In *The Lord God Made Them All,* however, Herriot showed new depths to Siegfried's generous, forward-thinking character, just as longtime partners who work well together continually find more and more aspects of each other's personality to respect. In *Every Living Thing,* Siegfried appeared mainly as the older partner who generally disapproves of Calum's unconventional approaches, but Siegfried's tirades were muted, as though age and fatigue were catching up with even his volatile temperament.

Herriot's wife, first seen as the serenely patient object of his often bumbling courtship, features importantly in *All Creatures Great and Small* and *All Things Bright and Beautiful.* Likewise, Herriot portrayed her as the adored wife, to whom Herriot so desperately wanted to return in *All Things Wise and Wonderful,* and the cherished mother of his children, but Helen is not shown so often or so intimately in Herriot's later work. She seemed to have been occupying herself at home as a wonderful cook and compulsive housekeeper, as Herriot noted in *Every Living Thing,*[14] while Jimmy and Rosie went along on their father's farm calls. Helen also appeared as the stabilizing influence in episodes of Herriot's fumbling attempts at home furnishing, even making a classic mistake of her own with the Kasbah carpet. She moved briefly into center stage at the close of *Every Living Thing,* when she tamed the little feral cats before Herriot could approach them. And in no uncertain terms, as Joan Wight did in real life, she set priorities for their life together, telling her husband that now he was middle-aged, he would have to cut back on his work and spend more time at home.

As the colorful old Dales characters who provided Herriot's favorite raw material passed away, he seemed to turn his attention increasingly toward the self-portrait he was creating in his successive books. At first, as he said, he had used the figure of the younger Herriot as only the skeleton that upheld and unified his various tales. However, starting with *All Things Wise and Wonderful*, Herriot the author became progressively more concerned with portraying his own emotional and psychological development. By the time he reached his last book, *Every Living Thing*, the James Herriot 30 or so years younger that Herriot the author fictionalized is a fully realized character, whose struggle to accept the inevitable process of aging forms the major tension of the book. Besides wanting to earn a little more cash, Herriot always said that he began to write to entertain his readers and memorialize the lifestyle of the Dales. Toward the end of his writing career, he seemed more willing to probe human motivations, including his own, than he had been initially. Unless or until all possible biographical materials become available for study, though, no definitive answer can satisfy either the question of the relationship between the successive James Herriots as younger protagonist, James Herriot the author, and the busy veterinarian who created them both, or the question of the degree of fictionalization to which Herriot subjected his material.

Herriot always insisted that he wanted to be remembered primarily as a veterinarian. Donald Sinclair did not record his memoirs of his famous partner; neither did Brian Sinclair, who in his latter years gave lectures about his association with Herriot, and Colum Buchanan, the world-traveling fancier of exotic animals, leave published recollections of Herriot. Two other veterinarians who knew Herriot well, however, agreed wholeheartedly with Herriot's estimate of himself. "In spite of Herriot's literary talents, [John] Crooks says he will remember him more for his ability to show animals respect and compassion without anthropomorphizing them: 'His books will be on the shelves with some of the great writers of the past, but I remember him as a vet, a competent, kind, caring vet' " (Daniel, 32). John Bower, another former president of the British Veterinary Association, also recalled an anecdote that Herriot treasured because it summed up his estimate of his own contributions: "Herriot was paying a visit to a farmer and had brought along a friend. The friend asked the farmer, 'Do you realize this is the world-famous author?' The farmer replied, 'He's not a bad veterinarian either' " (Daniel, 32). Herriot himself flatly declared, "If a farmer has a sick cow, they don't want Charles Dickens turning up, they want a good vet. And that's what I've tried to be."[15]

The technical aspects of veterinary practice today differ greatly from those in Herriot's heyday, but the profession's intangible challenges will probably never change: learning to treat several different species of animals and coping with the emotional needs of their owners; dealing with constant physical fatigue and emotional tension and balancing one's family life against the night-and-day demands of the profession. The graced individuals, and Herriot was one, who win respect as good vets must deal not only with the physical ailments of their animal patients, but with the emotional needs of their owners—as well as the emotional needs of the animals themselves.

In choosing a veterinarian, a genuine love of animals and flexibility with owners is the combination of qualities American animal owners rate most highly: most of them agree that "Nothing wins me over like someone who seems to like my animals as much as I do."[16] American veterinarian A. F. Hopkins observes, "To be flexible and sensitive, and thus tune-in to the relationship between a client and his animal, this is the essence of clinical practice."[17] Herriot's flexibility, sensitivity, and most of all his empathy toward the bonds between the humans and animals with which he worked daily not only made him a good vet but also enabled him to become the perceptive author that he was.

Taken as a whole, Herriot's work celebrates a growing realization that veterinary and human medicine are two sides of the same coin of healing, one that his published work burnished to a fine, soft glow. Both veterinarians and their M.D. colleagues are becoming increasingly aware of the interrelations between their work. A 1978 U.S. symposium, "Implications of History and Ethics to Medicine—Veterinary and Human," recognized that all "Medicine is a value-laden enterprise," taking into account the moral principles involved in both animal and human medical practice, and drawing upon the commonality of their historical origin: "the dignity and effectiveness of veterinarians and physicians rest, in part, on their willingness and ability to appropriate for themselves the legacy of their medical forebears and to evaluate and judge this legacy in relation to themselves, their profession and their times . . . giving it new forms, and, finally . . . hand it on to their own heirs" (M&M, xv). Herriot's books bring this process home to the general public, because he built upon the traditional veterinary medicine he found in the Dales, amalgamated its fascinating "old black magic" into the explosion of new scientific forms that greeted him after World War II, and in time handed his work over to his son Jim, a better vet, Herriot generously believed, than he had been.

Throughout his books, Herriot created a portrait of himself that exhibited qualities acknowledged since antiquity as the distinguishing marks of the healer—characteristics, interestingly enough, that also belong to the finest literary artists, whose work heals the human heart. In ancient Greece, the physician functioned as priest, purifying the patient physically just as the writer of tragedy helped his audience experience curative emotional catharsis; in today's more approachable fashion, Herriot produced a similar effect in such stories as his tale of the doomed dog Amber he had loved and lost. Both the epilogue of a Greek tragedy and the Greek physician exhorted hearers to lead a "good and clean life," just as Herriot's stories implicitly celebrate the healthy benefits of a hardworking country life. Because the ancient Greek physician considered himself only the instrument of healing, he possessed a deep sense of humility, a quality badly needed in modern medicine,[18] and in much the same spirit, Herriot often declared he wanted to be known simply as "not a bad veterinarian" (Daniel, 32).

Ranked second to physician-priests in ancient times were the artisan-physicians, "in the same social stratum as bakers, butchers, lampmakers, and masons"—like the British vets who, when they came to treat expensive hunters or lapdogs, were shown the back door of great houses. Like Herriot, who successfully saved Tricki Woo from pastry-induced terminal obesity, the artisan-physicians possessed "a keen empirical sense, and well-developed powers of observation, which allowed [them] to detect flaws in the physical workings of the body." Herriot's meticulous ability to observe and deftly describe his work lends enormous verisimilitude to his writing, just as humility provided one of his most endearing virtues as an autobiographer. Like Herriot, who for much of his practice lacked "miracle drugs" and technical surgical expertise, the artisan-physician had to be humble, because "he was essentially helpless before the onslaught of disease," and often had to stand by helplessly while a patient crumbled "into sickness, and oftentimes, ultimately into death" (M&M, 42–43). Herriot often had to do the same heartbreaking thing when he was faced with animal diseases such as bovine husk or Amber's demodectic mange for which no cures had then been found, instances of dramatic irony that deeply involve readers in his narrative.

The ancient tradition that overwhelmed the physician-priests and the artisan-physicians and became the ancestor of modern medicine was "the physician as natural philosopher and ultimately as a scientist." Despite the outcries of Hippocrates and his followers that the individual, not the general premise, had to be treated, natural philosophy and its practical corollaries dominated the medical profession for centuries until Herriot's own day with such remedies as draining off measures of blood to cure "imbalances of humors" as Siegfried successfully did with the gypsy pony, though such remedies risked killing off the patient in the process. Such procedures comprised much of the folk medicine that deeply intrigued Herriot and made his literary records of his early practice so absorbing. Despite all its drawbacks, however, natural philosophy "ultimately led to the basic understanding of physiology of cells and the germ theory of disease in the nineteenth century, and they in turn led to the scientific medicine which is characteristic of modern medicine today" (M&M, 44–45), the medicine that Herriot embraced.

While James Herriot grounded himself in the scientific advances of his day and practiced effectively for some 50 years, his unique gift was to blend modern knowledge with the older, intangible functions of the priestly healer and the artisan, the humble idealism of the one joining with the humble practical observation of the other. Herriot also had in abundance the gift of compassion, which made him seem to care for his patients every bit as much as their owners did. Herriot's genuine combination of high moral values, humility, keen observation, and compassion distinguished him equally as a physician and as a literary artist, making him one of the most beloved writers of his or any times, although the easygoing approachability of his writing proved the undoing of his own privacy, bringing his readers to his door in droves. His publisher Thomas McCormack recalled seeing a car full of Australian tourists pull up at Herriot's very driveway: "Because of the way he wrote, people thought they knew him. They were coming to have tea with Herriot" (Daniel, 32).

Herriot also had "an extraordinary impact on the future of the veterinary profession." He modestly insisted, "I've had nothing to do with it. It's the direct effect of the affluent society and the trend back to the land," but a 1979 American Gallup Youth Poll showed that "many more young people are considering veterinary careers as a result of reading his books" (Del Balso, 179). British veterinary professors coined the phrase "the Herriot factor" for a similar phenomenon that took place in the United Kingdom. According to British veterinarian John Bower, "Science is fine, but one must also have the ability to communicate with

clients. James Herriot elevated veterinarians to an almost superstar status by the way he handled animals and their owners" (Daniel, 33).

At the height of Herriot's popularity, American medical historian
James Polk Morris summed up Herriot's achievements for the veterinary
profession, claiming Herriot's books are responsible for

> Today's extraordinary public interest in animals and veterinary medicine
> . . . Herriot has accomplished many positive things for his profession, his
> colleagues, and the public. He strikes a chord in the public consciousness
> which relates to and reinforces their increasing perception of the value of
> animals in human terms. He provides a delightful, inspiring, and accu-
> rate glimpse into the life of the general vet practitioner. But perhaps
> most important is the fact that through the depiction of everyday inter-
> actions between the practitioner, the people of his community and their
> animals, he conveys a veterinarian's dedication to public service which
> equals that of his physician counterpart.
>
> Within the United States context some authorities note that his
> books describe a general veterinary practice most typical of about twenty
> years ago. But, they quickly add, that adds to the charm and value of the
> books in this country, because it further reinforces the veterinarian's
> indispensable role as a dedicated servant of the people for many genera-
> tions. Herriot's books have also helped close the gap between the public's
> favorable image of the physician and that of his professional cohort, the
> veterinarian. Thus, he has facilitated the movement toward one medi-
> cine.[19]

In the annals of human achievements, many compassionate physicians have graced the history of the healing arts, and many storytellers
and writers have endeared themselves to human hearts. James Herriot's
devotion to animals, whom he surely believed had both the gift of consciousness and the ability to use it to the benefit of mankind, allowed
Herriot to unite the talent of the healer with the charm of the tale spin-
ner, two of the civilizing roles that have brought humanity out of its
primeval caves onto whatever sunny heights of human dignity we may
have reached. This kind and decent man made his readers immeasurably
wealthier in spirit for having had their sympathies expanded and tender-
ness stirred by his stories about the animals who so deeply enrich our
lives (Sutherland and Arbuthnot, 383).

The fourth volume of Sir Frederick Smith's venerable *Early History of
Veterinary Medicine* is dedicated to the memory of William Youatt, an
early-nineteenth-century veterinarian, but Smith's words describe every
good vet like James Herriot:

A gentle, amiable man of great benevolence and humanity,
A prodigious worker, ever faithful to the cause he undertook to serve;
A pioneer of the veterinary art, whose name is written in letters of gold
upon the tablets of his profession.[20]

James Herriot's "letters of gold" remain bright. The Humane Society
of the United States gives an annual award in Herriot's name to the
individual "who through communication with the public has helped to
promote and inspire an appreciation of and concern for the animals of
the world."[21] Veterinary colleges are filled with young men and women
inspired by Herriot's stories, carrying on the hard dangerous work he
loved so much, and readers worldwide continue to cherish his books for
his examples of compassion toward every living being, the greatest
legacy of the gentle veterinarian from Darrowby. By depicting the stability of a rural society revolving around the virtues of integrity and
hard work, Herriot's stories offer the healing security to love and be
loved for all creatures, great and small. Herriot's wise portrayals of character, his self-portrait most of all, illustrate the human need to belong;
to achieve victories little or great; to change for good reason, not for the
sake of change alone; and to grasp as well as human beings can an
orderly meaning for their existence. Finally, by celebrating the bright
and beautiful Yorkshire Dales he loved, James Herriot allowed his readers to share the sense of wonder he felt at creation, reflected in every living thing.

" 'Oh aye,' said James Herriot simply, 'it's been a marvelous life' "
(*Life*, 69).

Notes and References

Preface

1. Quoted in Alice Daniels, "The Herriot Factor," *Animals* (May/June 1995): 32; henceforth cited in text.
2. James Herriot, *The Lord God Made Them All* (New York: St. Martin's Press, 1981), 28; henceforth cited in text as *LGMTA*.
3. Quoted in Asa Briggs, *A Social History of England* (New York: Viking, 1983), 312; henceforth cited in text.
4. Quoted in "In Search of the Simple," an interview with James Herriot by Arturo Gonzalez, which appeared excerpted from *Maclean's* in *Atlas World Press Review* 25 (September 1978): 38; henceforth cited in text as Gonzalez, *A.*
5. Quoted in "James Herriot," an interview by Arturo Gonzalez in *Saturday Review* (May–June 1986): 59; henceforth cited in text as Gonzalez, *SR*.

Chapter One

1. Timothy Green, "Best-Selling Vet Practices as Usual," *Smithsonian* (November 1974): 96; henceforth cited in text.
2. Lila Freilicher, "The Story behind the Book: *All Creatures Great and Small*," *Publishers Weekly* (8 January 1973): 53; henceforth cited in text.
3. *Publishers Weekly* (3 October 1994): 15. *Publishers Weekly* (20 March 1995): 55, 58. *Publishers Weekly* (15 July 1996): 61.
4. Sanford Sternlicht, *All Things Herriot* (Syracuse: Syracuse University Press, 1995), 16. Sternlicht feels that "this Herriot industry, created by astute publishers, will be self-perpetuating at least for a generation." This source is henceforth cited in the text.
5. James Herriot, "The Books I Almost Never Wrote," unpaginated introduction to *The Best of James Herriot* (New York: St. Martin's Press, 1982); henceforth cited in text as *BJH*.
6. Maurice Lindsay, *Glasgow*, 3d ed. (London: Robert Hale Ltd., 1989), 16.
7. Arturo F. Gonzalez Jr., "Interview with James Herriot," *Maclean's* 91 (29 May 1978): 4; henceforth cited in text as Gonzalez, *M*.
8. Briggs, 224–25. Briggs took his data from the New Doomsday Survey of 1873.
9. Wilfrid Mellers and Rupert Hildyard, "The Cultural and Social Setting," in *Early Twentieth Century Britain*, ed. Boris Ford (Cambridge: Cambridge University Press, 1992), 28–29.

10.   Harold D. Hughes and Edwin R. Henson, *Crop Production: Principles and Practices* (1930; reprint, New York: Macmillan, 1949), 11. By comparison, at that time 28 percent of German arable land was in farms of approximately 49 acres, and in the United States, the average farm was 148.2 acres. In 1930, England and Wales averaged 106 workers and 125 horses per 1,000 acres of cropland, while U.S. cropland averaged 40 persons and 80 horses per 1,000 acres. North Dakota cropland in 1930 averaged 12 persons and 45 horses per 1,000 acres (Hughes and Henson, chart 20a, p. 11).

11.   James Herriot, *All Things Bright and Beautiful* (New York: St. Martin's Press, 1974), 183; henceforth cited in the text as *ATBB*.

12.   James Herriot, *James Herriot's Dog Stories* (New York: St. Martin's Press, 1986), xii–xiii; henceforth cited in the text as *DS*.

13.   Leon F. Whitney and George Whitney, *Animal Doctor: The History and Practice of Veterinary Medicine* (New York: David McKay Company, 1973), xvi, henceforth cited in the text as W&W. Also see Frederick Smith, *The Early History of Veterinary Literature and its British Development,* vol. 11 (London: Bailliere, Tindall and Cox, 1919), vii.

14.   B. W. Kingrey, "Ethical Problems and Decisions in Food Animal Medicine," in *Implications of History and Ethics to Medicine—Veterinary and Human,* ed. Laurence B. McCollough and James Polk Morris (College Station, Texas: Texas A & M University, 1978), 115; henceforth cited in text.

15.   J. B. Priestley, *English Journey* (New York: Harper and Brothers, 1934), 316–17.

16.   Keith Robbins, "From Imperial Power to European Partner 1901–1975," in *The Cambridge Historical Encyclopedia of Great Britain and Ireland,* ed. Christopher Haigh (Cambridge: Cambridge University Press, 1985), 291.

17.   Sociologist Seebohm Rowntree, quoted in Briggs, 281.

18.   Frank Duerden, *Great Walks: Yorkshire Dales* (London: Ward Lock Ltd., 1986), 7; henceforth cited in text.

19.   Stanley Haggart and Darwin Porter, *England and Scotland on $20 a Day* (New York: Frommer and Pasmantier Publishing, 1980), 404, 412.

20.   Quoted in "James Alfred Wight," in *Something about the Author,* ed. Anne Conmire, vol. 55 (Detroit, Michigan: Gale Research, 1989), 17; henceforth cited in text as *SATA*.

21.   James Herriot, *All Creatures Great and Small* (New York: St. Martin's Press, 1972), 370; henceforth cited in text as *ACGS*.

22.   Frederick Smith, *The Early History of Veterinary Literature,* vol. 1 (London: Balliere, Tindall and Cox, 1911), 64–66.

23.   Mary Williams, *Witches in Old North Yorkshire* (Beverley: Hutton Press Ltd., 1987), 50; henceforth cited in text. Williams, an amateur Yorkshire historian, amassed anecdotal evidence about Yorkshire witches who functioned as recently as the 1940s.

24.   Without substantiation from British military sources or from Herriot himself, Sanford Sternlicht leaps to a dangerous insinuation: "A country

veterinarian could have remained in reserve occupation helping hard-pressed British agriculture . . . instead of this rational decision, Herriot enlists as an aircrewman in the RAF, ostensibly out of patriotism or need to prove 'manhood,' although he never directly states this." See *All Things Herriot* (Syracuse, N.Y.: Syracuse University Press, 1995), 80.

25. Roy and Gwen Shaw, "The Cultural and Social Setting," in *Modern Britain,* ed. Boris Ford (Cambridge: Cambridge University Press, 1988), 6; henceforth cited in text.

26. Stefan Kanfer, "The Marcus Welby of the Barnyard," review of *The Lord God Made Them All,* by James Herriot, *Time* (29 June 1981): 74; henceforth cited in text.

27. Ken Nickel, "James Herriot Revisited," *Dog World* (April 1992): 18; henceforth cited in text as Nickel, "Revisited."

28. James Herriot, introd. to *James Herriot's Cat Stories* (New York: St. Martin's Press, 1994), x.

Chapter Two

1. Quoted in Gilbert Phelps, "Literature and Drama," in *Modern Britain,* ed. Boris Ford (Cambridge: Cambridge University Press, 1988), 198; henceforth cited in text.

2. Quoted in Ken Nickel, "A Trek to Find James Herriot," *Dog World* (September 1985): 51; henceforth cited in text as Nickel, "Trek."

3. Monty Brower, "Long a Success as 'James Herriot,' Yorkshire Vet Jim Wight Says All Things Must Come to an End," *People Weekly* 23 (18 March 1985): 97; cited henceforth in text.

4. Arthur Marshall, review of *It Shouldn't Happen to a Vet, New Statesman* (10 March 1972): 317.

5. Quoted in David Taylor, "It Could Only Happen to a Vet," *Radio Times* (January 1978); cited in *Something About the Author,* ed. Anne Conmire, vol. 55 (Detroit, Michigan: Gale Research, 1989), 172.

6. William R. Doerner, "How Now, Brown Cow?" *Time* (19 February 1973): 88.

7. Nelson Bryant, "A Place Where the Wind Blows Clean," *New York Times Book Review,* 18 February 1973, 10.

8. Introduction to "James Herriot," *Contemporary Literary Criticism,* vol. 12 (Detroit, Michigan: Gale Publishing, 1980), 282.

9. David Llewellyn, review of *Let Sleeping Vets Lie, Books and Bookmen* 19 (October 1973): 118.

10. Simon Pepper, "Housing at Roehampton," in Ford, *Modern Britain,* 283. Andrew Saint, "The New Towns," in Ford, *Modern Britain,* 152.

11. Richard Gardner, "James Herriot (James Alfred Wight)," in *Beacham's Popular Fiction in America,* ed. Walton Beacham, vol. 3 (Washington: Beacham Publishing, 1988), 635.

12.   Quoted from a private letter to the author from Mrs. Harold Balas. Accompanied by her husband, a rural North Dakota veterinarian, Mrs. Balas visited with Brian Sinclair at Harrogate in 1985.

13.   Martin Seymour-Smith, *The New Guide to Modern World Literature* (New York: Peter Bedrick, 1985), 217.

14.   Charles Williams, *Witchcraft: A History of Black Magic in Christian Times* (London: Faber and Faber, 1941; New York: New American Library, 1959), 246.

15.   Konrad Lorenz, *Man Meets Dog* (in German) (Vienna: Verlag Dr. G. Borotha-Schoeler, 1953), (in English) (Kodansha International, 1994), xvi.

Chapter Three

1.   Review of *All Things Bright and Beautiful, Washington Post Book World,* 14 September 1975, 2.

2.   Michael Putney, "A Decent Man Records More 'Little Triumphs,' " *National Observer* 13 (28 December 1974): 17.

3.   "Best Book by a D.V.M.," *Washington Post Book World,* 8 December 1974, 1.

4.   Joni Bodart, review of *All Things Bright and Beautiful, School Library Journal* (March 1975): 114.

5.   Putney, 17. Many books about veterinarians have followed in Herriot's wake, and an interesting comparative study might be made of them.

6.   Dorothy L. Sayers, "An English War," quoted in James Brabazon, *Dorothy L. Sayers* (New York: Charles Scribners' Sons, 1981), 187. The poem was first printed in *The Times Literary Supplement* 2014 (7 September 1940): 445.

7.   Peter Lowe, "Warfare and International Relations: Empire, Commonwealth, Community," in *The Cambridge Historical Encyclopedia of Great Britain and Ireland,* ed. Christopher Haigh (Cambridge: Cambridge University Press, 1985), 314.

8.   Ibid., 315. Recent historians believe the issue is more complex than Chamberlain's personal desire for peace: "[T]he British and French overestimated the dangers before them, and were too quick to quail. But there is in conflicts of this kind, with their mixture of threat and bluff, a certain dynamic that eludes purely rational verdicts. Victory often goes not to the stronger antagonist, but to the one who cares (or seems to care) most passionately . . . real determination makes the less determined give way. These judgments, when they involve war or peace, are not a matter of reasonably deliberation . . . Chamberlain and Daladier were civilized men, and when they remembered the agony of 1914–18, and then imagined war, they imagined bombs falling on London and Paris, bombs and murderous clouds of poison gas. When Hitler imagined war, he remembered defeat on the Western Front and gloated at the opportunity for revenge." Otto Friedrich, "Appeasement at Munich—and the Way to War," *Smithsonian* (October 1988): 193–94.

9. Edwards Parks, *Fighters: The World's Great Aces and Their Planes* (New York: Barnes and Noble, 1990), 106.

10. Quoted from Dr. Raymond Russo, longtime Massachusetts State Chairman (canine) of the Morris Animal Foundation, in Darlene Arden, "Choosing a Veterinarian, Part II," *Dog World* (August 1992): 44. Also see Amanda Wray, "Animal Doctors," *Dog Fancy* (April 1991): 40.

11. Amanda Wray, "Animal Doctors," *Dog Fancy* (April 1991): 43.

12. According to Jeffrey M. Masson and Susan McCarthy in *When Elephants Weep: The Emotional Lives of Animals* (New York: Delacorte Press, 1995), Although most sensitive people believe that animals have emotions, "By dint of rigorous training and great efforts of the mind, most modern scientists—especially those who study the behavior of animals—have succeeded in becoming almost blind" to the emotions of animals (p. 43). Masson and McCarthy claim that studies such as Jane Goodall's chimpanzee research, however, indicate that popular wisdom is correct, and animals do feel much as humans do. This position is currently responsible for a shift in animal-training methods, especially in the sport of dog obedience, from harsh corrections to positive reinforcement incentives such as praise and food.

13. Certain episodes in Herriot's works, such as Tristan's pub visits and the Granville Bennett passages, involve drinking, sometimes to excess. When portrayed in the television series *All Creatures Great and Small*, these episodes drew criticism from British (especially Scottish) viewers (see chapter 9). In *All Things Herriot* (Syracuse, N.Y.: Syracuse University Press, 1995), Sanford Sternlicht declares flatly, "Herriot's main personal difficulty, presented humorously of course, is with alcohol" (p. 60). In a classic example of jumping to a unsupported conclusion without considering the possibility that Herriot may have exaggerated such episodes for fictional effect, and without taking into account the difference in American and British drinking habits of the 1930s, Sternlicht conjectures without any corroborating evidence whatsoever that "Tristan's drinking and frequent inebriation complements James and Siegfried's imbibing. It is possible that the author may be both encoding and denying a problem with alcohol shared with his pals, a problem that perhaps results from the homosociality of the pub, which is the chief place of recreation for the men of a somewhat sexually segregated community" (p. 61). Without factual support, Sternlicht's hypothesis of Thirsk's three problem-drinker veterinarians (who successfully carried on a heavy practice) seems ludicrous.

14. One of Herriot's most appealing devices is his constant reference to his patients by name, making them seem as much valued individuals to his readers as they were to himself. Other veterinarian fiction, such as Joyce Stranger's *Lakeland Vet* (New York: Viking, 1972), tends to refer to animal patients impersonally as "the black Persian," or "the little fox."

15. With only a small stretch of the imagination, "Mrs. Donovan" could well take her place among the formidable ladies described in Mary Williams's *Witches in Old North Yorkshire* (Beverley: Hutton Press Ltd., 1987).

16. The U.S. Delta Society indicates that current research into interaction between animals and human beings may have important, concrete health benefits such as a higher one-year survival rate after coronary heart disease; reduction in blood pressure, heart rate, and anxiety levels in healthy people; and success in psychotherapy sessions as well as helping patients work through anxiety and despair; developing more appropriate social behavior in prisoners and people with mental illness; and facilitating speech in children with language disorders. James Herriot demonstrated almost all of these benefits of pet ownership either explicitly or implicitly in his stories.

17. Jonathan Swift, "To Mr. Delany," 10 October 1718.

18. Edward Weeks, review of *All Things Bright and Beautiful*, *Atlantic Monthly* (October 1974): 114.

19. James Herriot, *James Herriot's Yorkshire* (New York: St. Martin's Press, 1979), 170, henceforth cited as *JHY*.

Chapter Four

1. "Famed Veterinarian-Author Herriot Visits AVMA," *Journal of the American Veterinary Medical Association* 164 (1 February 1974): 257.

2. Edwards Parks, *Fighters: The World's Great Aces and Their Planes* (New York: Barnes and Noble, 1990), 14. World War II fighter pilots were not large men. American pilots "who joined up after Pearl Harbor were selected as fighter pilots because we were no taller than 5'10",weighed no more than 160 pounds, had fast and decisive reactions, and were reasonably competent" (Park, 14).

3. James Herriot, *All Things Wise and Wonderful* (New York: St. Martin's Press, 1977), 440.

4. Gavin Lyall, *The War in the Air: The Royal Air Force in World War II* (New York: William Morrow and Company, 1968), xiv.

5. Group Captain J. E. ("Johnnie") Johnson, DSO, DFC, quoted in Lyall, 128–30.

6. "Horse Therapy Helps Patients," *The Forum* (27 March 1994): A 13.

7. Ann Gritt Ashby, "Healing War's Wounds," *Dog World* (July 1992): 42.

8. Joel Gavriele-Gold, "Dogs in a Psychologist's Office," *American Kennel Club Gazette* (July 1993): 77, 81.

9. Sharon Pflaumer, "Seizure-Alert Dogs," *Dog World* (January 1992): 42.

10. Cle Francis, "Dogs Energize Human Well-Being," *Dog World* (July 1992): 19.

11. Jack Butrick, "Therapy Dogs and the Power of Healing," *Dog World* (July 1993): 83–85.

12. Quoted in *The Battle of Britain* (New York: Time-Life Books, 1977), 57. Before World War II, Molders, one of Germany's top aces, had

flown in the Spanish Civil War, where many Luftwaffe pilots gained the experience that gave them an initial edge over untested RAF aircrews from 1939 to 1940.

13. Review of *All Things Wise and Wonderful, Virginia Quarterly Review* 54 (Winter 1978): 30.

14. Jane Manthorne, Review of *All Things Wise and Wonderful, School Library Journal* (October 1977): 131.

15. Richard R. Lingeman, "Animal Doctor," *New York Times Book Review,* 18 September 1977, 13.

16. Joy K. Roy, Review of *All Things Wise and Wonderful, English Journal* (March 1979): 57.

17. "AVMA Award of Appreciation Given to British Veterinarian-Author," *Journal of the American Veterinary Medical Association* 167 (15 October 1975): 704; henceforth cited in text as *JAVMA* 75.

Chapter Five

1. Suzanne Del Balso, "The Wise, Wonderful World of the Real James Herriot," *Good Housekeeping* (March 1979): 178.

2. Arturo F. Gonzalez Jr., "America's Favorite Animal Doctor," *50 Plus* 18 (September 1978): 45.

3. Ibid., 73. Although Herriot's manner with Ms. Del Balso was impeccably polite, she too rode in the backseat of his car (Del Balso, 177).

4. Ibid. Also see Gonzalez, "Animal Doctor," 42.

5. See Gonzalez, "Interview"; Gonzalez, "Animal Doctor,"; and Arturo F. Gonzalez Jr., "In Search of the Simple," *Atlas World Press Review* (September 1978): 37–38. Gonzalez's and Taylor's articles have many points in common (see bibliography).

6. Richard Lingeman, "Animal Doctor," *The New York Times Book Review,* 18 September 1977, 13.

7. Philip Johnson, Review of *The Lord God Made Them All, Saturday Review* (June 1981): 57.

8. Review of *The Lord God Made Them All, Booklist* (1 May 1981): 1174.

9. Peter Clarke, "Government and Politics in England: Realignment and Readjustment," *The Cambridge Historical Encyclopedia of Great Britain and Ireland,* ed. Christopher Haigh, (Cambridge: Cambridge University Press, 1985), 298.

10. Keith Robbins, "From Imperial Power to European Partner 1901–1975: Overview," in *The Cambridge Historical Encyclopedia of Great Britain and Ireland,* ed. Christopher Haigh (Cambridge: Cambridge University Press, 1985), 291.

11. In *All Things Herriot* (Syracuse: Syracuse University Press, 1995), 58–60, Sanford Sternlicht argues that Helen, in the "gender role" of a "Victorian good woman" "is not a viable role model for today's young women. Rather,

she is prototypical of a woman that contemporary feminism considers an anachronism." Further on in his book, Sternlicht observes that Helen "grows in stature" between *The Lord God Made Them All* and *Every Living Thing,* and comments "in fairness" that despite the "deeply patriarchal elements" he sees in the narrator's character, "Herriot does have many fine, redeeming traits that feminists and contemporary women in general can only admire" (126–27).

12. As an example of the reworking of Herriot's stories by television adapters, in the televised version of this episode, the actions of Norman Beaumont were given to Tristan in order to feature that continuing supporting character more strongly.

13. Brad Steiger and Sherry Hansen Steiger, *Strange Powers of Pets* (New York: Donald I. Fine, 1992), xii; also see Karen Pryor, *Don't Shoot the Dog! The New Art of Teaching and Training* (New York: Bantam, 1985). Pryor, an animal behaviorist, developed a workable method of animal training through positive reinforcement from her work with marine mammals, especially dolphins: "I had trained dogs and horses by traditional methods, but dolphins were a different proposition; you cannot use a leash or a bridle or even your fist on an animal that just swims away. Positive reinforcement—primarily a bucket of fish—was the only tool we had. . . . I found myself fascinated, not so much with the dolphins as with what could be communicated between us—from me to the animal *and* [italics in original] from the animal to me—during this kind of training" (Pryor, 13).

14. Gonzalez, M, 6.

Chapter Six

1. *Baedeker's Great Britain* (Englewood Cliffs, N.J.: Prentice Hall, 1990), 288–89.

2. Patrick Wormald, "Society: Warriors and Dependents," *The Cambridge Historical Encyclopedia of Great Britain and Ireland,* ed. Christopher Haigh (Cambridge: Cambridge University Press, 1985), 80.

3. The code of the *comitatus,* the mutual bond between an Anglo-Saxon chieftain and his warriors, is stirringly commemorated in the anonymous poem "The Battle of Maldon," written in A.D. 991 following the defense of a river ford near Ely Cathedral by Earl Byrthnoth and his men against Viking invaders. Byrhtnoth's body was buried at the cathedral, but the Vikings presumably took his head back to Norway as a trophy.

4. Albert C. Baugh and Thomas Cable, *A History of the English Language,* 4th ed. (Englewood Cliffs, N.J.: Prentice Hall, 1993), 100–101.

5. Reginald Hill, *Pictures of Perfection* (New York: Delacorte Press, 1994), 25. Hill won Britain's premier mystery award, the Golden Dagger, for this novel. Several other successful mystery authors have staked out colorful Yorkshire territories for their absorbing locales—Dorothy Sayers, Catherine Aird, P. D. James, Peter Robinson, and Elizabeth George, to name only a few.

6. James Herriot, *The Best of James Herriot* (New York: St. Martin's Press, 1982); henceforth cited in the text as *BJH*.

Chapter Seven

1. *The Standard,* quoted in Asa Briggs, *A Social History of England* (New York: Viking, 1983), 299.

2. Review of *The Market Square Dog,* by James Herriot, *Publishers Weekly* (13 October 1989): 51.

3. Rosemary Wells, "The Well-Tempered Children's Books," in *Worlds of Childhood,* ed. William Zinsser (Boston: Houghton Mifflin, 1990), 128.

4. Karen Hutt, review of *Smudge, The Little Lost Lamb,* by James Herriot, *Booklist* (15 January 1992): 951.

5. Leon Garfield, "The Outlaw," *Hornbook Magazine* (March–April 1990): 169–70.

6. J. R. R. Tolkien, "On Fairy-Stories," in *The Tolkien Reader* (New York: Ballantine Books, 1966), p. 38, note 23.

7. Robert Frost, "The Death of the Hired Man."

8. Hank Whitemore, "Pet Owners: Do the Right Thing," *Parade Magazine* (19 February 1995): 22.

9. James Herriot, *The Market Square Dog* (New York: St. Martin's Press, 1989), unpaginated. As a veterinarian, Herriot would also have been aware of the growing incidence of hereditary problems such as hip dysplasia and progressive retinal atrophy (PRA) which plague purebred dogs because of the narrow gene pool involved in their breeding. See "A Terrible Beauty," *Time,* 12 December 1994.

10. Review of *The Market Square Dog, Publishers Weekly,* 51.

11. James Herriot, *Oscar, Cat-About-Town* (New York: St. Martin's Press, 1992), unpaginated.

12. Stephen Carrin, "Children's Literature," *The Times Educational Supplement,* 22 January 1993, 10.

13. "James Herriot," *Publishers Weekly* (3 January 1986): 38.

14. Alvin A. Price, "An Implication of the History of Veterinary Medicine in Texas: Man and His Animals Inseparable," in *Implications of History and Ethics to Medicine—Veterinary and Human,* ed. Laurence B. McCullough and James Polk Morris (College Station, Tex.: Texas A & M University, 1978), 29. According to Price, "Artifacts of the Stone Age—20,000 years ago—indicate that by that time in human development the dog was a domestic pet and hunting companion. . . . the evidence is strong that man loved his dog more than he loved his wife. There is reasonable assurance that he traded wives more frequently but never his dog. He used his dog in the field for food procurement. After he and his dog had filled their bellies, the remains were lovingly distributed to his wife and children."

15. James B. Spencer, "The Flat-Coated Retriever Today," *Gun Dog* 14 (February–March 1995): 40.

16. Review of *Dog Stories,* read by Christopher Timothy, two audiocassettes, *Publishers Weekly* (1 December 1989): 30. The anonymous reviewer closes with an intriguing anti-British thesis evidently due to the "preachy tone" the reviewer finds in the performance by Timothy, "a narrator who is stiffly starched in his delivery": "The rural characters and animals encountered throughout offer a clear insight into the humility, humanity—and ultimately the hubris—of the British." I beg to differ: it is hard to imagine an author less possessed by hubris than James Herriot.

Chapter Eight

1. Kenneth Nickel, "A Trek to Find James Herriot," *Dog World* (September 1985): 50; henceforth cited in text as Nickel, "Trek."

2. James Herriot, *Every Living Thing* (New York: St. Martin's Press, 1992), 94; henceforth cited in text as *ELT.*

3. Wendell H. Hall, "Modern Chemotherapy for Brucellosis in Humans," *Review of Infectious Diseases* 12 (November–December 1980): 1060.

4. S. R. Damon, J. H. Scruggs, and E. B. Parker, "Brucellosis as an Occupational Hazard," *Journal of the American Veterinary Medical Association* 117 (1950): 40.

5. R. L. Cecil and R. F. Loeb, *A Textbook of Medicine,* 10th ed. (Philadelphia, Pa.: W. B. Saunders, 1959), 227.

6. Robert Berkow, ed., *The Merck Manual* (Rahway, N.J.: Merck Sharp and Dohme Research Laboratories, 1982).

7. Joyce Stranger, *Lakeland Vet* (New York: Viking, 1972). Intriguing parallels exist between this novel and Herriot's first book, *If Only They Could Talk,* published in London by Michael Joseph in 1970. In *Children and Books,* Zena Sutherland and May Hill Arbuthnot remark that "The English naturalist Joyce Stranger has, in *Lakeland Vet,* so skillfully woven incidents about animals into the fictional account of a veterinarian's hard life that his love and compassion for all living things are more impressive than the story line" (New York: HarperCollins, 1991), 382. A thorough comparative analysis is impossible here, but by comparison to Herriot's three-dimensional self-portrait, Stranger's hero seems deflated and fatigued.

8. Claudia Moore, review of *Every Living Thing, School Library Journal* (December 1992): 151.

9. Review of *Every Living Thing, Publishers Weekly* (20 July 1992): 238.

10. Debra Schneider, review of *Every Living Thing, Library Journal* 117 (1 October 1992): 110.

11. Maeve Binchy, "Make Way for Badgers," *The New York Times Book Review,* 6 September 1992, 2.

12. Review of *Every Living Thing, Kirkus Reviews* 60 (1 July 1992): 827.

Chapter Nine

1. Lila Freilicher, "The Story behind the Book: *All Creatures Great and Small*," *Publishers Weekly* (8 January 1973): 53.

2. Leslie Hallowell, *Hallowell's Film and Video Guide*, 6th ed. (New York: Charles Scribner's Sons, 1980), 23.

3. Leonard Maltin, *Leonard Maltin's TV Movies 1985–86* (New York: Signet, 1986), 15.

4. Anonymous review of the film *All Things Bright and Beautiful*, *50 Plus* (September 1978): 62.

5. "British Actor Brings James Herriot to Life on American Television," *Journal of the American Veterinary Medical Association* 175 (1 August 1979): 253; henceforth cited in text as *JAVMA* 79.

6. Christopher Timothy, *Vet behind the Ears* (London: Pan, 1979), 145–46; henceforth cited in the text.

7. Quoted in transcript of *All Things Considered*, 24 February 1995, National Public Radio.

8. Anonymous review of *Dog Stories*, audio recording, *Wilson Library Bulletin* (December 1990): 7.

9. Alexander Finlayson, review of *Every Living Thing*, audio recording, *Library Journal* (1 November 1992): 130.

10. Anonymous review of *Every Living Thing*, audio recording, *Wilson Library Bulletin* (May 1993): 70.

11. Anonymous review of *Every Living Thing*, audio recording, *Publishers Weekly* (2 November 1992): 73.

Chapter Ten

1. "Author Herriot Dies at Age 78," *The Forum* (24 February 1995): A13.

2. "So Much for the Young Vit'nery," *Duluth News-Tribune and Herald*, 5 July 1994, 3.

3. Martin Wainwright, "Sheep Take Revenge on James Herriot," *Manchester Guardian Weekly* 151 (10 July 1994): 8.

4. "British Author Attacked by Sheep," Segment 13 of *All Things Considered*, transcript from National Public Radio (5 July 1994): 24; henceforth cited in text as *ATC*.

5. From "Great God, What do I see," an anonymous hymn found in *Collyer's Hymns: Partly Collected and Partly Original*, 1812.

6. Herriot's success with cats in his practice seems to have been rooted in his sense of humor, as evidenced by the tale of the vengeful feline Boris, whom despite his terroristic activities Herriot refused to consign to the animal shelter. Cats are capable of driving the most devoted owners to such extremities, as the exasperated owner of Wilberforce did, chronicled in Peter Neville's *Do Cats Need Shrinks?* "Wilberforce . . . developed an insatiable lust for rubber

condoms. 'His career of lurking in the bedroom came to an abrupt end,' Mr. Neville writes, when the offender 'made the mistake of trying to capture his prize after it had been fitted but not yet employed for its intended function.' " Quoted in Susan Brownmiller, "Crazy Cats," *New York Times Book Review,* 14 December 1993, 56.

7. Review of *James Herriot's Cat Stories, Publisher's Weekly* (18 July 1994): 54.

8. "The Cat's Meow," *Publishers Weekly* (3 October 1994): 15.

9. Michele Slung, "Hairballs and Havoc," *The New York Times Book Review,* 11 September 1994, 12.

10. Cited from National Public Radio Morning Edition, 24 February 1995.

11. Matthew Arnold, quoted in Asa Briggs, *A Social History of England* (New York: Viking Press, 1983), 187.

12. Mircea Eliade, *The Myth of the Eternal Return, or Cosmos and History* (Princeton: Princeton University Press, 1954), 153. Eliade, a historian of religions, argues for two perceptions of time, the linear view of "historical man" who consciously creates history through the kind of change such as the modern bureaucratic war that Herriot abominated, and "traditional man" of agrarian societies: "by virtue of this view, tens of millions of men were able, for century after century, to endure great historical pressures without despairing, without committing suicide or falling into spiritual aridity" (152). Herriot and his readers seem to have taken a similar refuge from the terrors of history in the eternal values of the Dales world he immortalized.

13. Malcolm Crowthers, "All at Sea?" interview with John Tavener, *The Musical Times* (January 1994): 11–12.

14. James Herriot, *Every Living Thing* (New York: St. Martin's Press, 1992), 86. Citing this passage as evidence, Sanford Sternlicht accuses Herriot of male chauvinism and dismisses Helen as "a Victorian model 'good woman.' " See *All Things Herriot* (Syracuse, N.Y.: Syracuse University Press, 1995), 58–60.

15. "Small Wonders," *People Weekly* (13 March 1995): 104.

16. Amanda Wray, "Animal Doctors," *Dog Fancy* (April 1991): 40–41.

17. A. F. Hopkins, "Ethical Implications in Issues and Decisions in Companion Animal Medicine," in *Implications of History and Ethics to Medicine— Veterinary and Human,* ed. Laurence B. McCullough and James Polk Morris III (College Station, Tex.: Texas A & M University, 1978), 107; henceforth cited in text as M&M.

18. L. Pearce Williams, "History and Modern Medicine," in McCullough and Morris, 45.

19. James Polk Morris, introduction to McCullough and Morris, 10–11.

20. Dedication to vol. 4 of Sir Frederick Smith's *The Early History of Veterinary Literature* (London: Bailliere, Tindall and Cox, 1933). Spacing reproduced from original.

21. *Dog World* (March 1992): 54.

Selected Bibliography

PRIMARY SOURCES

Adult Works by James Herriot

All Creatures Great and Small (contains *If Only They Could Talk* and *It Shouldn't Happen to a Vet*). New York: St. Martin's Press, 1972; Book-of-the-Month and *Better Homes & Gardens* Book Club editions, 1973; large-print edition, G. K. Hall, 1973; Bantam paperback edition, 1973.

All Things Bright and Beautiful (contains *Let Sleeping Vets Lie* and *Vet in Harness*). New York: St. Martin's Press, 1974; Fall 1974 selection of the Book-of-the-Month, *Reader's Digest, Newsweek Condensed,* and *The Catholic Digest* Book Clubs; large-print edition, G. K. Hall, 1975; Bantam paperback edition, 1975.

All Things Wise and Wonderful (contains *Vets Might Fly* and *Vet in a Spin*). New York: St. Martin's Press, 1977; Literary Guild edition 1977; large-print edition, G. K. Hall, 1977; Bantam paperback edition, 1978.

Best of James Herriot. New York: St. Martin's Press, 1983; published as *The Best of James Herriot: Favorite Memories of a Country Vet.* London: Michael Joseph, 1982.

Every Living Thing. New York: St. Martin's Press, 1992; Bantam paperback edition, 1992; London: Michael Joseph, 1992.

If Only They Could Talk. London: Michael Joseph, 1970; large-print edition, G. K. Hall, 1977.

It Shouldn't Happen to a Vet. London: Michael Joseph, 1972.

James Herriot's Cat Stories. Illustrated by Lesley Holmes. New York: St. Martin's Press, 1994.

James Herriot's Dog Stories. Illustrated by Victor Ambrus. New York: St. Martin's Press, 1986; large-print edition, G. K. Hall, 1987; St. Martin's Paperbacks edition, 1987. London: Michael Joseph, 1986.

James Herriot's Favorite Dog Stories. Illustrated by Leslie Holmes. New York: St. Martin's Press, 1996. Contains Herriot's last writing, a six-page introduction.

James Herriot's Yorkshire. Photographs by Derry Brabbs. New York: St. Martin's Press, 1979; St. Martin's Paperbacks edition 1981; Bantam paperback edition, 1982. London: Michael Joseph, 1979.

Let Sleeping Vets Lie. London: Michael Joseph, 1973.

The Lord God Made Them All. New York: St. Martin's Press, 1981; large-print edition, G. K. Hall, 1982; Bantam paperback edition, 1983; London: Michael Joseph, 1982.

Vet in a Spin. London: Michael Joseph, 1977.
Vet in Harness. London: Michael Joseph, 1974.
Vets Might Fly. London: Michael Joseph, 1976.

Children's Books by James Herriot

Blossom Comes Home. Illustrated by Ruth Brown. New York: St. Martin's Press, 1988; London: Michael Joseph, 1988.
Bonny's Big Day. Illustrated by Ruth Brown. New York: St. Martin's Press, 1987; London: Michael Joseph, 1987.
The Christmas Day Kitten. Illustrated by Ruth Brown. New York: St. Martin's Press, 1986; London: Michael Joseph, 1986.
James Herriot Storybook. Illustrated by Ruth Brown. London: Michael Joseph, 1992.
James Herriot's Treasury for Children. Illustrated by Peter Barrett and Ruth Brown. New York: St. Martin's Press, 1992.
The Market Square Dog. Illustrated by Ruth Brown. New York: St. Martin's Press, 1989; London: Michael Joseph, 1989.
Moses the Kitten. Illustrated by Peter Barrett. New York: St. Martin's Press, 1984; London: Michael Joseph, 1984.
Only One Woof. Illustrated by Peter Barrett. New York: St. Martin's Press, 1985; London: Michael Joseph, 1985.
Oscar, Cat-About-Town. Illustrated by Ruth Brown. New York: St. Martin's Press, 1990; London: Michael Joseph, 1990.
Smudge, the Little Lost Lamb. Illustrated by Ruth Brown. New York: St. Martin's Press, 1991. Published as *Smudge's Day Out,* London: Michael Joseph, 1991.

Miscellaneous Work by James Herriot

James Herriot's Yorkshire Calendar. New York: St. Martin's Press. Yearly since 1983.

Audio Versions of James Herriot's Works

All Creatures Great and Small. Read by James Herriot. Audiocassette. Listen for Pleasure, 1980.
All Things Bright and Beautiful. This and all following cassettes read by Christopher Timothy, with exception of selections in *Dog Stories* and *Cats and Dogs,* which Herriot reads, and the following entry. Audiocassette. Listen for Pleasure, 1980.
All Things Wise and Wonderful. Read by Edmund Stoiber. Cassette Book Co.
Cats and Dogs. Audiocassette. Durkin Hays Publishing, 1989.
Dog Stories. Audiocassette. Durkin Hays Publishing, 1989.
Every Living Thing. Audiocassette. Audio Renaissance, 1993.
The Lord God Made Them All. Audiocassette. Listen for Pleasure, 1982.

Let Sleeping Vets Lie. Audiocassette. Listen for Pleasure, 1981.
Mrs. Beck and Georgina [and other stories.] Audiocassette. Durkin Hays Publishing, 1990.
Nip and Sam. Audiocassette. Paperback Audio, 1990.
Stories from the Herriot Collection. Audiocassette. Listen for Pleasure, 1985.
Summer's Bull and Other Herriot Stories. Audiocassette. Paperback Audio.

Cinema and Video Adaptations of James Herriot's Works

All Creatures Great and Small, motion picture starring Simon Ward, Anthony Hopkins, and Lisa Harrow, with screenplay by Hugh Whitemore adapted from Herriot's book *All Creatures Great and Small,* produced by David Susskind, EMI Productions, 1975; shown on Hallmark Hall of Fame, NBC-TV, February 4, 1975; also released as videocassette, CBS/Fox Video, 1992.
All Creatures Great and Small, motion picture starring Christopher Timothy, Robert Hardy, and Carol Drinkwater, dramatized by Brian Finch from material in *All Things Wise and Wonderful,* produced by Bill Sellars; BBC Video, 1983; released as videocassette, CBS/Fox Video, 1986.
All Creatures Great and Small, television series starring Christopher Timothy and Robert Hardy, beginning BBC, 1978, and PBS-TV, 1979, both continuing to be shown on PBS as of 1996.
All Things Bright and Beautiful, motion picture starring John Alderton, Colin Blakely, and Lisa Harrow, adapted by Alan Plater and produced by David Susskind; also released as *It Shouldn't Happen to a Vet,* BBC-TV, 1979.
James Herriot's Yorkshire—the Film, 55-minute 16 mm wide-screen travelogue-documentary video narrated by Christopher Timothy with an appearance by James Herriot; coproduced by Timothy and David Wilkinson, directed by Joy Perino; originally released in 1993 by Big Life Pictures in U.K. video format; according to Timothy, updated for rerelease in December, 1995.

SECOND ARY SOURCES
American Veterinary Medical Association. "AVMA Award of Appreciation Given to British Veterinarian-Author." *Journal of the American Veterinary Medical Association* 167 (15 October 1975): 703–4.
————. "British Actor Brings James Herriot to Life on American TV." *American Veterinary Medical Association Journal* 175 (1 August 1979): 153–56. Contains an interview with actor Christopher Timothy on his most famous role.
————. "Famed Veterinarian-Author Herriot Visits AVMA." *American Veterinary Medical Association Journal* 154 (1 February 1974): 257. Herriot's contact with U.S. vets on a rare trip away from Yorkshire.

Brower, Monty. "Long a Success as 'James Herriot,' Yorkshire Vet Jim Wight Says All Things Must Come to an End." *People Weekly* 23 (18 March 1985): 90–92, 97. Herriot's declaration that his personal life and vet work must come first.

Del Balso, Suzanne. "The Wise, Wonderful World of the Real James Herriot." *Good Housekeeping* (March 1979): 148, 178–81. Interview resulting from a day spent with Herriot on a typical day's calls.

Freilicher, Lila. "The Story Behind the Book: *All Creatures Great and Small*." *Publishers Weekly* (8 January 1973): 53. Description of the discovery of Herriot's work by St. Martin's Press's President Thomas McCormack and the derivation of Herriot's first four titles from an Anglican hymn.

Gardner, Richard. "James Herriot (James Alfred Wight.)" In *Beacham's Popular Fiction in America,* vol. 3, edited by Walton Beacham. Washington, D.C.: Beacham Publishing, 1986. A brief critical overview of Herriot's works to 1986, with discussion of themes, social concerns, and literary precedents.

Green, Timothy. "Best-Selling Vet Practices as Usual." *Smithsonian* (November 1974): 90–98. A rare interview with Herriot, containing Paul Conklin's photographs of Herriot's home and place of work.

Gonzalez, Arturo F., Jr. "America's Favorite Animal Doctor." *50 Plus* 18 (September 1978): 42–45. Freelancer Gonzalez's first interview with Herriot, stressing Herriot's nonmaterialist attitude toward his writing.

———. "In Search of the Simple." *Atlas World Press Review* 25 (September 1978): 37–38. Excerpt of interview published in *Maclean's* (Toronto, 29 May 1978); concentrates on the beginning of Herriot's writing career.

———. "Interview with James Herriot." *Maclean's* 91 (29 May 1978): 4–6. Question-and-answer format dealing with Herriot's unexpected early success.

———. "James Herriot." *Saturday Review* (May–June 1986): 56–59, 88–89. Later question-and-answer format focusing on Herriot's strong desire to preserve the Yorkshire he loved in his work.

Kelly, Catherine. "Home, James." *Yorkshire Sunday* (31 October 1993): 24.

Nickel, Kenneth. "A Trek to Find James Herriot." *Dog World* (September 1985): 14, 49–51. Interview by one of the first journalists to connect "James Herriot" with Thirsk veterinarian "Alf" Wight in 1978, according to Nickel's letter of July 25, 1994, to the author.

———. "James Herriot Revisited." *Dog World* (April 1992): 15–19. Nickel's second interview with Herriot, focusing on the dogs Herriot has owned and updating the real-life people Herriot made into characters in his books.

Nickson, Liz. "Life Visits Herriot Country." *Life* (March 1988): 66–69. Illustrated interview featuring Herriot's work in Yorkshire.

Simpson, Rachel. "Animal Magnetism." *Daily Express* (9 December 1993): 50.

Sternlicht, Sanford. *All Things Herriot: James Herriot and His Peaceable Kingdom.* Syracuse: Syracuse University Press, 1995. First full-length book on the subject; an example of often unfounded and undocumented weighty psychosocial American literary criticism about Herriot and his work, the kind Herriot once declared he was unable to understand (see Taylor, 75). Sternlicht's thesis is that both "James Herriot" the author and "James Herriot" the protagonist are dual faces of one character, James Alfred Wight, consciously constructed to achieve greater creative literary freedom.

"Wight, James Alfred (James Herriot)." In *Something About the Author,* vol. 55, edited by Anne Conmore. Detroit, Michigan: Gale Research, 1989. Overview of Herriot's work, including excerpts of autobiographical statements gleaned from his work and from published interviews.

Chronological Selection of Reviews of James Herriot's Works

Llewellyn, David. Review of *Let Sleeping Vets Lie. Books and Bookmen* 19 (October 1973): 118.

Doerner, William R. "How Now, Brown Cow?" Review of *All Creatures Great and Small. Time* (19 February 1973): 74.

Putney, Michael. "A Decent Man Records More 'Little Triumphs' " Review of *All Things Bright and Beautiful. National Observer* 13 (28 December 1974): 17.

Taylor, David. "It Could Only Happen to a Vet." *Radio Times* (January 1978): 72–77.

Review of *All Things Wise and Wonderful. Virginia Quarterly Review* 54 (Winter 1978): 30.

Kanfer, Stefan. "The Marcus Welby of the Barnyard." Review of *The Lord God Made Them All. Time* (29 June 1981).

Binchy, Maeve. "Make Way for Badgers." Review of *Every Living Thing. New York Times Book Review,* 6 September 1992, 5–6.

Slung, Michele. "Hairballs and Havoc." Review of *James Herriot's Cat Stories. New York Times Book Review,* 11 September 1994, 12.

Index

The Author

Mitzi M. Brunsdale received her B.S. with honors and her M.S. from North Dakota State University and her Ph.D. as a Danforth Fellow from the University of North Dakota. She has taught English since 1976 at Mayville State University near her husband's Red River Valley grain farm, an area like Herriot's Dales in many ways, both "sweet, safe" places to be.

WITHDRAWN